Critical Political Theory and Radical Practice

Series Editor
Stephen Eric Bronner
Department of Political Science
Rutgers University
New Brunswick, NJ, USA

The series introduces new authors, unorthodox themes, critical interpretations of the classics and salient works by older and more established thinkers. A new generation of academics is becoming engaged with immanent critique, interdisciplinary work, actual political problems, and more broadly the link between theory and practice. Each in this series will, after his or her fashion, explore the ways in which political theory can enrich our understanding of the arts and social sciences. Criminal justice, psychology, sociology, theater and a host of other disciplines come into play for a critical political theory. The series also opens new avenues by engaging alternative traditions, animal rights, Islamic politics, mass movements, sovereignty, and the institutional problems of power. Critical Political Theory and Radical Practice thus fills an important niche. Innovatively blending tradition and experimentation, this intellectual enterprise with a political intent hopes to help reinvigorate what is fast becoming a petrified field of study and to perhaps provide a bit of inspiration for future scholars and activists.

More information about this series at
http://www.palgrave.com/gp/series/14938

Beth M. Titchiner

The Epistemology of Violence

Understanding the Root Causes of Violence
in Schooling

Beth M. Titchiner
Norwich, Norfolk, UK

Critical Political Theory and Radical Practice
ISBN 978-3-030-12910-1   ISBN 978-3-030-12911-8   (eBook)
https://doi.org/10.1007/978-3-030-12911-8

Library of Congress Control Number: 2019934988

This Palgrave Macmillan imprint is published by the registered company Springer Nature Switzerland AG.
The registered company address is: Gewerbestrasse 11, 6330 Cham, Switzerland

For Katie and Lúcia

Acknowledgements

This research was funded by the University of East Anglia and conducted as part of a Research and Teaching Doctoral Studentship at the School of Education and Lifelong Learning, University of East Anglia, Norwich, Norfolk, UK. This research was approved, and reviewed prior to publication, by the School of Education and Lifelong Learning Research Ethics Committee at the University of East Anglia. The author is currently based at the University of Nottingham, Nottinghamshire, UK.

I would like to thank Dr John Gordon and Dr Bryan Maddox for their supervision, Dr Sarah Amsler and Dr Spiros Themelis for their invaluable feedback, and the following for their support: Robert C. Smith, Rose Titchiner, Gabriel Titchiner, Mark Titchiner, Dulcie and Jonny Crickmore, Jude Fitzgerald and Tove Nylund, Arnold DeGraaff and Rita Reitsma, Jeanne and Jack Titchiner, Belinda Loftus, Esther Priyadharshini, Claire Bennett, Sokratis Kioussis, Antoni Wojcik, Susanne Harris, Martin Scott, Rachael Quast, Tom Pablo Dalby, Nitasha Kul, Mirana Casali Silveira, Ozorio Passos Mendes, Luan Bushby, Sylvia Large, Georgie Murdoch, Anita Staff, Michael Parsons, Robert Lancaster, Flower Trower, Fiona Nairn, Beckie Davies, Eva van Eeghan, Mary Hogan, Sarah Cassels, Chris Edwards, Helen Sharp, Lisa James, Janet Cross, Stephen Spawls, Ian Cummings, and Benjamin Walker.

I would also like to thank all of the teachers and students who gave me their valuable time and energy, and Carlos Lima for facilitating my access to DCX School.

CONTENTS

LIST OF FIGURES

CHAPTER 1

Introduction

1.1 The Pedagogical Meeting[1]

Wedged-in behind a small Formica desk at the back of a classroom, I sat among a group of teachers and the school director in an otherwise empty municipal school in the centre of São Paulo. The plain white walls, pencil-scratched white desks, and our tired faces, all lay bare under the caustic fluorescent light. I stared wistfully up at the little shaft of sunlight just visible through the frosted glass vents at the top of the classroom wall, looking out at the crumbling, dilapidated apartment block looming over us.

Then I heard something that caught my attention. An elderly lady who taught year five was speaking. She leaned in towards the group, saying earnestly, 'I put tables against the door so they don't leave, because there's nobody in the corridor to ask for rescue. I go to the head teachers' room and there's nobody there…. They start throwing chairs and tables on the floor, laughing, they start dancing and there's nothing you can say…. If they get up and pull the tables away from the door and say "Teacher we're going now because the other classes have already gone"—is it worth holding the door?'

To either side of me, backed right up against the rear wall behind a barricade of tables, as if trying to protect themselves from the school director

---

[1] Held at intervals throughout the school year, pedagogical meetings (which are a common feature of Brazilian schooling) are intended to provide a space for teachers and school management to reflect on the overall progress, direction, and educational aims of the school.

© The Author(s) 2019

B. M. Titchiner, *The Epistemology of Violence*, Critical Political Theory and Radical Practice, https://doi.org/10.1007/978-3-030-12911-8_1

and possibly from the rest of the group, a small huddle of teachers sat at jaunty angles, various expressions of boredom, disbelief, scepticism, desperation, impatience, indignation, and doubt washing over their faces in waves. A group to my left sat muttering under their breath, suppressing laughs or shaking their heads in disbelief almost every time the school director spoke. A mix of disaffection, frustration, resignation, and a feeling of ridiculousness seemed to dominate the atmosphere in the room.

Following the elderly teacher's statement, a man in a wool sweater at the edge of the group sat up and raised his hands, a mix of tension and empathy in his voice. 'They invade the classrooms without asking to be excused. Sometimes they come into your lesson and turn off the light and start clapping their hands saying, "Come on! Let's mess about!" trying to work up the kids in the class. The other day they said, "Let's mess about!" They threw tables, turned off the light, swore at me.... And I didn't know whether to get the tables, turn on the light, hold the door.... They didn't do it because they don't like me, it's because they like to mess about. They apologised afterwards, and one boy came and put his hand on my heart and said, "Wow teacher you got really nervy!" and I said, "I did, but I'm calming down now." I get worked up and stressed, but I'm not going to let it get to me. I'm not going to get ill.'

Somewhere in the discussion, a younger woman piped in frustratedly, 'When some teachers get fed up and let their class out early, they all come banging on the doors of all the other classrooms that are still in lessons. We can't maintain the routine! They are out of control! JL[2] carries on being out of the classroom from 1.30 until 6.30. He isn't a criminal, he doesn't use drugs.... Why can't we reach him?'

A young man in a tracksuit spoke of how he had told a boy who was in the corridor to go back to his classroom a few days previously. 'He told me, "I'll go back, but only because it's you who's telling me." Sometimes I think they only respect me because I'm a P.E. teacher and P.E. is "cool". But you need to have a strong posture. If they find a millimetre of fear in you it's over.'

'They're not bad', another young teacher argued, 'they just need limits. They're children. They're not monsters. They just want limits. They want you to tell them where the limits are.'

The younger woman added, 'It's their way of saying, "we can be violent in the classroom too. We become animals if the teacher shouts."'

---

[2] All names have been changed to randomised initials for reasons of confidentiality.

Across the room, a tired-looking man in a leather jacket sighed. 'We come here in the morning, and when we leave this place it seems as if we're leaving a battle front.' Heads nodded in agreement, and it was clear that many in the group could relate to this sentiment.

The conversation moved to the topic of what could be done to improve discipline. An older man, who had been sitting in silence doodling on a notepad throughout the discussion, looked up and said calmly, 'Things that seem banal sometimes help a lot. For example, if the blackboard is by the door, the teacher can control the flow of entering and leaving. When I call the register I always stay by the door so as not to let the people who hang around hassling at the door come in.'

The school director stood up from her table in the middle of the room and tried to move the discussion on to the topic of next week's national test. But before she could continue, a new teacher who had been sitting meticulously filling out attendance registers from the start of the meeting looked up nervously. Tense, her hair awry from running her hands through it, she asked, 'Test? What test? When is it? Do I have to administer it? Because I don't know how … and I don't think I'll be able to….' She got out of her chair and walked halfway across the room, a look of panic on her face. 'In my class…. I don't think…. I already have so many problems with discipline….' She looked at the group, wide-eyed.

'Ask someone for help', the school director replied, rather shortly.

'But there's nobody to ask', the woman said desperately. 'Sometimes I look outside to see if there's anybody to help but there's never anybody there.'

'Well go to the head teacher's office.'

'But I can't leave the room; if I leave the room they start throwing tables and…'

'Well that's just the conditions we work under, we're understaffed', the school director replied. 'We should ask the DRE[3] for some help … we're alone here….' She paused for a few seconds in thought and then took a deep breath and carried on. 'And discipline is not my responsibility. I can't help you with that. It says so in my job description. I can go and get it and read it to you if you want. Come and see me afterwards and we'll go over the test.' The new teacher slid back into her chair with a meek nod of acknowledgement, evidently still extremely anxious.

The younger teacher who spoke earlier had been sitting with her head in her hands, shaking it from side to side and muttering, 'I don't believe

---

[3] Regional Directorate of Education.

this…' under her breath. Suddenly she burst out, 'People, there's no such thing as team work here! There's no such thing as interdisciplinary work here! We have a discipline of shouting!'

The man in the leather jacket cut in. 'We teachers don't know each other, we are strangers to each other. We sit together for forty minutes in the staff room, me here at the table and the other on the sofa over there. The two of us breathing for forty minutes. And then the bell rings and not even a "have a good class!" How am I going to ask for help from a person that is a stranger to me?' He was getting more and more worked up, his face becoming red and tense as he waved his arms emphatically in the air. He turned and pointed his whole arm at the man in the wool sweater. 'And you, who said that you won't get ill … you will! We don't know any more who are our colleagues and who aren't. Are we unbalanced? Are we? I came to this school balanced and healthy and now I'm ill, so-and-so is ill, you're going to get ill.' He brought his arms down decisively. Some of the others hid sniggers and looks of amused surprise at their colleague's outburst.

The director looked around at the entire group and said, 'We're all in this together. We're all going to get ill.'

The man in the leather jacket sighed and his shoulders slumped as if in defeat. 'I see the state of education as a silent scream', he said. '[W]e shout and shout and nobody hears.'[4]

The meeting carried on much to the same tune for a while longer and then disbanded along with a few complaints about the school director being up in the clouds and 'not having a clue', how it was another day wasted, and how perhaps a change in the time schedule for the year groups might help to improve discipline. On Monday, the children returned and it was business as usual until the next pedagogical meeting, which played out in much the same way.

1.2   THE PROBLEM OF CONCEPTUALISING AND ADDRESSING VIOLENCE

The vignette above contains many examples of manifestations and impacts of violence, although to some this may not obviously appear to be the case. Throughout this book, I will elucidate in detail how this is so, but for now, I have opened this book with this vignette because it illustrates a key

---

[4] Teacher's meeting at DCX, a Municipal School of Fundamental Education (EMEF) in São Paulo, 15 June 2011.

issue: the difficulty of clearly and sufficiently defining violence. Without a clear understanding and definition of what violence *is*, it is difficult to focus research on understanding its root causes. And without an under-standing of the factors leading to violence, it is difficult to design and implement meaningful, effective interventions and non-violent ways of working.

It is well known that violence is an issue in schools around the world. Few people have not heard of violent tragedies in the USA in which youngsters have taken guns to their peers, teachers, and themselves (Elliott et al. 1998). Indeed, while I was carrying out my research in 2011, a for-mer pupil returned to his school in Rio de Janeiro, gunning down 12 students and then killing himself (Phillips 2011). Sadly, such occurrences have not been infrequent news headlines since.

When considering the words 'violence in schooling', for many, school shootings will be the first thing to come to mind because of their sudden, extreme, tragic, and well-reported nature. However, as illustrated in the above vignette, violence can manifest in a much wider variety of ways. Common in some parts of the world is the use of corporal punishment in schools and the occurrence of sexual violence, often carried out by male teachers on female pupils (Harber 2002). Teachers can be victims of physi-cal attacks by pupils, and even more common are occurrences of physical conflict, verbal abuse, and bullying between pupils (as is the case in Brazil) (Smith 2003; Sposito 2001).

To varying degrees, all of the above are widely recognised and con-demned. Even more commonplace however, and particularly insidious because it largely goes unrecognised and unchallenged, is the bullying of students by teachers and the socially accepted forms of violence and abuse which are carried out by school institutions on pupils and teachers every day (such as the control, suppression, and neglect of physical, emotional, psy-chological, and intellectual needs) (Schostak 1986). This includes the less obvious, but pertinent, subtle forms of violence perpetrated by the institu-tional and pedagogical practices of schooling, and often unintentionally by well-meaning teachers (ibid.). The latter is so commonly engrained within the day-to-day functioning, rituals, and policies of the school day in tradi-tional schooling that it is normalised, and is therefore rarely recognised as a form of violence (Horta 2005).

Due to this normalisation, many of the more implicit, subtle, and insid-ious forms of violence embedded in institutional and pedagogical practices (and the contexts in which they are situated) are likely to go unrecognised as such, in the majority of contexts. This perhaps explains why much of the literature on violence in schooling published to date focusses on attempting to define and categorise violence rather than understanding its root causes. That is, in order to understand the root causes of violence, it is first necessary to define what is being investigated.

Definitions of violence in relation to schooling range from the very narrow to the relatively broad and far-reaching. At the narrower end of the spectrum, Elliott et al. state that 'violence refers to the threat or use of physical force with the intention of causing physical injury, damage, or intimidation of another person' (1998, p. 13). Based on this definition, the authors assert that 'historically, our schools have been relatively safe havens from violence. However, over the past decade there has been an epidemic of youth crime' (ibid.). This narrow perspective allows for the perception of physical acts of interpersonal violence in which the student is the perpetrator, but is blind to violence perpetrated by schools and those who work in them; to historical violence (such as corporal punishment or the use of schooling in colonial contexts to 'civilise' indigenous people); and to non-physical forms of violence. Hoffman (1996) also takes this narrow definition, writing that the perpetrators of violence in schools are either 'trespassers who enter the school building to steal, rob or assault someone' or 'students enrolled in the school' who commit violence 'against teachers, administrators, other staff members, or fellow classmates' (p. 11). Again, this definition does not allow for non-physical forms of violence, nor for the school or school staff to be perpetrators.

Harber (2002) offers a broader conceptualisation, stating that violence is 'behaviour by people against people liable to cause physical or psychological harm', defining this as 'how schools can be both violent towards pupils and can foster violent activity'. Ardizzone (2007) also argues for a broader definition of violence 'that includes not just war, torture, homicide, and other physical abuse but also emotional abuse, oppression and exploitation' (p. 2). These perspectives go beyond the purely physical understanding of violence, making possible the consideration of schools and teachers as potential perpetrators and the acknowledgement of less obvious forms of violence.

Galtung (1996) argues that it is important to distinguish between different types of violence, naming three in particular: direct violence, which is 'intended to insult the basic needs of others (including nature); structural violence which includes that exploitation and oppression built into social and world structures; and cultural violence—aspects of culture (such as religion and language) which legitimize direct and structural violence' (Galtung 1996, p. 40). Unlike Elliott and Hoffman's definitions, Galtung's formulation demonstrates that violence does not only occur on an interpersonal level.

Ross Epp (1996) also goes beyond the interpersonal and acknowledges that violence can function on a structural level. She speaks of 'systemic' violence, defining it as 'any institutional practice or procedure that adversely impacts on individuals or groups by burdening them psychologically, mentally, culturally, spiritually, economically or physically. Applied to education, this means practices and procedures that prevent students from learning, thus harming them' (p. 1). Harber (2002) also describes the 'structural violence' of the ways that poverty and global economic relationships affect schooling provision, and also proposes three additional ways of defining violence in relation to education. These include: how schools are affected by contexts of violent conflict; Bourdieu's 'symbolic violence' of schools imposing forms of dominant knowledge; and the way in which schools can be implicated in violence through omission by, for example, ignoring racism or bullying.

From the few authors cited above, we can already see that violence has been defined in many different ways, just within the field of education studies. Ralph (2013) argues that this broad variation is in part due to the multidimensional nature of violence. If we consider the definitions cited above, each one appears to focus on a different dimension (or selection of dimensions) of violence. On the one hand, there are physical dimensions, and on the other, psychological and emotional. There are also dimensions of violence functioning at the level of the individual (as victim or perpetrator) as well as at the institutional, societal, and global levels (in the forms of structural and systemic violence). Furthermore, there are explicit dimensions of violence (such as its expression through physical aggression) and more implicit dimensions (such as schools neglecting to act on bullying or enforcing authoritarian disciplinary regimes).

1.3   The Challenge of Addressing Violence in Schooling

As we have seen, manifestations of violence are commonly recognised in a piecemeal manner. This is problematic because, when it comes to planning and implementing interventions with the aim of reducing violence, seldom are interventions designed to address violence holistically. Taking the wide range of definitions and perspectives regarding the nature and causes of violence in schooling, the challenge facing practitioners when it comes to addressing the problem of violence in schools can be seen as a complicated one.

Practitioners are often faced with narrow definitions which do not fully encompass the complexity of how violence can manifest in schools—for example, by failing to acknowledge that schools and teachers can also be perpetrators of violence. In these instances, defensive and disciplinary measures are often employed, with the aim of preventing, protecting against, and punishing explicit acts of violence perpetrated by students. Such measures can include heightened security such as surveillance and control of access (e.g. security guards and gates) (Phaneuf 2009; Xaba 2014), the installation of metal detectors (Hankin et al. 2011), and campaigns to arm teachers (Rostron 2013). Punitive discipline is also common practice all over the world, including corporal punishment in many locations (Cameron 2006; González 2012). However, the use of security measures has been found to result in increased fear and reduced feelings of safety within schools (Perumean-Chaney and Sutton 2013), and the use of metal detectors has not been shown to reduce incidences of violence (Hankin et al. 2011), while corporal punishment and other punitive disciplinary action have been found to promote and perpetuate violent and antisocial behaviour (Mayer 1995; Noguera 1995; Hyman and Perone 1998; Cameron 2006; Skiba and Nesting 2014). These measures are superficial, and do not address violence at its root causes.

International organisations tend to promote rights-based and peace education approaches (UNESCO 2014; Council of Europe 2011). These approaches tend to take an educational, behavioural, and disciplinary stance. For example, teachers are encouraged to educate each other and students about children's rights and how violence infringes on these rights. Collaborative approaches to agreeing behavioural 'rules', and the use of disciplinary measures to respond to infringement of these rules, are encouraged. The development of skills such as conflict resolution and attitudes of tolerance is also promoted (UNESCO 2014).

While these frameworks can help to 'keep the peace' and reduce incidences of overt violence, they do not provide an understanding of, or address, the root causes of violence—especially more subtle and structurally engrained forms. This can result in what Galtung (2013) calls 'negative peace'—the removal of explicit, direct forms of violence without addressing issues of structural, implicit, and indirect violence. Gur-Ze'ev

(2010) argues that 'current peace education enables, serves, conceals and glorifies' existing oppressive power relations (p. 316), representing what Galtung (1975) calls 'peacekeeping'—the action of averting immediate conflict without addressing its roots. In this way, Gur-Ze'ev (2010) argues that peace education is actually 'one of the most advanced manifestations' (p. 319) of oppressive, implicit violence.

Approaches which do acknowledge the implicit, structural, and more complex nature of violence require the teacher to question not only established and accepted pedagogical practices to which they may be accustomed but also the entire structures of the institutions in which they work. Such approaches are often presented as a 'radical' alternative to mainstream pedagogical practices, which are seen in whole or in part to foster violence. This was the view of A. S. Neill, a 'founding father' of the international democratic education movement. Neill believed violence to stem from repression and conditioning, beginning at birth, in which he saw parenting as playing a significant role. But he also believed that the rigidity and discipline of schooling could amplify and perpetuate this. He writes, 'unfree education results in a life that cannot be lived fully. [It] ignores almost entirely the emotions of life, and because these emotions are dynamic and unkillable, their lack of opportunity for expression must and does result in cheapness and ugliness and hatefulness' (Neill 1953, p. 29).

Neill's approach was to isolate the child as much as possible from external influence (including the parents), providing them with a space at boarding school in which they could be free from repressive social structures, taboos, and authoritarian discipline (ibid.). This meant non-compulsory lessons and self-regulation within a democratically run school community, in which adults and children would have an equal vote in the day-to-day running of the school. Neill's view was that this scenario would enable children to experience their emotions freely, and 'if the emotions are free, the intellect will look after itself' (ibid., p. 29). Neill wrote that, in his school Summerhill, 'the children's reaction to emotional freedom [...] was a great increase in sincerity and charity, [and] a lessening of aggression' (ibid., p. 36). What Neill and other thinkers in democratic education have not managed to provide, however, has been an understanding of the specific mechanisms that lead from repression to violence.

In Brazil, including throughout the São Paulo Municipal Education Network, the concept and practice of Educommunication is employed with the aim of reducing violence, and is grounded in Paulo Freire's (1996) argument that the traditional 'banking' method of education is an 'exercise of domination [which] stimulates the credulity of students, with the ideological intent (often not perceived by educators) of indoctrinating them to adapt to a world of oppression' (p. 59). Rather than a distant and authoritarian relationship between teacher and students, he emphasised the importance of collective solidarity in learning (Freire 1973). Building on Freire's ideas, Educommunication theorists argue that the rapid expansion of media and communications technologies has created tensions between new and traditional 'schooled' practices of knowledge production and dissemination, which are believed to exacerbate the symbolic and epistemic violence already present in traditional schooling (Soares 2011).

Educommunication projects in schools aim to break down traditional nineteenth-century-style 'chalk and talk' pedagogical practice, by implementing participatory media production projects, the purpose of which is to address symbolic violence by 'open[ing] up channels of expression and participation, [and] spaces for the pronouncement of the subjectivity of all involved in the actions of the school' (Horta 2005, pp. 57–58). The aim is to promote the development of a type of 'communicative ecosystem' (Barbero 2002) in which all members of the school community can actively participate as subjects and agents in the production of knowledge, thus breaking down the symbolic violence inherent within the hierarchical, one-way transmission model of education (which posits the teacher as knower and the students as passive receptacles of knowledge). More overt acts of violence are seen to stem from this symbolic violence, and it is thus believed that reducing symbolic violence will in turn reduce all forms of violence within the school (Soares 2011). Proponents of Educommunication also propose that the encouragement of collaboration between teachers and students in the joint production of media outputs (e.g. videos, school radio stations, and newspapers) can increase contact and communication between different members of the school community, fostering horizontality and mutual understanding, and thus reducing conflict and prejudice (C. Lima, personal communication, 9 May 2011).

The participants in the case-study research upon which this book is based were also participants in an Educommunication project within the case-study school. However, analysis of this project (cf. Titchiner 2017) found that while pedagogical practice became more participatory within the project, this reach was limited to approximately 2% of the student population and did not extend into day-to-day classroom pedagogy, which retained its hierarchical 'banking' style. Within the project, students were encouraged to participate and work collaboratively as agents of knowledge and change. This led some students to report that they had learnt to work better in groups, had seen new ways to resolve conflict, and had gained increased respect for their teachers and peers. However, this was limited to around 1% of the total student population, with acts of bullying, violence, and aggression (on the part of both teachers and students) remaining a daily occurrence both inside and outside of the classroom, as well as during project activities.

While more 'radical' approaches to addressing violence in schooling may produce a more humane environment and some positive effects for participating individuals, their reach is limited for a number of reasons. Those which entail running the school in an entirely different manner (such as in the case of A. S. Neill type democratic schools) tend to operate in isolation from the social context in which the school is situated, and therefore do not engage with the broader contextual causes of violence beyond the pedagogical practices and structural factors of the school itself. There is also no clear definition of violence within the philosophy of democratic schooling which, considering that there is often support for rights-based education among democratic educators, makes such approaches vulnerable to the potentially superficial and oppressive 'peace education' type philosophies. When it comes to examining the role of epistemology in violence, as this book will, Neill's assertion that the intellect can 'take care of itself' is also insufficient. This is especially so because democratic schooling is just as vulnerable to ideological thought as other educational philosophies, and thus equally unprotected against the fostering of violence (see Chap. 4 for discussion on the relationship between violence and ideology).

Freirian-type interventions such as Educommunication limit their definition of violence to that of the symbolic violence inherent to a specific type of pedagogical practice. While this is helpful in understanding the role that traditional pedagogy can play in fostering violence, this definition fails to take into account or address the much broader and more complex landscape of violence and its root causes, such as institutional, structural, contextual, and historical factors. They also tend to pose a false dichotomy between 'oppressors' (teachers) and 'oppressed' (students), which does not take into account the complex interactions between structure and agency in which an individual can be both oppressor and oppressed, but in a more nuanced and inconsistent manner.

Fundamentally, while there are a wide range of approaches to addressing violence in schooling which draw on different definitions and philosophies, as yet there is no approach that fully encompasses violence from both a holistic and detailed perspective. That is, one which addresses the levels of individual subjectivity, actions and interactions, institutional structures and practices, and the community, societal, global, and historical contexts in which schools are situated, within a single conceptual framework. Aside from this, no current theory of violence in schooling offers a suitably detailed definition and understanding of the root causes and specific mechanisms of violence, rather than simply naming contributory and/or correlational factors.

1.4   Aims and Scope of This Book

In light of this context, this book aims to develop a suitably holistic conceptual framework for understanding violence in schooling. This framework intends to be both broad and specific, focussing on both the specific underlying mechanisms that result in violence at the level of individual consciousness, and the broader contextual factors that foster this. The purpose is not to provide a statistical analysis of factors correlational to the enactment of overt violence, but rather to develop a deep, detailed understanding of the complex interrelationships between individuals, the world in which they exist, and other beings. Deeper than this, the book aims to formulate a conceptualisation of the most irreducible root causes of the enactment of violence in its multiple (not just overt) manifestations.

This involves drawing on multiple disciplines to examine everything from cognitive processes, emotions, motivations, and learning theory to local and global histories, ideology, economic, social, political, and institutional structures, and the relationships between structure and agency. As the title of this book suggests, the core perspective from which this book will tackle all of the above is the lens of epistemology. The book is structured around two core pillars: conceptual formulation, and an in-depth case-study which demonstrates how the conceptual formulations presented apply in practice. While the case-study is a school, and this book is focussed on understanding the root causes of violence in schooling, my intention is that the conceptual frameworks (and methodologies) presented herein are broad enough in scope that they can be employed in analysing the root causes of violence in any context, not just in education. This book is fundamentally about deep-rooted problems of epistemology and their impact on the human condition—and thus aims to be of much wider and far-reaching applicability than the field of education studies alone.

1.5   CHAPTER-BY-CHAPTER OVERVIEW

This chapter has outlined the problems involved in conceptualising, and therefore addressing, violence in schools by examining the variety of ways in which violence in schooling is currently defined, and how these definitions influence current approaches to addressing violence in practice. The limitations of these conceptual frameworks and interventions have been briefly discussed, and the aims and scope of this book have been defined.

In Chap. 2, I will outline the epistemic and methodological framework developed and employed in conducting the research upon which this book is based. I dedicate an entire chapter to this because, being that this book argues for the conceptualisation of violence as a problem of a specific form of epistemology, the epistemic and methodological frameworks employed in the study of violence are important so as not to fall into the trap of reproducing violent epistemology during the research process. I have therefore shared my approach to researching this topic in detail, in the hope that it can be of use to other researchers in this area. In a nutshell, this involves an epistemic approach to analysis that overcomes the limitations of idealist epistemologies, without reverting to a strong foundationalism.

Chapter 3 presents the idea that the 'linchpin' for the manifestation of violence is a specific type of epistemology, which I term 'violent epistemology'. I outline in detail a conceptual framework for understanding the specific cognitive mechanisms of violent epistemology and how this is made possible by the nature of human consciousness and its agency. The chapter draws on neuroscience, psychology, learning theory, and philosophy (including phenomenology and early Frankfurt School critical theory) to delineate a specific concept of violent epistemology. This moves away from current relativistic definitions of 'epistemic violence', in which different epistemologies are perceived as having equal 'truth' (with the violence occurring when one group or individual's epistemology is afforded primacy over others), to the concept that some epistemologies can be more or less violent, and produce more or less 'truth' than others (with the violence occurring when a more violent epistemology is employed). This chapter also discusses the role of emotions and motivations in the enactment of violent epistemology.

Chapter 4 presents a definition of ideology, positing ideological thought as possessing a specific epistemic structure analogous to violent epistemology. The chapter outlines how the violent epistemology inherent to ideological thought shapes social structures and promotes ways of relating with the phenomenal world, ourselves, and others. This chapter also addresses the complex issue of the relationship between structure (social circumstances) and individual agency in the cyclic perpetuation of violence. This involves a discussion of the role that violent epistemology and 'non-conducive' circumstances play in the de-formation of subjectivity, and the role of subject deformation in the perpetuation of non-conducive social circumstances.

In Chap. 5, I begin to demonstrate how the conceptual framework developed in Chaps. 3 and 4 applies in practice, by showing how violent epistemology has shaped the global, national, local, and historical contexts in which schools are situated. Using the case-study school of DCX in São Paulo, Brazil, I demonstrate how violent epistemology can be seen to have shaped Brazil's colonisation and transformation into a society marked by extreme social inequality which, despite the country's economic growth, has persisted throughout the industrial and neoliberal eras, to produce a scenario in which social neglect, violent crime, poor quality housing, and destitution are actively perpetuated in inner-city neighbourhoods by the enactment of violent epistemology at a range of structural levels.

Chapter 6 demonstrates, through the example of the development of schooling in Brazil and São Paulo, how violent epistemology shapes schooling systems. The chapter discusses the historical shaping of schooling in Brazil and São Paulo, from the use of schooling to catechise the indigenous population and provide a pliant work force during the colonial era, through the failure to provide education from the mid-18th to late 19th centuries due to a lack of perceived economic need, the later development of schooling as a means to progress the ideological endeavours of an elite aspiring to 'civilise the nation' in the aftermath of slavery, the establishment of typical nineteenth-century-style schooling to meet the needs of industrial capitalism, to the introduction of neoliberal technocratic reforms aimed to depoliticise students and train them for the labour market, along with legal, physical, and coercive repression of teacher and student dissent. Aside from analysing the role of violent epistemology in these particular processes, the chapter highlights how violent epistemology has played a general role in the implementation of successive reforms in the name of ideological schema, without sufficient regard to particular contextual needs. I conclude by outlining how this has resulted in non-conducive circumstances within schools and neutralised attempts to enact less violent epistemic practice.

Chapter 7 concludes the case-study by focussing on the broad variety of ways in which violence manifests in DCX School. Drawing on a large body of qualitative data collected during a period of immersive field research, I analyse how these manifestations of violence can be seen to result from the multiple manifestations, enactments, and impacts of violent epistemology at all levels—from the individual to the collective, institutional, structural, and global scales. This chapter draws the analysis presented in the previous chapters down into the context of day-to-day life within the school, to highlight the impacts of pervasive violent epistemology at the micro level, concluding a complex yet detailed and holistic conceptualisation of the root causes of violence in schools as stemming from violent epistemology and the non-conducive circumstances that it fosters.

To conclude the book, Chap. 8 formulates a concept of less violent epistemology, and of the circumstances that might be conducive to fostering its enactment. The chapter discusses the implications of, and processes required to, transition towards non-violent epistemology from habitual enactment of violent epistemology. This includes a discussion on what this is likely to mean for individuals from an emotional, psychological, and practical standpoint, and how moving away from violent epistemology towards less violent epistemic practice is not a concept that can simply be 'adopted', but is rather a complex, whole-person approach which can have a deep and potentially transformative impact on how we relate with our selves, others, and the phenomenal world. The chapter ends with a discussion on the potential and possibilities for change within social systems and structures which have been built on violent epistemology, and possible future directions for research.

References

Ardizzone, L. (2007). *Getting My Word Out: Voices of Urban Youth Activists.* New York: SUNY Press.

Barbero, J. M. (2002). *La Educación desde la Comunicación.* Buenos Aires: Norma.

Cameron, M. (2006). Managing School Discipline and Implications for School Social Workers: A Review of the Literature. *Children & Schools, 28*(4), 219–227.

Council of Europe. (2011). *Tackling Violence in Schools: High-Level Expert Meeting Co-organised by the Government of Norway, the Council of Europe and the UN Special Representative of the Secretary-General on Violence against Children.* Resource Document. Retrieved July 20, 2018, from https://rm.coe.int/CoERMPublicCommonSearchServices/DisplayDCTMContent?documentId=090000168046cfcd.

Elliott, D. S., Hamburg, B. A., & Williams, K. R. (1998). *Violence in American Schools*. Cambridge: Cambridge University Press.

Freire, P. (1973). *Extension or Communication*. New York: The Seabury Press.

Freire, P. (1996). *Pedagogy of the Oppressed*. London: Penguin Books.

Galtung, J. (1975). Peace: Research, Education, Action. *Journal of Peace Research, 12*(3), 238–244.

Galtung, J. (1996). *Peace by Peaceful Means: Peace and Conflict, Development and Civilisation*. London: Sage.

Galtung, J. (2013). Positive and Negative Peace. In J. Galtung & D. Fischer (Eds.), *Johan Galtung: Pioneer of Peace Research* (pp. 173–178). Berlin: Springer.

González, T. (2012). Keeping Kids in Schools: Restorative Justice, Punitive Discipline, and the School to Prison Pipeline. *Journal of Law & Education, 41*(2), 281–335.

Gur-Ze'ev, I. (2010). Beyond Peace Education: Toward Co-poiesis and Enduring Improvisation. *Policy Futures in Education, 8*(3–4), 315–339.

Hankin, A., Hertz, M., & Simon, T. (2011). Impacts of Metal Detector Use in Schools: Insights from 15 Years of Research. *Journal of School Health, 81*(2), 100–106.

Harber, C. (2002). Schooling as Violence: An Exploratory Overview. *Educational Review, 54*(1), 7–16.

Hoffman, A. M. (1996). *Schools, Violence and Society*. London: Praeger.

Horta, P. (2005). Raízes Educomunicativas: Do conceito a prática. *Revista Comunicação e Educação, 7*(3), 1–17.

Hyman, I. A., & Perone, D. C. (1998). The Other Side of School Violence: Educator Policies and Practices that May Contribute to Student Misbehaviour. *Journal of School Psychology, 36*(1), 7–27.

Mayer, G. R. (1995). Preventing Antisocial Behaviour in Schools. *Journal of Applied Behaviour Analysis, 28*(4), 467–478.

Neill, A. S. (1953). *The Free Child*. London: Herbert Jenkins.

Noguera, P. (1995). Preventing and Producing Violence: A Critical Analysis of Responses to School Violence. *Harvard Educational Review, 65*(2), 189–213.

Perumean-Chaney, S. E., & Sutton, L. M. (2013). Students and Perceived School Safety: The Impact of School Security Measures. *American Journal of Criminal Justice, 38*(4), 570–588.

Phaneuf, S. W. (2009). *Security in Schools: Its Effect on Students*. El Paso: LBF Scholarly.

Phillips, T. (2011). Brazil Shooting: 12 Children Killed in School Rampage. *The Guardian*. Retrieved August 1, 2016, from https://www.theguardian.com/world/2011/apr/07/brazil-shooting-rampage-gunman.

Ralph, S. (2013). *The Archaeology of Violence: Interdisciplinary Approaches*. New York: SUNY Press.

Ross Epp, J. (1996). Schools, Complicity and Sources of Violence. In J. Ross Epp & A. M. Watkinson (Eds.), *Systemic Violence: How Schools Hurt Children*. London: Falmer Press.

Rostron, A. (2013). School Shootings and the Legislative Push to Arm Teachers. *University of Toledo Law Review, 45*(3), 439–456.

Schostak, J. F. (1986). *Schooling the Violent Imagination*. London and New York: Routledge & Kegan Paul.

Skiba, R. J., & Nesting, K. (2014). Zero Tolerance, Zero Evidence: An Analysis of School Disciplinary Practice. *New Directions for Youth Development, 2001*(92), 17–43.

Smith, P. K. (2003). *Violence in Schools: The Response in Europe*. London: RoutledgeFalmer.

de Soares, I. O. (2011). *Educomunicação: o conceito, o profissional, a aplicação*. São Paulo: Paulinas.

Sposito, M. P. (2001). Um Breve Balanço da Pesquisa Sobre Violência Escolar no Brasil. *Educação e Pesquisa, 27*(1), 87–103.

Titchiner, B. M. (2017). *The Epistemology of Violence: Understanding the Root Causes of Violence and Non-conducive Social Circumstances in Schooling, with a Case-Study from Brazil*. Digital Thesis, University of East Anglia. Retrieved from https://ueaeprints.uea.ac.uk/63644/.

UNESCO. (2014). *Stopping Violence in Schools: A Guide for Teachers*. Resource Document. Retrieved July 20, 2018, from http://unesdoc.unesco.org/images/0018/001841/184162e.pdf.

Xaba, M. I. (2014). A Holistic Approach to Safety and Security at Schools in South Africa. *Mediterranean Journal of Social Sciences, 5*(20), 1580–1589.

CHAPTER 2

A New Epistemic and Methodological Approach to the Study of Violence

2.1 A New Epistemic Approach

This book proposes that the reason we have so far struggled to arrive at a suitably holistic and in-depth conceptualisation of violence is due to a problem of epistemology—both lay epistemology and the specific, explicitly considered epistemologies employed by researchers. Without an adequate epistemology for considering, researching, and developing a conceptual framework for understanding violence, researchers, practitioners, policy-makers, and the general public have failed to perceive violence not just as a wide range of manifest phenomena but also as a specific epistemology in itself. This idea is the key notion that I will develop and illustrate in detail throughout this book. Not only has there been a failure to recognise violence as a problem of epistemology, but also a failure on the part of researchers to devise and employ a suitable epistemic and methodological framework for studying violence, leading to the distinct lack of suitably holistic theories of violence that we face today.

Post-structural epistemic frameworks are a common go-to for critical social science. However, my experience with this research was that post-structuralism failed in the face of my lived experiences in the case-study context. My epistemic framework has therefore been developed with a mind to do justice to these experiences. While I saw no value in reverting

B. M. Titchiner, *The Epistemology of Violence*, Critical Political Theory and Radical Practice, https://doi.org/10.1007/978-3-030-12911-8_2

to a positivist, rationalistic approach,[1] I found that while post-structural frameworks allowed for the expression of subjective experiences, they offered little in terms of interpreting these experiences within a broader, more concrete theoretical and contextual framework.

The epistemic framework that I have developed draws largely on early Frankfurt School critical theory and elements of post-Husserlian phenomenology. While I do not subscribe wholeheartedly to any one author or tradition, within these areas I have found a number of very useful strands of thought which, combined, served to provide an epistemic and methodological framework that I felt could do justice to my research data and experiences in a critical yet balanced and useful way. The key benefits of this framework are its ability to 'lend a voice to suffering' without decontextualising, neutralising, or depoliticising it; its ability to maintain a dialectical, balanced, and integrated relation between particularity/generality, individual consciousness/society, structure/agency, and subjective experience/sociohistorical context; and its ability to recognise (inter)subjective experience whilst also examining it from a critical perspective.

Allow me to explain. Some valuable work comes from strands of poststructural thought that challenge modernistic narratives of progress, and in doing so lend voice to the human suffering often hidden beneath such narratives. Post-structuralists also tend to criticise the 'repressive hierarchies' of the dualisms of modern philosophy (such as universal/particular, public/private, and subject/object) in which one pole is often afforded significantly more worth than its counterpart, leading to the marginalisation of the latter (Schick 2009; McLaren 1995; Hammer and McLaren 1991).[2] Post-structuralism aims to counter this by giving focus to the less-valued poles of traditional dualisms, celebrating the local and the particular, while eschewing the analysis of metanarratives. Some such authors argue that in modern philosophy particular experience of suffering is silenced to prevent it disrupting narratives of order and progress,[3] by reinserting survivors of suffering and trauma back into the established social order and encouraging them to 'forget' suffering or otherwise labelling them with mental illness (Edkins 2002). It is argued that the incorporation

---

[1] As Schick (2009) states, the rationalistic, positivist 'rush to "solve" the problem of suffering with the forward-looking articulation of an abstract, universal response skims too quickly over concrete human experience' (p. 138).

[2] Cf. Edkins (2002, 2003) and Zizek (2002a, b).

[3] I will illustrate examples of this later, as indeed, the motto emblazoned on Brazil's national flag is 'order and progress'.

of such experience into a broader historical narrative should be prevented, as it only contributes to this silencing (Schick 2009).

While this approach can be praised for challenging the unbalanced treatment of dualisms and the silencing of suffering, it can be criticised for tipping the balance too far in the opposite direction. By refusing to incorporate particular experiences of suffering into a broader social narrative, it fails to provide us with any means for understanding and addressing the causes of suffering, leading to something of a theoretical 'vacuum'. Adorno brings a valuable alternative to this approach. While he shares critical aspects with his emphasis on the importance of particularity (Horkheimer and Adorno 2002) and his refusal to forget suffering (Adorno 1973), he differs in one key aspect: he maintains a dialectical approach which 'attends to broader social processes and institutions and the ways in which these constitute (and are constituted by) particularity' (Schick 2009, p. 141). Adopting this dialectical approach enables the analysis of both particular, individual experiences and the sociohistorical context in which these experiences take place. What is particularly valuable about Adorno's work is that he does not prioritise one pole of a dualism over another, but rather advocates holding the two in balance—not synthesising or settling for a 'weak middle ground' but examining in detail the complex, co-constitutive relationships between the two.

These ideas allow for a comprehensive approach to studying violence, incorporating historical and contextual analysis with the study of individual consciousness and lived experience. In pursuit of the former, I have drawn on strands of critique from Adorno and his Frankfurt School contemporaries, as well as more recent authors who are contributing to a revival of Frankfurt School critical theory for the twenty-first century (Cf. Cook 2005; Sherman 2007; Smith 2011). In pursuit of the latter, I draw on strands from post-Husserlian phenomenology (Cf. Merleau-Ponty 2012, 1964; Sartre 1956; Wider 1997) and more contemporary works which highlight the links between Frankfurt School critical theory and phenomenology (Sherman 2007; Smith 2011).

The strengths of these works include: the understanding of consciousness as embodied and situated in the world (and as intentionally and inter-subjectively relating with that world, as opposed to more Cartesian strands of phenomenology); acknowledgement of the multidimensionality of consciousness and phenomena, and of the ever-changing nature of phenomena (as opposed to phenomena possessing immutable 'essences'); and its emphasis on the importance of a dialectical 'openness' to experience (as opposed to pure 'objectivity' or 'subjectivity').

Many equate 'openness' to experience with the phenomenological concept of 'bracketing' (Cohen et al. 2011). This has been criticised as an assumption that it is possible to 'set aside' our pre-existing experiences and concepts, positioning ourselves as a 'tabula rasa' and thus gain an objective view on phenomena (Hutchinson 1988). Contrary to this view, I have adopted a more dialectical interpretation grounded in Adorno's (1973) critique of 'identity thinking'. As Waring (2012) argues, bracketing is unrealistic if understood in the above way. However, by seeing 'bracketing' as temporarily 'suspending' one's pre-existing concepts and experiences and remaining open to new experiences, it becomes plausible to maintain a dialectical relationship between the former and the latter, thus preventing the subsumption of the latter by the former. In this way I have not subscribed either to the concept of pure objectivity or to subjectivism, but rather to an intersubjective, dialectical relationship between my own subjectivity as a researcher and my data/experiences in the field (what Sherman (2007) calls 'mediating subjectivity').

This attitude has been central to my analytical approach, which has been based in what Clough and Nutbrown (2012, p. 26) call 'radical enquiry'. Characterised by the 'arrest' or 'bracketing' of experience (which I employed in the dialectical manner described above), radical enquiry is defined as an 'exploration beyond the familiar and the (personally) known, to the roots of a situation'. While I have not adhered strictly to its specific procedures of data collection and analysis, and therefore cannot claim that my research has produced a 'Grounded Theory' in the traditional sense, I found several aspects of Grounded Theory useful and drew on these during my analytical process. Firstly, the intention of radical enquiry to get to the 'roots of a situation' is also reflected in Grounded Theory methodology, which asks 'what is happening and why is it happening?' (Waring 2012, p. 299). Secondly, Grounded Theory can be seen as compatible with my dialectical framework because it 'assume[s] the capacity of an agent to act in the world and be producers and well as products of social systems' (Bryant and Charmaz 2007, p. 21). Finally, the analytical methodology of Grounded Theory can be useful in aiming to understand the root causes of violence because it looks for 'a set of relationships among data and categories that proposes a plausible explanation of the phenomena under study' (Moghaddam 2006, p. 299).

Developing a new epistemic framework for the study of violence has not involved simply adopting a single set of concepts deriving from a pre-existing 'ism' (e.g. foundationalism, post-structuralism, etc.) but rather the selection of appropriate constructs and positions from a range of disciplinary/theoretical areas to compose a 'patchwork'[4] like epistemic framework. Pieces of this patchwork have been selected on the basis of how well they are able to accommodate the multidimensionality of my data and experience in the field. As Chap. 3 demonstrates, apart from early Frankfurt School critical theory and post-Husserlian phenomenology, these pieces have also been drawn from research in psychology, neuroscience, and learning theory to refine a holistic epistemic framework.

For those who might wonder where exactly this epistemic patchwork lies in relation to other existing frameworks: it can be seen as closely aligned with Critical Realism (Cf. Bhaskar 1979; Fletcher 2016; Fleetwood 2013). While foundationalist epistemologies presume that a concrete, phenomenal reality exists outside of human consciousness, and is fully accessible to that consciousness (Kurki 2008; Rockmore 2004; Cruickshank 2003), idealist epistemologies (e.g. postmodernism, post-structuralism) argue that this is a fallacy, and that reality is in fact socially constructed through language, discourse, and human subjectivity—meaning that 'objective' truth cannot exist (White 2006). In their most extreme forms, idealist epistemologies appear to promote the view that 'if we cannot have absolute untarnished access to knowledge, there can be no knowledge' (ibid., p. 54). White (ibid.) argues, however, that this position is untenable and unnecessary, quoting William James' argument that 'when we give up the doctrine of objective certitude, we do not thereby give up the quest or hope of truth itself' (ibid.). This latter view (which acknowledges a concrete reality existing outside of human subjectivity and accepts that we cannot 'have absolute untarnished access to knowledge', yet does not abandon the quest for understanding altogether) underpins both Critical Realism and the epistemic framework employed in this book.

Where foundationalist epistemologies emphasise the material dimension at the expense of the ideal (i.e. discursive) and social dimensions of reality and idealist epistemologies can be accused of doing the opposite, Critical Realism, like the approach employed here, recognises the material, ideal, social, and artefactual dimensions as being equally 'real' components of a multidimensional reality (Fleetwood 2013; Maxwell 2012). Critical Realism also recognises that 'existing theories may not necessarily reflect

---

[4] The use of the term 'patchwork' here is not to be taken to mean a lack of coherence, but rather a coherent framework pieced together from compatible elements of a variety of separate frameworks.

reality accurately' (Fletcher 2016, p. 184) and therefore argues that researchers should 'avoid any commitment to the content of specific theories and recognise the conditional nature of all [...] results' (Bhaskar 1979, p. 6). However, unlike idealism, Critical Realism assumes that, since there is a concrete reality to which our theories refer, 'some theories may be more accurate than others' (Fletcher 2016, p. 184). This position has been central to the elaboration of the theoretical dimension of this book: by assuming that 'some theories may be more accurate than others' whilst treating all theories as provisional, I have reviewed and selected theoretical constructs based on how well they are able to accommodate or represent my data and experience in the field, without attempting to squeeze my data into theoretical constructs into which it did not 'fit' (which is often a pressure applied by more prescriptive epistemic frameworks).

In line with the approach already outlined, Critical Realism also takes a dialectical attitude in which structure and agency are both recognised and seen as distinct yet interrelated—that is, agents are seen to interact with structures (which pre-exist their action) in a cyclical relation through which structures are reproduced or transformed (Fleetwood 2013). Extending beyond this, this book also explores how subjectivity can also be shaped by structures. The two core concepts that this book presents (violent epistemology and non-conducive circumstances) are products of employing this dialectical approach—the former represents a deep engagement with subjectivity (agency) and the latter with context (structure), while the relationship between the two is examined in detail.

This book presents a framework for understanding the 'root causes' of violence. But causality can be a contentious issue in social research, and I must therefore clarify my approach to this. Foundationalist/Empirical Realist social science has received heavy criticism for its Humean approach in which causality is seen as event regularity, laws, and law-like or functional relations operating in linear temporal 'causal chains' (Fleetwood 2013). Many argue that this approach, which emphasises statistical analysis and deterministic prediction, is inappropriate for understanding the social world in which the complexity of social phenomena cannot be reduced to numerical data, and in which human agency makes determinism a fallacy and prediction impossible (Kurki 2008; Fleetwood 2013; Fletcher 2016; Cohen et al. 2011). The idealist response to this has been to reject the notion of causality altogether, and consequently disengage from it (Fleetwood 2013). However, this is unhelpful because it does not help us to understand the mechanisms and processes contributing to the manifestation of social phenomena (such as violence), and without such understanding, it is very difficult to identify appropriate means to address social problems (Harich 2010).

As with my general epistemic framework, my approach to causality can be seen as aligned with Critical Realism. This approach engages proactively with causality by striving to develop 'causal explanations' through uncovering and understanding the 'causal mechanisms' underlying social phenomena (Fleetwood 2013), thus making the 'suggest[ion of] practical policy recommendations to address social problems' (Fletcher 2016, p. 181) more viable. Unlike strong empiricist or idealist social science, Critical Realism sees the social world as an open system in which prediction is impossible, but explanation still possible (Fleetwood 2013). Although it is not straightforward to demonstrate causality in social phenomena, as Cohen et al. (2011) argue, 'there are regularities, there are likelihoods based on experience, there are similarities based on situations and people' (p. 60), and therefore while inferring causation can be 'complex and daunting' (ibid.), it may still be possible.

This perspective frames causality as complex, tendential, and, at times, probabilistic, rather than deterministic (ibid.). According to this view, the best causal explanations are those which engage with 'the most comprehensive theory (e.g. that [...] which embraces intentionality, agency, interaction as well as structure, i.e. micro- and macro-factors), that explain all the elements of a phenomenon, that fit the *explanandum* (that which is to be explained)' (Cohen et al. 2011, pp. 61–62). Rather than aiming to isolate decontextualised variables and identify statistical association based on correlation or event regularity, and rather than aiming to uncover 'regimes of truth' using discourse analysis alone (Fleetwood 2013), Critical Realism employs abductive and retroductive analysis in aiming to 'understand the emergent history of a phenomenon or whole' (Cohen et al. 2011, p. 71).

This 'emergent history' considers all dimensions of reality from the material to the discursive (Fletcher 2016) and can involve multiple and simultaneous causes and sub-causes, processes, effects and sub-effects, operating in causal chains, feedback loops, and holistic webs of connections involving interactions between agency, intentionality, and structural constraints (Morrison 2009; Cohen et al. 2011; Harich 2010). As Cohen et al. (2011) and Fletcher (2016) argue, elucidating these complex relations is where qualitative data can come into its own and hold pre-eminence over quantitative/statistical analysis. This is because understanding causal processes involves understanding 'how macro- structural features from society actually enter into individuals' actions and interactions and how individuals' actions and interactions determine social structures' (Cohen et al. 2011, p. 63). These processes are often opaque and need cautious elucidation—something that qualitative analysis tends to be better suited to because experimental methods 'tend to overlook the significance of context and conditions, of processes, of human intentionality, motives and agency' (ibid., p. 66).

As Pearl (2009) writes, it is also important to consider circumscription in research seeking causal explanations. This involves deciding how far back in time and how far out into the 'causal space (how many conditions and circumstances contribute to the causation at work [...])' to go (Cohen et al. 2011). The factors included or excluded can affect judgements of causality: casting the net too widely or narrowly can make it difficult to differentiate the wood from the trees (Pearl 2009). To address this issue I centred on the concept of 'root' causes. Harich (2010) differentiates between 'intermediate', 'apparent', 'interim', or 'pseudo root' causes and 'true root' causes. The former can be seen as sub-causes in a causal (not necessarily linear) chain, or as 'coincident occurrence[s] that, like the trouble symptom itself, [are] being produced by the feedback loop dynamics of a larger system' (Forrester 1971, p. 95), whereas a 'root cause' can be defined as 'a portion of a system's structure that "best" helps to explain why the system's behaviour produces a problem's symptoms' (Harich 2010, p. 57).

'Difficult problems', Harich (2010) explains, 'usually have multiple [...] causes' (p. 58) and 'asking why a phenomenon is the way it is, often leads to the identification of more fundamental causes further down the causal chain' (p. 57), highlighting that a phenomenon is actually a symptom or 'an intermediate, rather than a root, cause' (ibid.). Harich argues against stopping at intermediate causes, and instead for treating them as 'starting points for deeper analysis' (ibid.) in a process of asking a series of 'why is this happening?' (ibid., p. 58) questions until the root cause(s) are found.

But how can we know when we have arrived at a root cause? Harich (ibid.) proposes that a root cause has three identifying characteristics: firstly, it is clearly a (or the) major cause of the symptoms (e.g. manifestations of violence); secondly, it has no worthwhile deeper cause; and thirdly, it can be resolved. There may be deeper, unchangeable causes (in the model presented in this book, these are identified as emotions and to some degree motivations), and Harich (ibid.) states that it may be useful to emphasise these for greater understanding, and to determine the point at which intervention can effectively be targeted (i.e. at the level of the root cause, rather than at deeper, unchangeable, or higher, symptomatic levels). Guided by this formulation, this book identifies 'violent epistemology' as the root cause and 'non-conducive circumstances' as the causal conditions (Cohen et al. 2011) of violence in a case-study school.

Rejecting post-structuralism and adopting the above epistemic approach raises the question of epistemic justice (Fricker 2013; Anderson 2012).[5] Fricker (2013) defines epistemic injustice as when 'someone is wronged in their capacity as a knower' (p. 1317). This concept requires researchers to ask questions about the credibility afforded to research participants' knowledge, and about the balance of power between researchers and participants in terms of whose theoretical concepts are deployed (Anderson 2012). When assessing theoretical frameworks to support the process of analysis, I considered the ways in which teachers and students in the case-study school expressed their interpretations of the challenges they faced, and of the phenomenon of violence in the school, neighbourhood, and broader society. These ranged from rather traditionalist to strong Marxist perspectives among teachers, and among students ranged from beliefs that they needed to try harder and be more obedient and collegiate to frustrations with broader structural factors such as low staffing; parental poverty; violence in the neighbourhood; social inequality in São Paulo; and the government's perceived lack of interest in meeting their needs.

A key concept in relation to epistemic justice is that of recognising research participants as credible 'knowers' (Fricker 1999; Anderson 2012). This combines well with interpretivist research grounded in subjectivist epistemologies, in which the researcher's core focus is to understand the different ways in which participants perceive a phenomenon. However, the ontological and epistemic foundations of my Critical Realist approach (i.e. that 'there is a 'real' world and it is theory-laden, not theory-determined' (Fletcher 2016, p. 188)), and my desire to really understand the root causes of violence in schooling, not just how participants perceive this, have required me to balance the question of epistemic justice with the need to develop a comprehensive and coherent theoretical model (Nurjannah et al. 2014). No single theory or participant explanation could fully explain the multiple dimensions and complexities of the phenomenon of violence in schooling, let alone get at its root causes.

---

[5] See Chap. 3 for further discussion on epistemic justice.

Unlike interpretivist approaches, by assuming that a reality exists to which (sometimes competing) explanations refer, Critical Realism allows the researcher to make judgements about which explanations appear to better reflect that reality (Fletcher 2016). This 'may be seen as disempowering for participants' through the implication that the researcher 'knows best' (ibid., p. 188). However, because Critical Realism also treats all explanations of reality as fallible (Bhaskar 1979), 'including [those] provided by research participants, theorists and scientists' (Fletcher 2016, p. 188), participants' interpretations and explanations are carefully considered, and certainly not summarily dismissed. Rather, Fletcher (ibid.) argues that 'participants' experiences and explanations of a phenomenon may in fact prove most accurate', while Redman-MacLaren and Mills (2015) explain that in Critical Realist research, research participants' experiences and understandings can also challenge existing theory. This approach cannot therefore be seen as contrary to the ideals of epistemic justice, but it may not sit comfortably with strong idealists because it does allow the researcher to 'practice rational judgment, wherein [they] may need to elaborate upon (or deviate from) participants' own interpretations' (Fletcher 2016, p. 190) in order to provide 'fuller or more adequate interpretations of reality' (Parr 2013, p. 10).

This expresses how I have aimed to balance tensions between doing justice to participants' diverse and particular perspectives, with making coherent, broad, and holistic theoretical and interpretive assertions. On the one hand, I fully considered and integrated into my analysis, the experiences and interpretations expressed by teachers and students at DCX School. I also carefully considered locally constructed theoretical frameworks. However, I have also made judgements about which explanations and theoretical concepts appeared to most accurately reflect the reality (albeit a complex and multidimensional reality) expressed in the data, and allowed myself to elaborate on and deviate from participants' own interpretations in order to construct a comprehensive theoretical model.

2.2   A New Methodological Approach[6]

The primary data on which this book is based was collected during a period of immersive field research conducted in a case-study school between December 2010 and July 2011. The case-study, which will be

---

[6] A more detailed discussion on methods, methodology, and ethics in relation to this study can be found in Titchiner (2017).

referred to as DCX, is a Municipal School of Fundamental Education (EMEF) situated in a run-down neighbourhood in the centre of São Paulo, Brazil. The core participant group was comprised of 21 students participating in an Educommunication violence reduction project within the school, and the three teachers running the project. I spent several hours a day with this group, on five days a week, for the duration of the field work period. Other teachers and staff within the school, as well as the school director, also participated in the research on an occasional basis through attendance at discussion meetings and occasional interviews.

The core student participants were mostly fifth-year students aged between ten and twelve, but included a handful of older students aged thirteen to seventeen. Children self-selected to participate, with no selection criteria imposed other than a requirement for parental/guardian consent. Almost all student participants lived within walking distance of the school, and all came from low-income families (characteristic of the overall student population at DCX). Approximately 45% were housed in (often overcrowded and insalubrious) tenement accommodation. Like the rest of the student population, many of the children had experienced difficult family circumstances such as relationship breakdowns, disability, poverty, illness, incarceration, dislocation, or bereavement. A number of children were living with friends or extended family rather than with their parents, and many had one absent parent. Many were regularly left unsupervised for long periods while parents or carers were at work, and undertook significant responsibilities in the home such as cooking, cleaning, and caring for younger siblings.

The experience of the three core teacher participants ranged from six to twenty-five years of teaching, and all held either an undergraduate or master's degree. All lived outside of the local neighbourhood, commuting up to 1.5 hours each way to teach at DCX. All three also taught in at least one other state or municipal school.

The primary data collection method was participant observation. Ethnographic data collection methods were chosen because of their ability to provide 'in-depth description and understanding of the human experience' (Lichtman 2006), and a case-study approach because of its ability to provide 'powerful human-scale data on macro-political decision making' (Cohen et al. 2011, p. 291). Case-study methodology was also chosen because of its usefulness for answering 'how' and 'why' type questions and for generating theories about the behaviour of individuals, groups, organisations, communities, and societies (Yin 2009, pp. 27–35), because of its ability to capture unique features that might hold the key to understanding a situation (Nisbet and Watt 1984), and its ability to produce data that is 'strong in reality' (Adelman et al. 1980).

The benefit of a single case-study design was that immersing myself in, and concentrating my attention on, just one school and its surrounding context enabled me to 'intensively investigate the case in-depth, to probe, drill down and get at its complexity' (Ashley 2012, p. 102). While I did not set out to select an extreme case (Patton 1980), DCX can be seen as lying closer to the severe end of the spectrum due to its location within a neighbourhood marked by extreme degradation and social neglect. This meant that students came to school having experienced more difficult life events and circumstances than average. Rather than undermining the relevance of my findings to other contexts, I found this beneficial because it shed light on the potential extent of the impact of a wide variety of factors contributing to school violence, where a less extreme case would not have provided the same quantity and richness of relevant data. While there are some more extreme cases than DCX, and while DCX's location makes it more extreme than the average São Paulo municipal school, social inequality is pervasive in Brazil and thus there are numerous schools situated in similar locations of socio-spatial segregation. As such, many of the issues highlighted by this case can be considered relevant to other contexts.

For both ethical and methodological reasons, I was interested in a Chicago School-style naturalistic approach (Bogdan and Biklen 2007; Lichtman 2006) with its emphasis on understanding social phenomena by studying them in 'natural, uncontrived, real-world settings with as little intrusiveness as possible by the researcher' (Cohen et al. 2011, p. 220). For this reason, I chose participant observation as my core data collection method. As Marshall and Rossman (2006) attest, immersive participant observation can allow the researcher to learn directly from reflecting on their own experience and interactions in the field, and thus develop a deeper understanding of how participants perceive their world. This enabled me to gain a strong feeling (Agrosino 2012) for the day-to-day struggles and contradictions of life in São Paulo, the Baixada, and DCX School and, while still an 'outsider' in many respects, aided the approximation of an 'insider's perspective' to complement my 'outsider's overview' (ibid., p. 166).

In line with my naturalistic affinities I aimed to hang closer to the 'observer' end of the observer-participant spectrum (Cresswell 2014) and made a point of being non-directive (Bogdan and Biklen 2007) by following the lead of teachers and students. However, for ethical reasons I also aimed to be a helpful presence by supporting the teachers and students in their daily activities, and to balance my 'observer' role by participating just enough so that my presence would not feel unnatural. Rather than assuming a single role, I shifted roles depending on what felt appropriate, ethical, and useful for my research in each situation. Sometimes I assisted students with their work, and sometimes I took part as if I were a student. At other times, I accompanied activities as a friendly presence without taking on any particular role.

All data was collected in Portuguese and later translated by myself. Data consisted largely of observational notes focussing on activities, conversations, interactions between teachers and students, appearance and behaviour of teachers and students, the environment, my own thoughts and feelings, and anything else that stood out to me (Bogdan and Biklen 2007). Notes were not written in front of teachers or students so as not to interrupt our interactions and rapport. For conversation-rich activities, such as meetings and discussion groups, audio recordings were taken and later transcribed. I conducted a small number of interviews with people whose view I considered relevant to the research but with whom I did not interact often, such as the school director. I also employed the ethnographic method of keeping a field diary, in which I recorded and from which I generated some 'thick descriptions' (Geertz 1973) of my experiences in the wider metropolis, the school, and its surrounding neighbourhood.

While ethnographic methods have made a valuable contribution to this research, the work is broader and rather different in scope than a traditional ethnography. Aside from the fact that my analysis has been influenced by other approaches (viz. critical theory, Critical Realism, phenomenology, and Grounded Theory), unlike many ethnographies (Cohen et al. 2011), my intention was not to study the culture of a specific context but rather to investigate a particular phenomenon (violence) which involved an openness to allowing anything relevant to understanding the phenomenon to be considered. This meant making use of what ethnographic case-studies afford through their ability to capture the particularities of a specific context in detail (Dobbert and Kurth-Schai 1992), but also broadening my focus to allow more explicit consideration of 'regularities, order and pattern within such diversity' (ibid., p. 150) that extend beyond issues of 'culture' and the specificity of the particular case.

Ethnography and naturalistic enquiry are often conflated because the former is by nature naturalistic and the latter utilises ethnographic data collection methods (Cohen et al. 2011). However, while ethnographers tend to emphasise the production of descriptive cultural knowledge of a specific group (Hitchcock and Hughes 1989), naturalistic enquiry tends to emphasise investigating the characteristics, causes, and consequences of a specific phenomenon in its real life context (Lofland 1971; Arsenault and Anderson 1998). In this sense, the case-study presented in this book can be seen to operate more as an example of naturalistic enquiry than ethnography. On the other hand, naturalistic enquiry has been criticised for failing to engage adequately with social theory (Norris and Walker 2005). I have broken away from this by looking far beyond the immediate context of the case-study to the broader municipal, national, and global contexts and by engaging in depth with both historical analysis and theory (including social theory) from a wide range of disciplines. Rather than being a narrowly defined ethnography of a particular context, the DCX case-study both aided the development of a theoretical model for understanding violence as a global phenomenon and served to illustrate how this model can broaden our understanding of violence in specific contexts.

Data analysis combined methods from ethnography and Grounded Theory. This began with taking a break to gain some emotional distance from the data (Bogdan and Biklen 2007), followed by a re-familiarisation with the data during which memos were written on initial themes. This was followed by a period of wide reading in order to increase theoretical sensitivity. Glaser (1998) argues that by studying many themes across different disciplines, researchers may identify numerous theoretical codes embedded in these theories, and thus enhance their own knowledge base of theoretical codes. With this in mind, I read widely in sociology, psychology, neuroscience, history, learning theory, education, and philosophy. Working part-time supporting young people in situations of risk during data analysis also helped to increase my theoretical sensitivity by offering insight into issues such as vicarious traumatisation, burnout, organisational change, and the interrelationships between precarious housing, poverty, mental health, and violence.

I took an abductive approach to relating theory to data, following what Thornberg (2012b) and Douven (2011) describe as a selective and creative process in which the researcher carefully investigates which hypothesis explains a particular segment or set of data better than any other hypothesis. As Thornberg (2012a) advocates, I treated pre-existing theories and concepts as provisional, disputable, and modifiable conceptual proposals. Following the advice of Strauss and Corbin (1990, p. 23), I did not 'begin with theory, and then prove it', but rather began with an area of study (the root causes of violence), allowing what was relevant to that area to emerge. I found, as Kelle (1995) argues, that the ability to draw good abductive inferences was dependent on my previous knowledge (theoretical sensitivity), rejection of dogmatic beliefs, and the development of open-mindedness (through my dialectical approach to 'bracketing').

Transcribed audio recordings were collated with observational notes in chronological order. Various cycles of coding and analysis were then conducted by hand in order 'to be close to the data and have a hands on feel for it' (Cresswell 2014, p. 264). Beginning with the question 'what are the root causes of violence in the DCX School?' I read through the raw (Portuguese) data to identify regularities, patterns, and topics, then assigned words or phrases to these which became my initial codes (Bogdan and Biklen 2007, p. 173). I specifically looked in the data for indicators of manifestations of violence in any form, and potential factors contributing to such manifestations. Initial codes were then arranged into themes (such as 'student experience brought from outside of school') and each code given an abbreviation and colour (Cresswell 2014). I then read through the data again, marking relevant sections with the appropriate code abbreviation and colour, and adding any new codes that arose. All coded data was then translated into English and reorganised by theme and sub-code. The data was then read again, new sub-codes added, and reorganised again according to the now complete list of themes, codes, and sub-codes (see Titchiner (2017) for full list). While I did not follow the Grounded Theory open, axial, and selective coding phases as distinct processes, I integrated aspects of these into the overall analytical process, and used techniques such as memos and diagrams to aid analysis (Thornberg 2012a).

Aside from a substantial list of themes, sub-themes, and codes, these initial rounds of coding also revealed indications of feedback loops (Forrester 1971) (e.g. 'vicious cycle of low staffing') and a wide range of potentially causal relations between different factors (e.g. 'low self-esteem linked to low literacy'; 'exhaustion results in lower quality engagement with students'; and 'pressure on teachers to be in control results in aggressive and controlling behaviour by teachers'). When taken together these indications, combined with the many identified manifestations of violence and numerous causal/contributing factors that emerged from the coding process, represented a broad 'network' (Cohen et al. 2011) of causal factors and relations. However, a clear picture regarding exactly how these many factors related to each other was not evident at this stage, and while many intermediate causal factors were apparent, there was no clear differentiation between 'intermediate' and 'root' causes, or between causal and merely contributory factors (Harich 2010).

The next stage, therefore, was to develop a clearer picture of this network of causal relations and to differentiate between intermediate and root causes. To achieve this I began with the manifestations of violence in DCX identified during the coding process, and taking each, followed Harich's (2010) process of asking a series of 'why is this happening?' (p. 58) questions, again looking to the data and coding results to formulate answers. Each 'Why?' question often resulted in more than one answer, reflecting Harich's (2010) assertion that 'difficult problems usually have multiple [...] causes' (p. 58). Answers that arose during this questioning process were treated as intermediate causes, and as 'starting points for deeper analysis' (ibid., p. 57). Taking each answer, I then asked 'and why is *this* happening?' This questioning cycle was repeated multiple times, resulting in the delineation of various causal chains such as that illustrated in Fig. 2.1.

While not uniformly the case, there was a tendency that with each cycle of questioning the analysis was drawn further out into the causal 'space' (Cohen et al. 2011) to incorporate local, national, and global factors.

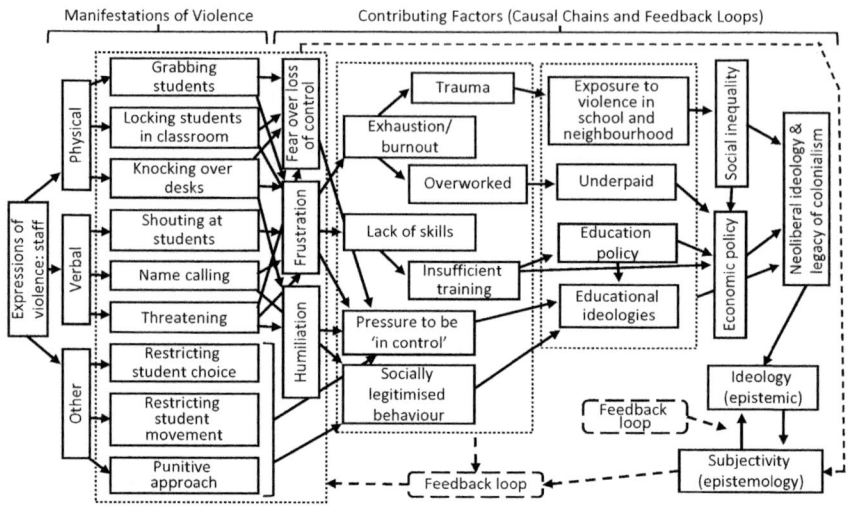

Fig. 2.1 Example of causal chain analysis

Since the data was strongly concentrated on DCX School itself, to some degree the local neighbourhood, and to an even lesser degree the city of São Paulo, there was a need to supplement primary data with reading from historical, contextual, and theoretical literature in order to formulate answers as the questioning cycles continued. At this stage Bronfenbrenner's (1944, 1979, 2005) bioecological model of human development became useful as a means to structure the spatial and contextual aspects of the analysis (see Chap. 5). After beginning with the manifestations of violence that largely occurred at the level of individuals, the cycle of questioning drew analysis all the way out to the scale of global issues such as neoliberal economic ideology. At this point, asking 'and why is *this* happening?' led quickly to ideology as both a collectively affirmed phenomenon and a phenomenon of individual thought. This in turn resulted in the scale of the causal chain collapsing right back down to the level of the individual (since, as discussed in Chap. 4, ideology is born from the subjectivity of individuals). At this stage, a feedback loop could be drawn from 'subjectivity' (at one end of the causal chain) to the violent behaviour at the other, which had constituted the starting point for enquiry.

However, it was not sufficient to conclude at this stage that 'ideological subjectivity' was the root cause of violence in the case-study school. As the data illustrated, a variety of different ideological schema were at play, resulting in a range of different effects at different contextual levels. Aside from this, teachers and students did not share any overarching ideology (nor did they engage in significant ideological conflict), and often violent or aggressive behaviour was motivated by frustration, exhaustion, anxiety, humiliation, or practical and material factors, rather than by explicitly ideological thinking. This meant that the dimension of 'subjectivity' needed to be investigated further in order to understand its relationship to ideology, contextual factors, and the motivations and emotions that often appeared to fuel teachers' and students' violent/aggressive behaviour.

To achieve this I drew on the Grounded Theory concept of 'axial coding' using the 'paradigm model', described by Waring (2012) as the relating of sub-categories to categories which entails the 'identification of the causal conditions associated with the occurrence or development of a phenomenon; the specification of a category for the phenomenon; the specific set of properties that pertain to a phenomenon; the structural conditions bearing in action/interaction strategies that pertain to the phenomenon; action/interaction strategies devised to manage/respond to a phenomenon under certain circumstances; and the consequences of action and interaction' (p. 303). As Waring (ibid.) states, this process requires complex abductive thinking.

Having used the above-described process to identify the causal factors associated with the occurrence and development of different types of violence in DCX, these causal chains were sub-divided into categories such as 'situation' (the immediate situation or context in which the violent or aggressive behaviour took place); 'circumstances' (broader contributory circumstances in the fostering of such behaviour); and 'emotions and motivations' (the emotions and motivations fuelling such behaviour). Codes categorised under 'situation' and 'circumstances' (both treated as Waring's (2012) 'structural conditions') were then investigated in more depth, to better understand the roots, history, and particularities of each factor. This involved both collating and examining evidence from the data and also wider reading to fill gaps not fully covered by the data itself (e.g. the history and causal factors in the degradation of the local neighbourhood; and the history of public education in Brazil and São Paulo).

The third category, 'emotions and motivations', was then taken along with 'subjectivity', and examined from the perspective of aiming to delineate how the structural conditions (situations and circumstances) described above bore on the action and interaction strategies that resulted in teachers and students enacting violent or aggressive behaviour,[7] and the action and interaction strategies devised by teachers and students to respond to violence in the different circumstances and situations that were evidenced in the data. This resulted in the identification of two core themes: the mediation of subjectivity in interaction with specific situations and circumstances; and the mediation of subjectivity in interaction with ideology. I then returned to the literature, reading in philosophy, psychology, neuroscience, learning theory, sociology, and critical social theory to better understand the emotional, motivational, and cognitive processes underpinning teachers' and students' enactment of violence (whether explicit or implicit).

Theoretical constructs were then selected, adapted, and combined based on how well they were able to explain the teachers' and students' emotions, motivations, behaviours, and experiences, as demonstrated by the data. This involved a normative process of employing constructs to best fit the data, not of squeezing data into theories that did not accurately or

---

[7] Remembering that I was working with a broad definition of violence that included both implicit and explicit forms of violence.

adequately reflect the phenomenon at hand. Through this process, particular common themes became evident. Under the category of motivations, the themes of self-preservation and self-actualisation emerged. Under the category of emotions, fear, shame, anger, and desperation were common. Under the cognition dimension of subjectivity, certain thinking patterns became evident that were also highlighted by a number of authors in a range of fields with concepts such as 'type α behaviour' (Piaget 1977); 'non-learning' (Jarvis 2009); 'identity thinking' (Adorno 1973); 'everyday consciousness' (Leithäuser 1976); and 'Stage One' (Rogers 1961). It became evident that these thinking patterns were not only discernible in individual teachers' and students' responses to specific situations, but were also analogous to the ways in which some authors conceptualised the cognitive structure of ideological thought. This led me to consider the possibility of a single underlying structure of thought, a particular epistemic practice, which might underpin both ideology and the mediation of teacher and student subjectivity that resulted in the many different manifestations of violence evidenced in the data. This led me to formulate the concept of 'violent epistemology'.

Further exploration of the mediation of teacher and student subjectivity with ideology revealed that while violent behaviour was often directly influenced by ideological thought (e.g. the subscription (even momentarily) to collectively affirmed ideology, especially (in this case) educational ideology), this was not always the case. Often teachers would behave violently even though they were making a conscious effort to try not to subscribe to traditional educational ideology, and both teachers and students would often behave violently out of sheer desperation, frustration, or exhaustion. In these situations, teacher and student subjectivity could be seen as mediated not only by ideology, but also often by situations and circumstances which pushed them to their emotional and psychological limits. As the causal chain analysis highlighted, the circumstances themselves were often shaped by ideology even if the individuals within did not prescribe to that ideology. This led me to formulate the concept of 'non-conducive circumstances'—circumstances that are often shaped by ideology, and not conducive to the enactment of non-violent epistemology.

Finally, I examined the consequences (Waring 2012) of both non-conducive circumstances and the epistemically violent action and interaction strategies enacted by teachers and students. This entailed identifying a range of additional feedback loops within the data (such as the vicious cycle of teacher absenteeism, classroom violence, and its impact on student learning and teachers' physical and mental health), and also examining how both enacting violent epistemology and being exposed to violence and non-conducive circumstances could impact on subject development. This resulted in the formulation of the concept of 'learnt violent episte-mology' (e.g. evidenced in the data by students mimicking teachers' and parents' violent or prejudicial behaviour and language), and the integra-tion of the concepts of 'thwarted self-actualisation' and the 'de-formation of subjectivity' into the overall analysis.

In Grounded Theory, the axial coding phase is followed by 'selective coding', which involves 'the selection of a core category and systematically relating it to other categories' (ibid.). Glaser (2010) states that the core category should be a concept related to a behaviour that applies in not only one context or situation. In line with this, 'violent epistemology' was selected as the core category, because of how it could be seen as implicated (either directly or indirectly) in the numerous manifestations and types of violence evidenced in the data. This core category was then examined against each element within the causal chains (and the associated data), to confirm and refine the overall theoretical model of violence presented in Chaps. 3 and 4. This process confirmed that the concept of 'violent epis-temology' did indeed operate as a core category (Glaser 2010), but also reaffirmed the central importance of the concept of 'non-conducive cir-cumstances' in understanding violence within its context. Finally, return-ing to Harich's (2010) concept of 'root cause', I found that the core concept of 'violent epistemology' also operated as a root cause according to this definition.

REFERENCES

Adelman, C., Kemmis, S., & Jenkins, D. (1980). Rethinking Case Study: Notes from the Second Cambridge Conference. In H. Simons (Ed.), *Towards a Science of the Singular* (pp. 45–61). Norwich: University of East Anglia.

Adorno, T. W. (1973). *Negative Dialectics*. London: Routledge.

Agrosino, M. V. (2012). Observation-Based Research. In J. Arthur, M. Waring, R. Coe, & L. V. Hedges (Eds.), *Research Methods and Methodologies in Education* (pp. 165–169). London: Sage.

Anderson, E. (2012). Epistemic Justice as a Virtue of Social Institutions. *Social Epistemology, 26*(2), 163–173.

Arsenault, N., & Anderson, G. (1998). *Fundamentals of Educational Research*. London: Taylor & Francis.

Ashley, L. D. (2012). Case Study Research. In J. Arthur, M. Waring, R. Coe, & L. V. Hedges (Eds.), *Research Methods and Methodologies in Education* (pp. 102–107). London: Sage.

Bhaskar, R. (1979). *The Possibility of Naturalism: A Philosophical Critique of the Contemporary Human Sciences.* Atlantic Highlands: Humanities Press.

Bogdan, R. C., & Biklen, S. K. (2007). *Qualitative Research for Education: An Introduction to Theories and Methods* (5th ed.). London: Pearson.

Bronfenbrenner, U. (1944). A Constant Frame of Reference for Sociometric Research: Part II. Experiment and Interference. *Sociometry, 7,* 40–75.

Bronfenbrenner, U. (1979). *The Ecology of Human Development: Experiments in Nature and Design.* London: Harvard University Press.

Bronfenbrenner, U. (2005). *Making Human Beings Human: Bioecological Perspectives on Human Development.* London: Sage.

Bryant, A., & Charmaz, K. (2007). *The Sage Handbook of Grounded Theory.* London: Sage.

Clough, P., & Nutbrown, C. (2012). *A Student's Guide to Methodology* (3rd ed.). London: Sage.

Cohen, L., Manion, L., & Morrison, K. (2011). *Research Methods in Education.* London: Routledge.

Cook, D. (2005). From the Actual to the Possible: Nonidentity Thinking. *Constellations, 12*(1), 21–35.

Cresswell, J. W. (2014). *Educational Research: Planning, Conducting and Evaluating Quantitative and Qualitative Research.* London: Pearson.

Cruickshank, J. (2003). *Realism and Sociology: Anti-Foundationalism, Ontology and Social Research.* London: Routledge.

Dobbert, M. L., & Kurth-Schai, R. (1992). Systematic Ethnography: Toward an Evolutionary Science of Education and Culture. In M. LeCompte, W. L. Millroy, & J. Preissle (Eds.), *The Handbook of Qualitative Research in Education* (pp. 93–160). London: Academic Press.

Douven, I. (2011). *Abduction.* Retrieved June 17, 2016, from http://plato.stanford.edu/entries/abduction/.

Edkins, J. (2002). Forget Trauma? Responses to September 11. *International Relations, 16*(2), 243–256.

Edkins, J. (2003). *Trauma and the Memory of Politics.* Cambridge: Cambridge University Press.

Fleetwood, S. (2013, September 20). *What Is (and What Isn't) Critical Realism?* [Research Seminar]. Centre for Employment Studies, University of West England.

Fletcher, A. J. (2016). Applying Critical Realism in Qualitative Research: Methodology Meets Method. *International Journal of Social Research Methodology, 20*(2), 181–194.

Forrester, J. (1971). *World Dynamics.* Cambridge: Wright-Allen Press.

Fricker, M. (1999). Epistemic Oppression and Epistemic Privilege. *Canadian Journal of Philosophy, 29*(sup1), 191–210.

Fricker, M. (2013). Epistemic Justice as a Condition of Political Freedom? *Synthese, 190*(7), 1317–1332.

Geertz, C. (1973). *The Interpretation of Cultures.* New York: Basic Books.

Glaser, B. (1998). *Doing Grounded Theory: Issues and Discussions.* Mill Valley: Sociology Press.

Glaser, B. (2010). *Grounded Theory Is the Study of a Concept.* [Video Lecture]. Retrieved June 17, 2016, from http://www.youtube.com/watch?v=OcpxaLQDnLk.

Hammer, R., & McLaren, P. (1991). Rethinking the Dialectic: A Social Semiotic Perspective for Educators. *Educational Theory, 41*(1), 23–46.

Harich, J. (2010). Change Resistance as the Crux of the Environmental Sustainability Problem. *System Dynamics Review, 26*(1), 35–72.

Hitchcock, G., & Hughes, D. (1989). *Research and the Teacher.* London: Routledge.

Horkheimer, M., & Adorno, T. W. (2002). *Dialectic of Enlightenment.* Stanford: Stanford University Press.

Hutchinson, S. A. (1988). Education and Grounded Theory. In R. R. Sherman & R. B. Webb (Eds.), *Qualitative Research in Education: Focus and Methods* (pp. 123–140). London: RoutledgeFalmer.

Jarvis, P. (2009). Learning to Be a Person in Society: Learning to Be Me. In K. Illeris (Ed.), *Contemporary Theories of Learning: Learning Theorists… In Their Own Words* (pp. 21–23). London: Routledge.

Kelle, U. (1995). Theories as Heuristic Tools in Qualitative Research. In I. Maso, P. A. Atkinson, S. Delamot, & J. C. Verhoeven (Eds.), *Openness in Research: The Tension Between Self and Other* (pp. 33–50). Assen: Van Gorcum.

Kurki, M. (2008). *Causation in International Relations: Reclaiming Causal Analysis.* Cambridge: Cambridge University Press.

Leithäuser, T. (1976). *Formen des Alltagsbewusstseins.* Frankfurt: Campus.

Lichtman, M. (2006). *Qualitative Research in Education: A User's Guide.* London: Sage.

Lofland, J. (1971). *Analyzing Social Settings.* Belmont: Wadsworth.

Marshall, C., & Rossman, G. B. (2006). *Designing Qualitative Research.* Newbury Park: Sage.

Maxwell, J. A. (2012). *A Realist Approach for Qualitative Research.* Thousand Oaks: Sage.

Mclaren, P. L. (1995). Collisions with Otherness: "Travelling" Theory, Postcolonial Criticism, and the Politics of Ethnographic Practice – The Mission of the Wounded Ethnographer. In P. L. McLaren & J. M. Giarelli (Eds.), *Critical Theory and Educational Research* (pp. 271–300). New York: SUNY Press.

Merleau-Ponty, M. (1964). *The Primacy of Perception.* Evanston: Northwestern University Press.

Merleau-Ponty, M. (2012). *Phenomenology of Perception.* New York: Routledge.

Moghaddam, A. (2006). Coding Issues in Grounded Theory. *Issues in Educational Research, 16*(1), 52–66.

Morrison, K. R. B. (2009). *Causation in Educational Research*. London: Routledge.

Nisbet, J., & Watt, J. (1984). Case Study. In J. Bell, T. Bush, A. Fox, J. Goodey, & S. Goulding (Eds.), *Conducting Small-Scale Investigations in Educational Management* (pp. 79–92). London: Harper and Row.

Norris, N., & Walker, R. (2005). Naturalistic Enquiry. In B. Somekh & C. Lewin (Eds.), *Research Methods in the Social Sciences* (pp. 131–137). London: Sage.

Nurjannah, I., Mills, J., Park, T., & Usher, K. (2014). Conducting a Grounded Theory Study in a Language Other Than English. *SAGE Open, 4*(1), 1–10.

Parr, S. (2013). Integrating Critical Realist and Feminist Methodologies: Ethical and Analytical Dilemmas. *International Journal of Social Research Methodology, 18*, 193–207.

Patton, M. Q. (1980). *Qualitative Evaluation and Research Methods*. Beverley Hills, CA: Sage.

Pearl, L. (2009). *Causality*. New York: Cambridge University Press.

Piaget, J. (1977). *The Development of Thought: Equilibration of Cognitive Structures*. New York: Viking Press.

Redman-MacLaren, M., & Mills, J. (2015). Transformational Grounded Theory: Theory, Voice, and Action. *International Journal of Qualitative Methods, 14*(3), 1–12.

Rockmore, T. (2004). *On Foundationalism: A Strategy for Metaphysical Realism*. New York: Rowman and Littlefield.

Rogers, C. R. (1961). *On Becoming a Person*. London: Constable.

Sartre, J. P. (1956). *Being and Nothingness: An Essay in Phenomenological Ontology*. New York: Washington Square Press.

Schick, K. (2009). To Lend a Voice To Suffering Is a Condition For All Truth: Adorno and International Political Thought. *Journal of International Political Theory, 5*(2), 138–160.

Sherman, D. (2007). *Sartre and Adorno: The Dialectics of Subjectivity*. Albany: SUNY Press.

Smith, R. C. (2011). *Consciousness and Revolt: An Exploration Toward Reconciliation*. Holt: Heathwood Press.

Strauss, A., & Corbin, J. (1990). *Basics of Qualitative Research*. Newbury Park: Sage.

Thornberg, R. (2012a). Grounded Theory. In J. Arthur, M. Waring, R. Coe, & L. V. Hedges (Eds.), *Research Methods and Methodologies in Education* (pp. 85–93). London: Sage.

Thornberg, R. (2012b). Informed Grounded Theory. *Scandinavian Journal of Educational Research, 56*(3), 243–259.

Titchiner, B. M. (2017). *The Epistemology of Violence: Understanding the Root Causes of Violence and Non-conducive Social Circumstances in Schooling, with a Case-Study from Brazil.* Digital Thesis. University of East Anglia. Retrieved from https://ueaeprints.uea.ac.uk/63644/.

Waring, M. (2012). Grounded Theory. In J. Arthur, M. Waring, R. Coe, & L. V. Hedges (Eds.), *Research Methods and Methodologies in Education* (pp. 297–308). London: Sage.

White, C. (2006). *Agents, Structures and International Relations: Politics as Ontology.* Cambridge: Cambridge University Press.

Wider, K. (1997). *The Bodily Nature of Consciousness: Sartre and Contemporary Philosophy of Mind.* Ithaca: Cornell University Press.

Yin, R. K. (2009). *Case Study Research: Design and Methods.* Beverley Hills, CA: Sage.

Zizek, S. (2002a). *For They Know Not What They Do: Enjoyment as Political Factor.* London: Verso.

Zizek, S. (2002b). *Welcome to the Desert of the Real! Five Essays on September 11 and Related Dates.* London: Verso.

CHAPTER 3

Conceptualising Violence as a Problem of Epistemology

3.1   Beginning with Epistemology

As discussed in Chap. 1, violence has been defined and conceptualised in many ways—and often such definitions are limited to categorising the ways in which violence manifests, without reaching further to understand its root causes. This book aims to develop an understanding of the root causes of violence underlying and encompassing the multiple and diverse ways in which it manifests. As explained in Chap. 2, this involves getting to the 'heart' of things—looking for patterns or phenomena that can be found underlying all of the many different forms of manifest violence. On the basis of my analysis (as described in Chap. 2), my proposal in this book is that the best place to begin in aiming to understand violence is the locus of human agency in relating with the phenomenal world, ourselves, and others. As I will explain in this chapter, the locus of this agency can be found in our 'phenomenological freedom', and the specific ways in which we orientate ourselves towards our experiences—in other words, our epistemic behaviour.

When hearing the words 'epistemology' and 'violence' together, many will think of the term 'epistemic violence' (often also termed 'epistemic injustice') (Fricker 1998, 1999). The term 'epistemic violence' is common in post-colonial discourse, and refers to the legitimisation and imposition of one person or group's knowledge and way of knowing over and above that of another. The most obvious example of this is the imposition of the epistemology of the coloniser over that of the colonised (Foucault 1980;

© The Author(s) 2019
B. M. Titchiner, *The Epistemology of Violence*, Critical Political Theory and Radical Practice, https://doi.org/10.1007/978-3-030-12911-8_3

Spivak 1988). Similarly, the term 'epistemic injustice' 'concerns the process of credibility conferral upon knowledge claimants' (McConkey 2004, p. 198). According to McConkey, the contention of the latter term is that 'individuals belonging to marginalised or underprivileged groups may suffer from a lack of credibility when they deserve to be counted as credible knowers' (ibid.). Along these same lines, Young (2001) describes the experience of epistemic injustice as when 'dominant meanings of a society render the particular perspective of one's own group invisible at the same time as they stereotype one's group and mark it out as Other' (pp. 58–59).

Many concepts of violence (and violence-reduction interventions designed on the basis of these concepts) do not consider epistemology at all. Some, such as those based on Freire's (1973) critique of 'banking' style education, can be seen as aiming to address epistemic injustice or epistemic violence, through their aims to address 'symbolic violence'. Considered in this way, we can argue that the Educommunication project in the case-study school aimed to address epistemic violence, by increasing space for students to express their own perspectives, experiences, and interpretations of the world through participatory media production. However, discourse about epistemic violence and epistemic injustice tends to be rather relativistic, and does not consider the extent to which different epistemologies may be more or less violent *in themselves*. Also, when discussion remains at the level of whose knowledge or way of knowing is afforded more status or credibility, questions about what violence is, where it comes from, how it manifests in schools, and why it manifests are overlooked. Even though interventions such as Educommunication are considered to be innovative in their breaking away from traditional disciplinary approaches, by perceiving overt student violence as simply a response to implicit epistemic violence carried out by the teacher and the institution, the focus on whose voice is afforded more space and credibility blinds us to these questions, and also to the possibility of answering them.

While the concepts of epistemic violence, epistemic injustice, and symbolic violence are all useful for highlighting specific phenomena which are often the result of unequal power relations, and which foster and perpetuate oppression, these concepts alone are not sufficient to understand the root causes of violence, or to fully understand the complex relationships between violence and epistemology. This book presents instead the concept of 'violent epistemology', which I propose to be much broader in scope and capable of encompassing the diverse and multiple ways in which violence manifests. This is to be seen as distinct from 'epistemic violence', although the latter can be considered to be one (particularly insidious) manifestation of the former. Violent epistemology is presented as a specific type of epistemic behaviour, possessing very specific structures and patterns, and producing specific types of concepts about ourselves, others, and the phenomenal world, upon which violent action is often predicated. This is very different from the relativistic concept of 'epistemic violence'. In this chapter, I will outline this proposed concept of violent epistemology in detail.

3.2   The Historical Problem of Violent Epistemology: A Matter of Agency

It is common to hear advocates of traditional (authoritarian/disciplinary) schooling hark back to a 'golden age' in which the problems faced in schools today (violence, chaotic relations, disengagement) did not exist because students were kept firmly under control and 'respected authority' (Lowe 2007; Schostak 1986). This view can be traced back to views of human nature such as that of Hobbes (1996), who saw people as inherently prone to violence unless kept under control by the rule of a higher power, and religious beliefs that children are born in original sin and need to be 'civilised' through strict education (Francesco 1976). In so-called radical and alternative education spheres, another phenomenon is the formation of a rather romanticised ideal that looks to 'primitive' societies with envy, and views the educational practices of indigenous communities as free from the violence and corruption of the modern world (Eisler and Miller 2004). This view, in which primitivism is seen to bring with it peace, equality, and harmony with nature, can be traced back to Rousseau's notion of the 'noble savage' where he writes 'nothing is more peaceable than man in his primitive state' (Rousseau 1984, p. 115).

However, evidence suggests that neither view of human nature is correct. While violence is recognised as a problem in contemporary 'civilised' societies (Elliott et al. 1998; Hoffman 1996), archaeological and historical records show us that violence has been present throughout human history (Ralph 2013; Flannery and Marcus 2012; Wu et al. 2011), and that the so-called primitive communities so idealised by Rousseau were, and are, not immune to violence. Studies of human consciousness (Trevarthen and Reddy 2007; Trevarthen 1998, 2004) also debunk the notion that humans are inherently violent, by showing that we have conscious agency and an ability to choose how we think about and respond to our experiences of the world, ourselves, and each other. This suggests that interventions based on the concept of human agency and the ability to choose violent or non-violent responses are more likely to be effective than those based on concepts of educating individuals out of original sin/disciplining an inherently violent being into 'civility', or of nurturing/allowing the inherently peaceable nature of the individual to emerge. This goes against the ideas of both traditionalists and liberal 'alternative' education supporters (such as democratic education, peace education, and critical pedagogy).

Considering a conceptual foundation based on conscious agency requires a closer examination of epistemology. Epistemology is formally defined as 'the theory of knowledge, especially with regard to its methods, validity, and scope, and the distinction between justified belief and opinion' (Oxford English Dictionary 2014). The term is also used in reference to 'personal epistemology', meaning 'the beliefs we hold about knowledge and knowing' (Hofer 2002), and 'epistemic cognition', meaning individual reflection on 'the limits of knowing, the certainty of knowing, and criteria of knowing' (Kitchner 1983). All of the above definitions frame epistemology and epistemic thought as explicit thinking *about* the nature of knowledge and knowing. This view, which is common to cognitive science and contemporary psychology, presents epistemic thought as something that operates outside the domain of situated cognition, and only within cognition *about* cognition (Shanon 2002; Praetorius 2000).

Hofer (2002), however, presents an understanding of epistemology as integral to daily acts of thought—cognitive processes that we employ to define 'truth' for ourselves. Similarly, Shanon (2002) and Praetorius (2000) propose that epistemology is not only present in explicit reflective thought *about* the limits, criteria, and certainty of knowing, but that it is integral to *all* cognition. As Kant (1953), Heidegger (1962), and Merleau-Ponty (2012) affirm, cognition is grounded in 'the interface between organism and the world' (Shanon 2002), and it is via this interface (via the mediation between subject and object as Adorno (1973) and Sherman (2007) would say) that we experience conscious awareness of, and create what we believe to be knowledge about phenomena. In other words, as Shanon (2002) concludes, 'ipso facto cognition involves epistemology'.

In this book I use the terms 'epistemology' and 'epistemic cognition' to refer not only to explicit thinking about the limits of knowing, certainty of knowing, and criteria of knowing (Kitchner 1983), but also to refer to the experiential and cognitive processes through which we engage and relate with the phenomenal world, and to how we create what we believe to be 'knowledge' or 'truth' via these processes.

3.3   THE HUMAN CAPACITY FOR VIOLENCE: THE EPISTEMIC RELATIONSHIP BETWEEN CONSCIOUSNESS AND PHENOMENA

Returning to the argument that humans are neither inherently violent nor non-violent, but that the capacity for violence lies in our agency, we can consider Smith's (2011) assertion that certain 'fundamental epistemic conditions' (p. 24) lie at the roots of violence and violent regimes. These conditions, he argued, relate to the 'epistemic relation' between human consciousness and the phenomenal world (including other people and organisms). If this assertion is correct, then it follows that an examination of this relation could help us to better understand the root causes of violence.

The relation between human consciousness and the phenomenal world is one that philosophers have argued over for centuries, as it entails discussion about the nature of consciousness itself, the nature of the phenomenal world, and to what extent human consciousness can 'know' that world (Velmans and Schneider 2007). For centuries, as Trevarthen and Reddy (2007) write, 'the nature of consciousness defined in subtle ways has frustrated the understanding of philosophers' (p. 54). These authors suggest that this difficulty has been due to two related habits of thought which are deeply embedded in our language and meta-theoretical assumptions. These are, firstly, thinking of organisms as separate from the environment in which they exist, and secondly, assuming a categorical division between the intentional/mental and the physical/behavioural. This latter distinction can be traced back to the influential Cartesian strain of philosophy grounded in mind-body dualism, and subsequent representationist and behaviourist theories which present an individualistic view of consciousness (ibid.).

However, various authors including James (1918), Vygotsky (1978), and Dewey (1997) have pointed out problems with this dualistic way of thinking. Namely, that it leads us to believe that consciousness can live as thoughts, locked away inside the brains of each organism, rather than in dynamic interrelation with the physical and social world. Contrary to the traditional Cartesian dualism, Thompson (2001) proposes that 'human consciousness is formed in the dynamic interrelation of self and other, and therefore is inherently intersubjective' (p. 1). However, it is important to remember that 'other' does not simply mean 'other humans' and that 'intersubjective' does not purely mean 'knowledge formed in intersubjective relation with other humans', as this negates the role of interoception and other non-human phenomena as reference points for the formation of concepts (as explained below). Another problem created by the age-old mind/body dualism is the view that consciousness exists as separate from the body. More recent authors such as Wider (1997) and Searle (2007) have contested this theory, arguing that consciousness is grounded in the physiological and neurological operations of the body. In this book, I adopt these latter views—that is, consciousness is intersubjective and embodied.

Let us look at the intersubjective and bodily nature of consciousness in more detail. Firstly, we can discern the existence of a phenomenal and social world in which we (as conscious beings) are situated, acting within and on that world. Considering the phenomenal world, we can discern that it is incredibly diverse, complex, and ever-changing. Bauman (2000) uses the metaphor of liquid. This is reinforced by contemporary physics which at its present level of understanding tells us that matter and energy are in constant flux and that even apparently static objects change over time (Taube 2012). Our everyday experiences also confirm this: the changing seasons, plants growing and dying, people growing and changing, and the simple fact that the same water never passes under the same bridge twice (Jarvis 2009). Kierkegaard (1989) also argued that 'existence is continually in the process of becoming' (p. 82). For him, our essential existential position in the world is that there is no resting place, and no end point.

Existing and acting within this ever-changing phenomenal world, we find ourselves. Psychologists and neuroscientists now commonly accept that our consciousness operates *intentionally* (Graham et al. 2007; Siewert 2003; Chalmers 2004), meaning that it is always directed towards something, and it is always conscious *of* some thing or things as they present themselves to our awareness, whether these be phenomena external to our body (such as a landscape) or internal to our body (such as bodily sensations, emotions, and imaginings). While the concept of intentionality is used to express how our consciousness is always directed towards some thing or things, the term is also used to represent our ability to *focus* our attention and the power that we have, through *conscious agency* (Trevarthen and Reddy 2007; Trevarthen 1998, 2004) to give a *focus* and a *margin* to consciousness through voluntary effort (James 1918; Sully 1890; Posner 1978).

Conscious intentionality, by its nature, involves sense perception. Dainton (2007) and Chalmers (2007) speak of how phenomena become available to our consciousness via 'different sensory modalities'. As Tye (2007) illustrates:

Attending to the phenomenology of a perceptual experience, to its felt character, is a matter of attending to the way things look, smell, taste, sound or feel by touch. In the case of bodily sensations, the object of your attention is the way a certain part of your body feels. With emotions and moods, the attention and focus is often on things outside—things perceived as dangerous, foul or pleasing—but there is also attention to the ways in which one's body is changing (pounding heart, shaky legs, higher blood pressure). (p. 47)

From this passage, we can discern that via our different sensory modalities and awareness of both internal (interoception) and external (exteroception) phenomena (Rothschild 2006), our conscious experiencing is complex, diverse, multidimensional, and ever-changing. Rather than experiencing all of these different phenomena and dimensions of experience as separate, we experience them together, in unified, continuous experience. As Dainton (2007) illustrates:

You are, let us suppose, studying a landscape painting hung on a museum wall; while so doing you are absentmindedly playing with a pen, exploring its shape with your fingers, and over to your right you can hear a murmured conversation. The painting, as it features in your consciousness, is a complex of many parts all of which are unified in a distinctive way: you see the depicted tree—covered mountains, the bubbling brook, the frame and surrounding wall. The same applies to your experiences of the pen and the conversation: these too are unified complexes—albeit in different sensory modalities. [...] Your experience of the painting is experienced along with your tactile explorations of the pen, but also with the remainder of your bodily experience, your conscious thoughts, mental images, and your current emotional feelings. (pp. 209–210)

This description illustrates how we are continuously embedded in unified and multidimensional conscious experience, composed of an intersubjective interrelation between our exteroception (awareness of the multidimensionality and diversity of phenomena external to our body) and interoception (the multidimensionality and diversity of feelings and sensations that occur within our body).

3.4   The Role of Phenomenological Freedom

As mentioned previously, our ability to focus attention on particular phenomena or to push them to the margins of our awareness is something that numerous philosophers and cognitive scientists have recognised.

While James (1918) recognised the power of attention to give a focus and a margin to consciousness, Broadbent (1958) argued that we 'selectively attend' to sensory inputs in order to prevent overload of our information-processing system. Treisman (1964) also suggested that we 'attenuate', or 'turn down the volume' of certain sensory inputs so as to move them to the background of our awareness. While this process is thought necessary for preventing sensory overload, it is also important to be aware of when considering epistemology: as I have already mentioned, deploying selective attention and attenuation requires voluntary effort—that is, agency (Posner 1978). Because of its interaction with cognition, this agency can be considered 'epistemic'.

A characteristic of consciousness in which we find epistemic agency relates to Sartre's (1956) 'phenomenological freedom', which is found in the interrelationship between what he called 'prereflective' and 'reflective' consciousness. These can be seen as two 'interactive structures' of conscious experience (Smith 2011, p. 69). *Prereflective* consciousness consists of the bodily/tacit dimension (Wider 1997), which comprises the 'immediate, instantaneous, immersed, embedded, unabashed level of phenomenological experience' (Smith 2011, p. 69)—that is, the immediacy of sensory input—whereas *reflective* consciousness consists of the mechanisms by which we process, interpret, and reflect on sensory inputs. Reflective consciousness also consists of our ability to reflect on our own reflecting, constituting a 'third person perspective' type of thought that enables us to evaluate our own thoughts and actions (ibid.). As Sartre (1956) wrote, we experience ourselves as experiencing.

Analogies to Sartre's concepts of prereflective and reflective consciousness have been identified by other philosophers and cognitive scientists. Locke (1990) contrasted 'outer sense' (the mind's experience of things) with 'inner sense' (the mind's reflective experience of its own experience of things). Block (1998) spoke of 'phenomenal consciousness' (which consists of immediate, subjective experience, and feelings) and 'access consciousness', which consists of information globally available in the cognitive system for the purposes of reasoning, speech, and high-level action control, while Jarvis (2009) writes of 'primary experience' (experiencing with the senses) and 'secondary' experience (that which occurs as a result of language and other forms of mediation). According to Jarvis, primary and secondary experiences occur as a complex process of simultaneously experiencing 'both sensations and meanings' (p. 30). Sartre presented the *prereflective* and *reflective* dimensions of consciousness as ontologically distinct from each other—as opposite poles with little interaction between the two. In a retrieval of Sartre's work, Sherman (2007), like Jarvis (2009) argues that there is in fact a much more fluid, constant, interactive relation between prereflective and reflective consciousness, in what he calls 'mediating subjectivity' (p. 6).

By drawing a distinction between the prereflective and instantaneous level of consciousness and the explicitly reflective level, Sartre enables us to consider that in order for one to reflect upon the other, there must be a certain degree of 'space' between the two. This space, which enables us to be conscious of our own conscious experiencing and of our own reflecting on that experiencing, allows for what Sartre (1956) calls 'phenomenological freedom'. Phenomenological freedom, defined as freedom of conscious thought and reflection, is one of the great gifts of human intelligence. It gives us agency and allows us to learn. However, and this is of crucial importance, it is this (and not a vague instinct of human nature) which makes us capable of choosing whether or not to behave with violence.

As Smith (2011) explains, 'In experiential experience there is just enough space between our being embedded in a situation and our ability to reflect on that situation, and it is this space that makes possible the act of self-deceptive thought' (p. 70). Smith is highlighting a crucial point: whilst affording the amazing capacity of reflecting on our experiences, phenomenological freedom also makes us capable of lying to ourselves about our own experiences, by enabling us to choose to believe something even when our experiences prove otherwise. For example, when teaching I can tell myself that I am knowledgeable and my students are not, and I can uphold that belief by consciously attenuating all aspects of my experience that might suggest otherwise. In this sense, I am using my epistemic agency to manipulate the focus of my attention in order to actively close myself to experiences that might challenge my preconceived belief. But this alone does not stop me from experiencing phenomena that challenge my truth claim. Therefore, in order to uphold my belief, I need not only to choose 'not to focus' on certain aspects of my experience but also to lie to myself about these experiences (e.g. by telling myself that the student who disagrees with me in class is 'petulant', rather than knowledgeable in their own right). On the one hand, at the immediate, embedded level of experiencing, I am aware of aspects of the experiences that challenge my belief, and on the other hand, I can utilise my focusing and reflective abilities to 'push to the margins' and deny their existence or distort their significance. Therefore, as Sartre (1956) puts it, I can simultaneously believe (know) something whilst not believing it. Sartre (ibid.) calls this 'Bad Faith', while Smith (2011) calls it 'self-deception'.

3.5   ORIENTATIONS

As I have already established, consciousness is commonly understood as being intentional. One function of intentional agency is what phenomenologists such as Merleau-Ponty (2012), Husserl (1973), and Heidegger (1962) identified as a constant process of orientating ourselves by 'turning toward' phenomena. This 'turning toward' can be the simple focussing of our attention 'without moving our eyes' (Sully 1890), or the physical act of moving our eyes, turning our body, or approximating ourselves to our chosen subject (Ahmed 2006). As discussed earlier, we exist in a dynamic and intersubjective interrelation with the world, and both the world and ourselves are multidimensional and ever-changing. Considering this, it is fair to say that we can never *absolutely know* the world, nor ourselves or others. However, considering that consciousness is intentional and we are constantly *orientating* ourselves towards phenomena, even if we cannot absolutely know, we are still continuously engaged in a process of *trying* to understand the world.

Trevarthen and Reddy (2007) state that 'conscious awareness is adapted to detect the prospects for action that have definite purposes in the outside world' (p. 54). *Orientating* can therefore be seen as an integral mechanism through which we try to understand the phenomena that we become aware of (and focus our attention on), in order to inform our decisions about how to act in the world. Orientation, as Ahmed (2006) writes, 'is about making the strange familiar' (p. 11). It also entails processes of storing (remembering), reflecting on, and interpreting our immediate experience in order to create and recreate concepts, mental constructs, or 'orientations' to help us identify and develop a sense of understanding towards phenomena (ibid.). The act of orientating and the orientations that we create for ourselves in relation to our experiences are considered by contemporary learning theorists to be integral to our very being. Jarvis (2009) uses the term 'biography' to refer to our entire history of orientations, which can be thought of as the memories that we have of our past experiences and the mental structures and meanings that we have developed in order to make sense of those experiences. As Merleau-Ponty (2012) states, 'we cannot dissociate being from orientated being' (p. 295). However, considering the assumption that we can never absolutely know the world, ourselves, or others as these are constantly in flux, it may be more correct to think of our being as in a constant process of orientat*ing* and re-orientating, rather than in a static state of being orientat*ed*.

The need to be constantly orientating and re-orientating ourselves springs from the fact that our orientations will never be identical to the phenomena of our experience, because we cannot simultaneously access all dimensions of a phenomenon with our consciousness, and that phenomenon will be in a constant process of change (however fast or slow). Because of this, there will always be a discord between our orientations and phenomena themselves. Ahmed (2006) states that when we become aware of this discord we experience a sense of *dis*orientation, or what Piaget (1977) calls *disequilibrium* and Jarvis (2009) calls *disjuncture*. This is particularly evident when we are faced with new, unknown, or unexpected phenomena, and as Jarvis (ibid.) argues, this sense of disjuncture, felt as a gap between our existing orientations and our lived experience, is unavoidable and central to how we learn.

In line with Trevarthen and Reddy (2007), Illeris (2009) writes that 'The endeavour of the learner is to construct *meaning* and *ability* to deal with the challenges of practical life' (p. 10). Because of the nature of our consciousness, we all engage in informal learning as an integral element of our day-to-day, lifelong experience (Jarvis 2009). In line with the recognition that we are multidimensional beings, Piaget (1953) wrote that learning begins with the body and takes place through the brain, which is also part of the body, and only gradually is the mental side separated out as a specific but never independent area or function. In contrast to the mind-body dualism of Cartesian philosophy, learning can be seen as happening on many bodily and sensory dimensions, and not as a purely cognitive process. As Illeris (2009) describes:

> Human learning is the combination of processes throughout a lifetime whereby the whole person—body (genetic, physical and biological) and mind (knowledge, skills, attitudes, values, emotions, beliefs and senses)—experiences social situations, the perceived content of which is then transformed cognitively, emotively or practically (or through any combination) and integrated into the individual person's biography resulting in a continually changing (or more experienced) person. (p. 23)

Like many others, Illeris sees learning as socially mediated. This 'social constructivist' model of learning is valuable because it acknowledges the collective affirmation of constructs or orientations. However, it misses out a crucial and ethically relevant point when it comes to a discussion of epistemology. That is, although we are capable of agreeing on collective 'truths' through communication, dialogue, and discourse, our capacity for self-deceptive thought means that unless these truths are also developed in intersubjective relation with the phenomena to which they refer, they run the risk of not doing justice to these phenomena. This is something commonly seen in racist discourses, for example. This social constructivist model also leaves out the recognition that learning can, and often does happen outside of immediate social situations, in direct relationship with our sensory experience (e.g. when a child learns by playing alone outside—exploring textures, smells, sights, sounds, and movements).

While it is essential to remember that learning entails the multidimensionality of bodily experience as well as the mind, in seeking a deeper understanding of violence I propose that it is most beneficial to place a central focus on the *cognitive* dimension of learning because, being essential for concept-formation, the cognitive dimension is central to our epistemic relating with the phenomenal world. Illeris (ibid.) writes how 'the learner him—or herself actively builds up or construes his/her learning as mental structures' (p. 23). Piaget (1977) called these structures 'schema', influencing the contemporary psychological metaphor of 'schemes'. Illeris explains that rather than being some kind of archive, brain scientists believe schemes to be analogous to what they call 'engrams', which are 'traces of circuits between some of the billions of neurons that have been active at earlier occasions and therefore are likely to be revived, perhaps with slightly different courses because of the impact of new experiences or understandings' (ibid.). In order to deal with them more practically, Illeris suggests that we think of schemes as 'what we subjectively tend to classify as belonging to a specific topic or theme and therefore mentally connect and are inclined to recall in relation to situations that we relate to that topic or theme' (ibid.).

If we consider 'schemes' and 'orientations' to be analogous, then we begin to see a connection to categorisation and generalisation as cognitive processes that we employ in creating and recreating orientations. Ahmed (2006) writes, 'we think with and through orientation'. If this is true, the implications of creating orientations that do not do justice to the phenomena they intend to represent are ethically concerning. If categorisation and generalisation is central to how we orientate ourselves and therefore how we choose to act in the world, then a quest to develop a deeper understanding of violence demands a more detailed examination of these processes.

3.6   THE IMPORTANCE OF HOW WE GENERALISE

So far I have proposed that epistemic agency lies in the ability to pay selective attention to or attenuate phenomena in our awareness, and in the interrelation between reflective and prereflective consciousness, which enables us to form schema/orientations. It is now necessary to examine in more detail how these two important functions of consciousness also enable us to enact self-deceptive thought, and how the particular cognitive behaviours and structures that define this type of thinking can define a concept of 'violent epistemology'.

Kegan (2009, p. 44) argues that '"Epistemology" refers to [...] not *what* we know but our way of knowing'. I propose that the core difference between 'violent' and 'non-violent' epistemology can be seen as stemming from two different 'ways of knowing'. These two different ways of knowing can be distinguished by how we relate the *general* and the *particular* in our experience, or rather, how we generalise. Illeris (2009) writes (my interpretations are presented in square brackets):

> In relation to learning, the crucial thing is that new impulses [experiences] can be included in the mental organisation [schemes] in various ways [different epistemologies], and on this basis it is possible to distinguish between [...] different types of learning [epistemic processes] which are activated in different contexts, imply different kinds of learning results [violent or non-violent] and require more or less energy. (p. 13)

My proposal is that different epistemic processes or 'types of learning' can be more or less violent, depending on the ways in which we do or do not acknowledge and integrate the particulars of our experience into our general schemes/orientations.

As already discussed, our epistemic relation with the phenomenal world, ourselves, and each other entails a constant process of orientating ourselves towards our experiences through conscious intentionality. Central to how we orientate ourselves is the practice of generalisation. We can discern this quite practically using a simple example given by Polanyi (1969):

> The traveller who admires a landscape sees a particular image of trees, fields, rivers and peaks, and nearer his position he hears church-bells ringing and sees villagers walking to attend service. His experience is composed of particular instances of the classes denoted by the terms 'tree', 'river', 'peak', 'church-bell', 'villagers', 'walking', and 'religious service', etc. (p. 190)

Polanyi describes this process of orientating within an experience, of interpreting particular sensory impulses in relation to pre-existing general categories or concepts, as *sense-reading*. Polanyi highlighted how, when we have a first-hand experience such as that of the traveller described above, we witness 'particular instances' of phenomena, or 'aggregate[s] of objects that differ in every particular' (ibid.). This view is compatible with my earlier point that the phenomenal world is diverse, multidimensional, and ever-changing, and in light of this, no two phenomena can be experienced as absolutely identical. Waismann (1945) argued that the general terms or categories we use to identify phenomena have an 'open texture' which admits differences in the instances to which they apply. Another example from Polanyi (1969) illustrates this well:

> Our conception of a tree, for example [...] arises in a tacit integration of countless experiences of different trees and pictures and reports of still others: deciduous and evergreen, straight and crooked, bare and leafy. All these encounters are included in forming the conception of a tree; they are all used subsidiarily with a bearing on the conception of a tree, which is what we mean by the word 'tree'. (p. 191)

Polanyi argued that there is no 'explicit procedure' by which we form these general orientations, however he did begin to point towards certain cognitive procedures when he wrote that 'when groping for words to describe an experience, we [...] use the particulars we have seen and heard as clues to conceptions covering them, and we then designate these particulars by the names of these conceptions' (ibid.). Piaget, on the other hand, has provided us with research that has expanded the possibility of discerning such 'explicit procedures' by which we form orientations in relation to our experience—something I will get to in a moment.

Polanyi's work does present one useful concept for delineating such 'explicit processes' however—the notion of 'conceptual subsumption'. Citing Kant, Polanyi (op. cit.) writes that subsuming particular instances (of experience) under a general term or concept (such as 'tree') is a 'skill so deeply hidden in the human soul that we shall hardly guess the secret that Nature here employs' (pp. 105–106). He presents this as a rather mysterious yet neutral and unavoidable procedure which enables us to communicate such experiences to others via language. This 'tacit integration' of particular experiences into general, 'open-textured' orientations towards phenomena (e.g. 'trees', 'villagers', etc.) can be seen as a necessary and organic cognitive process which enables us to orientate ourselves towards our experience. However, it may not be as mysterious as Polanyi makes out, and when considering the ethics of epistemic processes, I propose that this practice needs to be examined more critically. Falzon (1998) writes how:

> Encountering the world ... necessarily involves a process of ordering the world in terms of our categories, organising it and classifying it, actively bringing it under control in some way. We always bring some framework to bear on the world in our dealings with it. Without this organisational activity, we would be unable to make any sense of the world at all. (p. 38)

While being a necessary action that helps us to understand and makes sense of our experiences, Jarvis (2009) writes of how the process of categorisation also makes it possible for us to impose general categorisations upon the particulars of our experience in a way that minimises our perception of diversity and particularity. This is where we begin to see the potential for violation. In such instances, it becomes easy to 'take for granted' that the world is identical to the concepts and categories that we have created. Jarvis writes:

> We assume that the world as we know it does not change a great deal from one experience to another similar one (Schutz and Luckmann 1974), although as Bauman (2000) reminds us, our world is changing so rapidly that he can refer to it as 'liquid'. (p. 26)

In other words, in this 'taken-for-grantedness', we tend to focus more on what we perceive to be general and presume to 'already know' in our experience, rather than on what is particular—those new and diverse encounters that may pose a challenge to our existing categories and schema.

Cook (2005) reminds us that 'the polarity between universal and particular takes a cognitive form' (p. 24). That is, while we can discern phenomenologically that general similarities between phenomena do not cancel out or override the diverse particularity of the phenomenal world, there appears to be a cognitive tendency in humans to sever the organic and dynamic interrelation between generals that we can perceive in our experience and the particular instances that those generals are comprised of. Instead, generality and particularity tend to be perceived as two opposing and irreconcilable poles (as can be seen in the epistemic feud between positivism and relativism).

Adorno (1973) cautions us against imposing general categories on diverse phenomena in a manner that tries to make phenomena identical to our concepts of them. He is especially concerned with what happens when phenomena are subsumed by 'their concepts without leaving a remainder' (p. 5). That is, using our general concepts to negate or override any particularities which do not fit neatly into them. When we negate or override particularities of our experience, we fail to do justice to the phenomenon of that experience, 'violating its condition' as Horta (2007, p. LVII) would say. Adorno heavily criticised this epistemic mode of thought, which he called 'identity thinking'.

However, as Sherman (2007) writes, 'Adorno does not want to discard the moment of identity altogether' (p. 240). To the contrary, Adorno (1973) is clear that 'the appearance of identity is inherent in thought itself', or, put more simply, 'to think is to identify' (p. 5). Therefore, while Adorno is not arguing that we should give up on constructing concepts and categories to make sense of our experience,[1] he is arguing 'the need for conceptual fluidity to adequately (and therefore never completely) describe the actual [phenomena] of a fluid reality' (Sherman 2007, p. 240). This type of conceptual fluidity that Adorno advocates is perhaps something more like Polanyi's 'open-textured' concept. The greatest epistemic error that we make, according to Adorno (1973, p. 12), is falling into the trap of identity thinking: tricking ourselves into believing that phenomena are identical to our conceptualisations of them. He argued that we should 'respect the nonidentity of objects with concepts' (Cook 2005, p. 24).

Adorno wrote that 'To gain [...] perspectives without velleity or violence' is the 'task of thought' and that such perspectives could only be gained 'from felt contact with objects' (2005, p. 247). That is, in order to enact a non-violent epistemology it is necessary to be normatively attentive to the particularities of our first-hand experiences with phenomena so as to assimilate particularities into our general concepts and adapt our concepts accordingly, rather than paying little attention to or rejecting particularities, and negating them by subsuming them under general concepts, which we take for granted as being identical to our experience. In sum, Adorno argues that in order to overcome the violence of identity thinking, we need 'to change the direction of conceptuality, to give it a turn toward nonidentity' (1973, p. 12).

---

[1] Throwing the baby out with the bathwater, as postmodernism could be criticised for having done.

In line with Polanyi and Adorno, Piaget (1977) also recognised that the identification and categorisation of phenomena into mental schema is central to how we orientate ourselves. However, it was Piaget who made most clear that the relating of particularities and generalities in our experience is a central and unavoidable aspect of the formation and re-formation of schema. He explained how, as we encounter new experiences and phenomena, we sort them according to what we perceive to be similar (general) between them and other phenomena that we have experienced, and what we perceive to be different (particular). We use our analysis of the generalities and particularities of phenomena to orientate ourselves—to decide what they might be and where they ought to fit within our schema in relation to other phenomena that we have experienced both past and present. This process is at its most intense during childhood, but as Jarvis (2009) highlights, it continues until the moment we die.

Importantly, Piaget identifies different ways of relating with the phenomena of our experience. One, 'assimilation', involves the integration of new experiences into existing categories and schema without changing the schema themselves. Another, 'accommodation', involves adapting schema to account for the particularities of experience as observed. As Jarvis (2009) writes, assimilative epistemic relating demands little energy as it does not require the subject to de-construct and reconstruct any aspect of the concept, but rather simply identifies phenomena with a pre-existing concept as with identity thinking. Piaget (1977) writes of how he has witnessed something in his experiments that he calls 'assimilative distortion'. When the subject experiences particularities which appear to contradict or not to fit into already existing conceptualisations, this causes the feeling of 'disequilibrium' (or 'disjuncture' as Jarvis (2009) calls it)—a sense of 'not knowing' or 'disorientation'.

Piaget (1977) identifies different ways in which the subject tends to respond, in order to regain a sense of equilibrium. One of these, he calls 'type α behaviour'. This is when 'the form [conceptualisation] rejects certain elements [particularity] of the content [phenomenon as experienced], so that the force exerted by the form [concept] in its rejection is opposed to that which is characteristic of the content [phenomenon]' (p. 150). In essence, Piaget appears to be describing the subsumption of particularities under general concepts to make the phenomenon identical to the concept, as in Adorno's concept of identity thinking. Piaget (ibid.) writes that in the process of constructing or adapting a scheme, what the subject has retained of his experience and conceptualised, amounts to what the subject has 'centred [focussed on], valued, and not dismissed' (p. 148). In type α behaviour, in the attempt to regain a sense of equilibrium, 'what the subject retains [of his experience] is reduced entirely to what at first was assimilable and comprehensible' (ibid.). The 'remainder' (to use Adorno's terminology), is 'somewhat removed from awareness [as] the objects [phenomena] of a kind of repression or inhibition' (pp. 149–150).

As Piaget writes, 'in these examples, it is clear that the subject does not simply neglect elements or make incomplete conceptualisations [...]. [Rather,] a greater [selective] focussing is apparent. The missing perception [that which was not integrated into the scheme] was actually dismissed because it was contradictory to a frequently used conceptual scheme' (Piaget 1977, p. 149). What Piaget appears to be describing is how an individual can perceive something and then pretend that they had not actually perceived it by rejecting or 'neglecting observables' (ibid.) so that they do not have to undertake the demanding work of accommodation (adapting or reconstructing the scheme in order to accommodate the particularity). This is a prime example of how our epistemic agency (our ability to focus on certain particularities of experience and push others to the margins of awareness, as well as the 'space' between prereflective and reflective consciousness) enables us to deceive ourselves about what we have experienced.

According to Piaget (1977), the sense of equilibrium achieved by type α behaviour is unstable, because 'neglected observables' have a tendency to 'exert [...] pressure in opposition to th[e] resistance' of the form [conceptualisation] (p. 150). In other words, the subject will most likely continue to re-encounter those 'remainders' or particularities which have been consciously rejected, and is therefore faced with the challenge of either continually upholding that rejection so as to protect the structural integrity of the concept, or admitting that they have lied to themselves and making the effort to adapt the concept to account for those particularities which had been repressed. As Illeris (2007) writes, individuals can become invested in the concepts that they have worked so hard to protect, which can contribute to the subject 'blocking' themselves from acknowledging and learning from new and rejected particularities. Adorno refers to this as 'guarding the old particularity' (1973, pp. 283–284), meaning that the subject refuses to acknowledge any new particularities which challenge their existing petrified concepts. We can imagine how 'guarding the old particularity' could perpetuate type α behaviour.

The severing of the organic interrelationship between general and particular that occurs in Piaget's type α behaviour and Adorno's identity thinking can also be seen as analogous in some ways to Jarvis' (1987) concept of 'non-learning', Leithäuser's (1976) theory of 'everyday consciousness', and Rogers' (1961) 'Stage One' of the process from 'fixity' to 'flowingness'. I will outline each of these briefly. Jarvis proposes that there are three broad types of non-learning. The first, *presumption*, implies that one already thinks one has an understanding of something and, therefore, does not register new learning opportunities. This appears analogous to the 'taken-for-grantedness' (as described by Illeris 2007) that we enact when imposing pre-existing general categories or concepts onto new experiences.

The second, *Non-consideration*, implies that one might register new opportunities (particularities), but not accommodate them into one's orientation perhaps through being too busy or too nervous of what they might lead to (Jarvis 1987). The latter part of this sentence (fear of what integration might lead to) brings to mind the act of lying to oneself so as to protect the comfort and security of the 'old particularity'. The final type of non-learning outline by Jarvis (ibid.) is *Rejection*. This means that, on a more conscious level, one does not want to learn something new in a particular context. This also brings to mind 'guarding the old particularity', and the rejection of new particularities because of the effort involved in integrating them into a restructured scheme.

Leithäuser's (1976) theory of everyday consciousness is based, among other things, on the idea that we adopt a fragmented, impoverished, prejudicial, and automatic manner of conceptualising our everyday experience as a way of coping with the modern world. He writes of how in modern life we are held to strict time-constraints and routines, and bombarded with overwhelming amounts of information and sensory impulses, such as the atrocities that appear every day on our television screens, and the numerous irresistible offers surrounding us in the supermarket. In such an environment, it is incredibly challenging to remain open and candid, to the degree that psychological and emotional defence appears necessary in order to cope. As a result, we feel the need to rationalise our consciousness, developing an 'everyday consciousness' that is characterised by fragmentation, stereotypes, and unmediated contradictions. Leithäuser describes this as a psychological structure comprised of limited schema by which we are able to routinely interpret the themes we come across in our everyday lives without reflecting on them or integrating new impulses.

This is a form of 'filtering' which Illeris (2007) describes as functioning similarly to Piaget's type α behaviour. In this way, we avoid relating to the huge stream of new impulses to which we are subjected in contemporary society, and part of our life fulfilment is confined in routines, impoverishment, falsity, and prejudice (Illeris 2007; Leithäuser 1976).

Finally, Rogers (1961) proposed a seven-stage process by which, through the therapeutic process, people could progress from 'fixity' to 'flowingness' in their way of relating to the world, themselves, and others. It is not difficult to see that each one of these stages is also analogous to an epistemic way of relating with one's experience. What Rogers describes as 'Stage One' is particularly interesting as it appears analogous to Adorno's identity thinking and is characterised by a similar rigidity and closure as that found in Piaget's type α behaviour. Rogers describes this stage as marked by 'fixity and remoteness of experiencing' (p. 132), in which:

> The individual has little or no recognition of the ebb and flow of the feeling of life within him. The ways in which he construes experience have been set by his past, and are rigidly unaffected by the actualities of the present. He is (to use the term of Gendlin and Zimrig) structure-bound in his manner of experiencing. That is, he reacts "to the situation of now by finding it to be like a past experience and then reacting to the past, feeling *it*". [...] There is much blockage of internal communication between self and experience. The individual at this stage is represented by such terms as stasis, fixity, the opposite of flow or change. (p. 133)

Rogers appears to be describing the failure of the subject to attend to, acknowledge, and accommodate the particularities of present experience into their general orientations. Instead, the subject severs the organic general-particular relation by imposing a fixed general orientation onto the particularities of experience in a manner which negates the ways in which they may be different from past experience. In short, the subject subsumes particularity under general concepts.

3.7   A New Concept: 'Violent Epistemology'

While I have not encountered any authors who use the term 'violent epistemology', and many of those cited in this section do not explicitly acknowledge the potential for violation within the concepts they present, I have demonstrated how a variety of research and concepts exist which point towards the same set of conclusions:

1. Through our epistemic agency (our ability to focus on and push particularities of experience to the margins of our awareness, and to reflect on our immediate experience), we are able to enact different epistemic behaviours while forming and maintaining schema.
2. Relating generalities and particularities of our experience is an essential cognitive behaviour which allows us to create and recreate schema, but the way in which we do this can impact the degree to which we do justice to the phenomena of our experience.
3. The concepts of type α behaviour (Piaget 1977), identity thinking (Adorno 1973), non-learning (Jarvis 2009), everyday consciousness (Leithäuser 1976), and Stage One (Rogers 1961), all point towards a similar type of epistemic behaviour which is marked by the pushing of certain particularities to the margins of awareness and the subsumption of those particularities under general concepts, so as to maintain those concepts in their rigid and unchanging form.

I propose that this type of epistemic behaviour can be integrated into the single concept of 'violent epistemology'. Some of the authors cited in this section present this epistemic behaviour as ethically neutral (Polanyi, Piaget, Jarvis, Rogers), while others (Adorno, Sherman, and Leithäuser) demonstrate more explicit consideration of its ethical implications. If we analyse this behaviour while trying to understand the root causes of violence (as this book will do in detail), then we begin to perceive the crucial importance of considering its ethical implications.

To briefly illustrate this before delving into more detail in the following chapters, let us return to the teacher who shut her students in the classroom, from the opening vignette in Chap. 1. We may imagine that she could have developed, over time, a scheme that relates to the role of 'good teacher' and with which she identifies—that is, she has subsumed the particularities of her own being into that scheme, 'objectifying herself into character' as Sherman (2007) would say. The scheme may contain certain generalisations that she has assimilated over time through her own experience of schooling and through teacher training, working in schools, and societal discourse about teachers. If we consider that one such generalisation may entail the common association of 'good teacher' with the characteristic of commanding a high level of control over the students in class, then we can imagine how she, wanting to be a 'good teacher', may strive to attain/maintain this generalised characteristic.

When the children start acting out—throwing chairs, dancing, laughing—the structure of this scheme and her identification with it are placed under threat (into disequilibrium) by the particularities of the situation, which threaten the stability of her generalised, rigid scheme. In a desperate effort to maintain her control over the students and therefore her ability to identify with her 'good teacher' scheme, she places tables against the door to stop the children spilling out into the corridor where her inability to control them will become evident to her colleagues, threatening her perceived ability to identify with that scheme even further. Thus, the teacher enters into a desperate panic in which she tries to keep the children locked in the classroom by any means possible, in order to 'guard the old particularity'. To maintain the integrity of her existing scheme she must push certain particularities of her experience to the margins of her awareness (such as the students' needs), because recognising and integrating them into her scheme could force her into further disequilibrium and necessitate the energy-consuming effort of deconstructing and reconstructing the scheme and her own identification with it altogether. The disequilibrium could be so intense that it forces her into an identity crisis—a terrifying prospect for most. The result of maintaining the integrity of her pre-existing scheme and using that as a guideline for action is that she has failed to do justice to particularities of her experience with herself and others, and acted violently by locking the children in the classroom with tables against the door.

Through this one example (more are provided throughout Chaps. 5 and 6), we can see how the epistemic behaviours described in this section can act as precursors to violent action. For this reason, I propose that it is necessary to explicitly recognise the ethical implications of these cognitive behaviours, by integrating them into the single concept of 'violent epistemology'.

3.8   Motivations and Emotions

So far, I have presented a detailed outline of a new concept of 'violent epistemology', by focussing on the capacity of human consciousness to enact certain cognitive behaviours. I have emphasised the crucial importance of integrating specifics pertaining to the cognitive and epistemic dimensions of experience into an understanding of the root causes of violence. As I have highlighted, the cognitive dimension is also home to the agency that enables us to choose which cognitive and physical behaviours to enact. Understanding this is vital because our agency can provide the linchpin for change. However, I mentioned earlier that phenomena (ourselves included) are multidimensional, citing Dainton (2007), Chalmers (2007), and Tye (2007) to illustrate that one important dimension of our experience, aside from our cognition, is our emotions. Further, achieving the goal of taking a multidimensional approach to understanding violence cannot be achieved without discussing the role of emotions.

Research has found that what we usually term 'reason' (i.e. the cognitive dimension) cannot function independently of emotions (Illeris 2007, p. 13). Thus, as Kant (1953) suggested more than 200 years ago in his *Critique of Pure Reason*, the Western and scientific ideal of 'pure reason', unaffected by emotion, is an illusion. Many psychologists have also been aware of the close connection between emotion and cognition (Vygotsky 1978; Furth 1987) and neurology has also confirmed this (Damasio 1994). In relation to violent epistemology, a number of authors point to emotion as the driving force for the cognitive acts of severing the generals from the particulars of experience—including the acts of self-deceptive thought, of blocking ourselves from honouring the diversity and new particularities of experience, and from integrating new particularities into our conceptual orientations. It stands to reason then, that we must examine the relationship between emotions and violent epistemology in more detail.

Before launching into a discussion of emotions however, it is necessary to first address a phenomenological category that is inextricably intertwined with the emotions, but which can be seen as somewhat distinct. This is the category of motivations. Psychological and sociological literature identifies certain phenomena which are often described as 'drives' or 'motivating forces'. These are usually divided into two core concepts: 'self-preservation' (Hobbes 1996; Spinoza 1985; Freud 1910; Adorno 1973), and 'self-actualisation' (Goldstein 1939; Maslow 1954; Rogers 1961). In examining this literature, there appears to be a strong interaction between these motivating forces, our emotions, and the enactment of violent or non-violent epistemology. I will outline each of the two concepts in a little more detail.[2]

Early discussions on the theme of self-preservation can be found in the work of Hobbes (1996) and Spinoza (1985). Arguing that 'the passions that incline men to peace are fear of death, desire of such things as are

---

[2] By discussing core motivations or 'drives', I am not attempting to make ontological assertions about 'human nature', but rather to identify what appear to be pertinent themes for the study of violence as a historical human problem.

necessary to commodious living, and a hope by their industry to obtain them', Hobbes (1996, p. 78) proposed that individual self-preservation is the primary motivating factor behind both the actions of individuals and the formation of societies. Spinoza (1985) wrote of a 'striving by which each thing strives to persevere in its own being' (p. 20). He refers to this as 'conatus'—a striving of the whole being of the person, both body and mind, to persevere in its existence. Freud (1910) later elaborated on this theme when he spoke of 'those [...] instincts, which have as their aim the self-preservation of the individual, the ego instincts' (p. 214). He believed self-preservation (particularly of the ego) to be a 'primal instinct' of humankind (Freud 1915).

Later, Adorno (1973) and Horkheimer and Adorno (2002) continued with, and elaborated on, the theme of self-preservation—in particular, exploring its relation to violence and epistemology. In his explanation of Horkheimer and Adorno's use of the concept of self-preservation, Sherman (2007) employs italics to clarify the two ways in which the authors use the term. Essentially, *self*-preservation refers to the 'preservation of the particular ego-structure which separates a human being from both nature and other human beings'[3] (p. 185), and self-*preservation* relates to the preservation of the biological organism (p. 184). Horkheimer and Adorno (2002) explored various ways in which the drives for egological *self*-preservation and biological self-*preservation* serve as a core theme in the history of human violence, domination, and repression (which I will come to in a moment).

The term 'self-actualisation' is thought to have been coined by Goldstein (1939), who saw humans as possessing innate 'capacities' or 'potentialities' which:

> Belong to the nature of the organism, but [...] are utilized only by the organism in the course of its encounter with the outer world and its coming to terms with external stimuli. Thus, they develop with the attempt of the organism to adjust itself to the environment in a certain way. The development of these capabilities is dependent on the possibility of a specifically formed environment suited to the use of such capacities. (p. 158)

In this sense, self-actualisation means the 'tendency to actualize, as much as possible, [the subject's] individual capacities [...] in the world' (ibid., p. 162). Goldstein presents the 'drive' for self-actualisation as a characteristic of a

---

[3] This is not a presumption that humans *are* separate from nature, but rather refers to when a person perceives himself as such.

healthy human organism. He contrasts this to self-preservation, which he describes as being a pathological phenomenon (self-actualisation which has undergone a characteristic change), marked by:

> The tendency to maintain the existent state [which] is characteristic for sick people and is a sign of anomalous life, of decay of life. The tendency of normal life is toward activity and progress. For the sick, the only form of self-actualization that remains is the maintenance of the existent state.[4] (p. 162)

In short, Goldstein sees self-actualisation as the action of a healthy subject who is constantly changing, growing, and developing in interaction with its environment. This interaction 'corresponds to a continual change of tension of such a kind that over and again that state of tension is reached that enables and impels the organism to actualize itself in further activities' (ibid., p. 163).

This is analogous to Piaget's continual process of equilibration in which the subject constantly experiences new feelings of 'disequilibrium' as it encounters new experiences, and works to equilibrate itself to its experience through continuous assimilation and accommodation of those new experiences into its schema/orientations. Similar to type α behaviour in which the subject attempts to resolve all disequilibrium by rejecting rather than accommodating new experiences, Goldstein (1939) proposes that self-preservation is marked by 'The tendency to discharge any tension whatsoever [...] even if in an imperfect way' (p. 161). Just as in type α behaviour, in Goldstein's self-preservation 'the tendency to remove any arising tension prevails' leading to 'the process of equalisation [being] disturbed' (ibid.) because the subject reduces his 'scope of life' (p. 162) as 'he is driven to maintain a certain state of living and not to be disturbed in this condition' (ibid.). This is a marker of what Goldstein calls 'sick life' and can be seen as analogous to Rogers' 'Stage One'.

Later, the term 'self-actualisation' was adopted by Maslow (1943, 1954), who described it as 'the desire for self-fulfilment, namely, [...] the tendency for [the subject] to become actualized in what he is potentially. This tendency might be phrased as the desire to become more and more what one is, to become everything that one is capable of becoming' (1943, p. 10). According to Maslow, the emergence of the self-actualising tendency 'rests upon prior satisfaction of the physiological, safety, love and esteem needs' (p. 11). He writes:

---

[4] This is a reference to an unhealthy psychology, rather than physical disease.

> We shall call people who are satisfied in these needs, basically satisfied people, and it is from these that we may expect the fullest (and healthiest) creativeness. Since, in our society, basically satisfied people are the exception, we do not know much about self-actualization. (ibid.)

From this statement, we can imagine how a lack of basic (including emotional) need satisfaction could (though not deterministically) result in the subject acting in more of a 'self-preserving' rather than a 'self-actualising' manner, leading to a violent epistemic relationship between the subject and themselves, the world, and others. Rogers (1980), who also engages with the theme of self-actualisation, suggests something very similar when reflecting on his experience with clients during therapy:

> The actualizing tendency can [...] be thwarted or warped, but it cannot be destroyed without destroying the organism. [...] Life would not give up, even if it could not flourish. [...] So unfavourable have been the conditions in which [some] people have developed that their lives often seem abnormal, twisted, scarcely human. Yet, the directional tendency in them can be trusted. The clue to understanding their behaviour is that they are striving, in the only ways that they perceive as available to them, to move toward growth, toward becoming. To healthy persons, the results may seem bizarre and futile, but they are life's desperate attempt to become itself. (p. 118)

We can imagine the teacher putting tables against the door, and the children throwing chairs as 'life's desperate attempts' to become itself, or in such difficult circumstances to at least preserve itself—even though to an observer these acts may have appeared futile and self-destructive.

As we can see, motivations to enact certain epistemic patterns of thought are deeply intertwined with emotions. In reviewing relevant literature, I uncovered numerous mentions of fear and anxiety in patterns of behaviour and thought that appear to match what I have termed 'violent epistemology'. Smith (2011) explores how anxiety, if not managed effectively, can lead us to enact self-deceiving thought. He writes of how the phenomenal world as we experience it is so complex that it does not provide us with any kind of absolute orientation that we can rely upon to know how to act in any given situation. Rather, it provides us with incredible amounts of sensory information that we must process and interpret ourselves. Smith calls this the 'lack of an absolute orientation', arguing that it is inherent to our epistemic relation with the phenomenal world. Horkheimer and Adorno (2002) spoke of a similar concept when discussing the 'nonconceptual', or 'remainder' of experience which cannot be conceptualised:

Primal and undifferentiated, it is everything unknown and alien; it is that which transcends the bounds of experience, the part of things which is more than their immediately perceived existence. What the primitive experiences as supernatural is not a spiritual substance in contradistinction to the material world but the complex concatenation of nature in contrast to its individual link. The cry of terror called forth by the unfamiliar becomes its name. (p. 10)

Building on this idea, Smith (2011) uses the term 'nonconceptual moreness' to describe the fact that there is always 'something more' to our experience which we cannot absolutely know. This stems from the nonidentity of objects [phenomena] with our concepts of them, as observed by Adorno (1973) and explained earlier.

Both Adorno (1973) and Smith (2011) propose that this nonconceptual moreness has historically stirred a deep-rooted fear or anxiety in humans. Adorno (ibid.) speaks of how it was our fear (for our self-preservation) in the face of the threat of nature that spurred the beginnings of abstract identity thinking. As he put it, 'abstraction is the medium of self-preserving reason' (ibid., p. 179). He is referring to his argument that, in the face of the unpredictability or 'moreness' presented by nature, upon which early civilisations depended for their self-preservation, humans responded by enacting 'a thinking that tolerates nothing outside it' (ibid., p. 172). Put crudely, humans created and sustained absolute, rigid schema in the form of myths and religions to satiate this fear and regain a sense of absolute security through those orientations, which was not provided by nature (Horkheimer and Adorno 2002). As we know, many atrocities (such as slavery and ritual sacrifices) were carried out in the name of these early myths and religions. Adorno's argument provides an age-old example of violent epistemology being enacted as a means of biological self-*preservation*.

As we know, the Enlightenment was an attempt to overcome our dependence on myth and religion. Adorno (1973) argues that in striving to break free from this dependence, Enlightenment thinkers transferred our search for absolute security from the creation of abstract myths, to the painstaking and 'rational' study of nature itself. However, rather than freeing us from our dependence on myth, Adorno proposes that Enlightenment thought actually created just another set of myths by using identity thinking and instrumental rationality in its effort to create an absolute orientation towards nature upon which we could ultimately depend. Essentially, in order to reduce the anxiety of not being able to absolutely know the phenomenal world, Enlightenment thought tried to subsume nature under 'identical' categories and concepts in order to absolutely know and dominate it (1973). As Horkheimer and Adorno (2002) state, 'humans believe themselves free of fear when there is no longer anything unknown' (p. 11).

In sum, in the age of myth humans responded to the anxiety induced by the 'disequilibrium' of not knowing, by trying to find absolute security in the creation of myths. In the Age of Enlightenment humans continued to seek security in an absolute orientation—only this time to be created through scientific study. Both responses, according to Adorno, involved the enactment of identity thinking (violent epistemology), hence Adorno's famous assertion that myth is already enlightenment and enlightenment reverts to mythology (Horkheimer and Adorno 2002), because both employ the same violent epistemic structure of thought.

The theme of anxiety has also been highlighted by Maslow (1943) in his discussion of the human need for safety, in which he outlines how some people act neurotically in effort to feel safe in the face of overblown fear. Fromm (2013) also discussed how:

> Any threat against vital (material and emotional) interests creates anxiety, and destructive tendencies are the most common reaction to such anxiety. [...] The threat can be circumscribed in a particular situation by particular persons [where] destructiveness is aroused towards these persons [or] be a constant [...] anxiety springing from an equally constant feeling of being threatened by the world outside. (p. 213)

Rogers (1959) also engages with this theme. In relation to egological *self-preservation*, he discusses the relationship between anxiety, the preservation of the ego-structure, and the enactment of behaviours that correlate with the above formulation of violent epistemology:

> [A]s the organism continues to experience, an experience which is incongruent with the self-structure (and its incorporated conditions of worth) is subceived[5] as threatening. The essential nature of the threat is that if the experience were accurately symbolized in awareness,[6] the self-concept would

[5] The term 'subceive' refers to perception that is not necessarily experienced as an explicit awareness—that is, the subject may feel threatened but not explicitly admit this to themselves, may deny awareness of the feeling, or may tell themselves that this is something other than threatenedness.

[6] The idea of 'accurate symbolisation' points towards the concept of non-violent epistemology. I discuss this in more detail in Chap. 8. The behaviour of the teacher who trapped

no longer be a consistent gestalt [integrated or unified whole], the conditions of worth would be violated, and the need for self-regard would be frustrated. A state of anxiety would exist. The process of defence is the reaction which prevents these events from occurring. (p. 227)

The paragraph above illustrates how threat to the self-concept (especially if that concept is a rigid scheme, highly protected by the subject) can cause the subject to experience anxiety.

Below, Rogers continues with a clear explanation of how, on a cognitive/epistemic level, this anxiety can fuel violent epistemic thought:

This process consists of the selective perception or distortion of the experience and/or the denial to awareness of the experience or some portion thereof, thus keeping the total perception of the experience consistent with the individual's self-structure, and consistent with his conditions of worth. […] The general consequences of the process of defence, aside from its preservation of the above consistencies, are a rigidity of perception, due to the necessity of distorting perceptions, an inaccurate perception of reality, due to distortion and omission of data, and intensionality.[7] (ibid.)

In essence, anxiety in relation to egological *self*-preservation can motivate the subject to use his or her self/identity-concept as a criterion by which to 'screen out experiences which could not comfortably be permitted in consciousness' (Rogers 1959, p. 251), resulting in a violent epistemic behaviour analogous to Piaget's type α.

More recently, other emotions have been linked to the *self*-preservation motivation, in the formation of Social Self-Preservation Theory (Gruenewald et al. 2004). Research in this field suggests that the creation and maintenance of a positive 'social self' is a primary human goal. Gruenewald et al. (ibid.) conducted experiments which found that situations where the subject perceived their 'social self' to be under threat engendered both psychological reactions (feelings of low social worth, shame, humiliation, embarrassment, and reduction in self-esteem) and

---

the children in the classroom with tables can be seen as one example of a *self*-preserving 'process of defence'.

[7] Rogers defines 'intensionality' as when the subject 'tends to see experience in absolute and unconditional terms, to overgeneralise, to be dominated by concept or belief, to fail to anchor his reactions in space and time, to confuse fact and evaluation, to rely upon abstractions rather than upon reality-testing' (1959, p. 205).

physiological reactions (higher levels of cortisol). In their research into the relationship between emotions and violence, Scheff and Retzinger (2001) identified unacknowledged shame as the primary emotion experienced by individuals before feeling rage and behaving violently. However, considering that Gruenewald et al. found that shame followed the experience of threat to the social self, it may be more correct to propose the following pattern: threat to the social self elicits anxiety, which if unacknowledged can be felt as shame, which, in turn, if unacknowledged, can be felt as rage.

Adorno (1973) also proposed that unacknowledged fear (and perhaps also shame) related to the preservation of the social self could precede the projection of rage onto others, whilst acknowledging the epistemic consequences of negating these more primary emotions:

> The "rational animal" with an appetite for his opponent is already fortunate enough to have a superego and must find a reason. The more completely his actions follow the law of self-preservation, the less can he admit the primacy of that law to himself and to others; if he did, his laboriously attained status of a *zoon politikon* would lose all credibility. The animal to be devoured must be evil. The sublimation of this anthropological schema extends all the way to epistemology. (p. 22)

This example contains similarities to Reich's (1972) concept of 'character armour'—a kind of attitude which an individual develops to act as a defence against the breakthrough of unwanted or intolerable feelings, sensations, emotions, or experience (Appleton 2002). It is also similar to Smith's (2011) concept of 'conscious evasion',[8] which has clear emotional roots and epistemic consequences, and to the theme of mechanisms of defence (especially ego defence) in the psychoanalytic tradition.

Aside from anxiety, another emotion is highlighted by a number of authors as playing a role in behaviour analogous to what I have termed violent epistemology. This is the feeling of 'being overwhelmed'. Whether this feeling is thought to contain an element of fear or anxiety is unclear. However, like anxiety it is often associated with defensive behaviour. Freud (1942) saw defence mechanisms as being active in specific personal relations. However, Illeris (2009) argues that in today's complex late-modern societies, these defence mechanisms 'must necessarily be generalised and take more systematised forms because nobody can manage to remain open to the gigantic volumes and impact of influences we are all constantly faced with' (p. 15).

---

[8] Characterised by closure to, and rejection of, certain particularities of experience.

This relates back to Leithäuser's 'everyday consciousness', in which 'people develop a kind of semi-automatic sorting mechanism vis-à-vis the many influences' (Illeris 2009, p. 15) that they encounter in everyday experience. Illeris argues that this sorting mechanism may serve as a means to protect ourselves emotionally from the sheer volume of cruelty, wickedness, and negativity that we are bombarded with every day either in firsthand experience or in the media, because 'people who cannot protect themselves from this are doomed to end up in some kind of psychological breakdown' (ibid.). However, one could also argue that the closure inherent to 'everyday consciousness' and its 'automatic sorting mechanisms' through which general concepts undoubtedly subsume or cause the subject to reject certain new particularities could also result in what Horkheimer and Adorno (2002) called a 'hardened' or 'callous' subject who is no longer able to allow themself to be open to, and to reflect on, the pain and suffering witnessed in social life.

Similar behaviour is witnessed in those experiencing secondary traumatic stress, vicarious trauma, or 'compassion fatigue', all of which result from the psychological and emotional strain of witnessing and imagining the suffering of others (Rothschild 2006). As mentioned previously, we rely on past experiences (often processed into orientations/schema) to make sense of sensory information received in the present. To consider possible connections between past experiences and present sensory information, we must undertake what Graeber (2011) calls 'labour of the imagination'. This is similar to Piaget's (1977) type γ behaviour, which relies on existing schema to try to predict the possible or likely outcomes of present experiences and actions. However—and for example—while we may have formed schema relating to the possible meanings of facial expressions, tone of voice, body language, and so on based on past experience, we can never absolutely know what another person is thinking and feeling. Therefore, in trying to understand another person, we must also draw on the sensory information we are perceiving in the present to *imagine* what the other person may be thinking or feeling. Psychologists call this 'mentalization' (Fonagy et al. 2002).

As Graeber (2011) writes, interpersonal relationships 'require a continual and often subtle work of interpretation; everyone involved must put constant energy into imagining the other's point of view' (p. 48). Because we cannot absolutely know phenomena, one of our core resources for approximating understanding is our imagination. The role of imagination in this sense, as Graeber writes, is not that referred to (since Descartes) as transcendental, in which imagination relates to that which we know is not real (i.e. fantasy, fiction, or mythical abstraction). Rather, the role of imagination is conceived here as a more immanent dimension of experience which helps us draw connections between past orientations and the particularity of our present experience, in order to interpret what might be happening. For example, a teacher might draw on past experiences and studies (existing orientations) as well as present information (such as the behaviour of a student) to imagine what that student might be feeling.

According to Graeber, Smith (1761) first made note of our capacity to empathise with others through imaginative labour, when he observed that humans 'appear to have a natural tendency not only to imaginatively identify with their fellows, but also, as a result, to actually feel one another's joys and pains' (ibid., p. 51). When faced with the suffering of others, a person who wants to be caring, compassionate, and non-violent will often draw on their own experience of suffering, undertaking imaginative labour to empathise with the other. However, this practice makes the 'imaginer' vulnerable to experiencing emotional distress themselves, sometimes even resulting in 'vicarious traumatisation' (McCann and Pearlman 1990; Pearlman and Saakvitne 1995). Empathic feeling can become overwhelming, causing the subjects to feel a need to withdraw or shut down in order to protect their own psychological and emotional health. Graeber (2011) gives an example of this in modern society, writing of how, 'the poor, however, are just too consistently miserable, and as a result, observers, for their own self-protection, tend to simply blot them out' (p. 51).

Suppressing, evading, and ignoring the suffering of others have been identified as primary symptoms of compassion fatigue, secondary traumatic stress, and vicarious traumatisation (Figley 1995; Meadors et al. 2008; Van Hook and Rothenberg 2009). According to these authors, when overwhelmed by the suffering of others we can experience a strong desire or need to safeguard our own emotional stability and psychological energy reserves causing us, just like sufferers of primary trauma, to avoid experiences that might trigger distressing emotions. While it is well known that trauma sufferers often avoid 'triggering' stimuli, and can sometimes become very aggressive when 'triggered' (behaviours that could possibly be linked back to violent epistemic behaviour motivated by self-preservation), the possibility of violent epistemic behaviour being enacted by those who have become overwhelmed after witnessing the suffering of others has received very little attention outside of traumatology research in the USA. However, research in this field has identified that teachers are particularly vulnerable to this phenomenon (Rothschild 2006).

3.9   Thwarted Self-Actualisation

The ideas presented thus far regarding the relationship between motivations, emotions, and epistemology have all been related to biological self-*preservation* and/or social and psychological *self*-preservation. Earlier, I introduced self-actualisation as another core human motivation. However, I have not yet discussed how this can be related to violence. Regarding this, I propose two possible scenarios. Firstly, in line with Rogers' own views (1980, p. 118), I suggest that a neurotic response (or pattern of neurotic responses which become habitual) to fear or anxiety felt in relation to self-preservation can result in the 'thwarting or warping' of self-actualisation. Secondly, I propose that when social or practical circumstances are not conducive to healthy self-actualisation and severely restrict the subject's ability to self-actualise or 'flourish freely' (Smith 2011), this can cause the subject to experience a strong sense of frustration[9] and/or helplessness. We can imagine how the individual could respond to these emotions with aggression in an attempt to alleviate frustration, or turn feelings of frustration and helplessness inwards upon themselves, experiencing diminished self-worth, and/or depression. The former involves violence towards phenomena outside of the subject; the latter involves the subject enacting violence upon themselves. I explore these scenarios in more detail in the next chapter, and provide some case-study examples to illustrate this in Chap. 7.

References

Adorno, T. W. (1973). *Negative Dialectics*. London: Routledge.

Adorno, T. W. (2005). *Minima Moralia: Reflections from Damaged Life*. London: Verso.

Ahmed, S. (2006). *Queer Phenomenology: Orientations, Objects, Others*. Durham: Duke University Press.

Appleton, M. (2002). *Summerhill: A Free Range Childhood*. Loughton: Gale Centre Publications.

Bauman, Z. (2000). *Liquid Modernity*. Cambridge: Polity.

Block, N. (1998). On a Confusion About a Function of Consciousness. In N. Block, O. Flanagan, & G. Guzeldere (Eds.), *The Nature of Consciousness: Philosophical Debates* (pp. 375–415). Cambridge: MIT Press.

Broadbent, D. (1958). *Perception and Communication*. London: Pergamon Press.

---

[9] For a discussion on frustration, see Fromm (1973).

Chalmers, D. (2004). The Representational Character of Experience. In B. Leiter (Ed.), *The Future for Philosophy* (pp. 153–180). Oxford: Oxford University Press.

Chalmers, D. (2007). The Hard Problem of Consciousness. In M. Velmans & S. Schneider (Eds.), *The Blackwell Companion to Consciousness* (pp. 225–234). Oxford: Blackwell Publishing.

Cook, D. (2005). From the Actual to the Possible: Nonidentity Thinking. *Constellations, 12*(1), 21–35.

Dainton, B. (2007). Coming Together: The Unity of Conscious Experience. In M. Velmans & S. Schneider (Eds.), *The Blackwell Companion to Consciousness* (pp. 209–222). Oxford: Blackwell Publishing.

Damasio, A. R. (1994). *Descartes' Error: Emotion, Reason and the Human Brain.* New York: Grosset/Putnam.

Dewey, J. (1997). *Experience and Education.* New York: Touchstone.

Eisler, R., & Miller, R. (2004). *Educating for a Culture of Peace.* Portsmouth: Heinemann.

Elliott, D. S., Hamburg, B. A., & Williams, K. R. (1998). *Violence in American Schools.* Cambridge: Cambridge University Press.

Falzon, C. (1998). *Foucault and Social Dialogue: Beyond Fragmentation.* London: Routledge.

Figley, C. R. (1995). *Compassion Fatigue: Coping with Secondary Traumatic Stress Disorder in Those Who Treat the Traumatized.* New York: Brunner/Mazel.

Flannery, K., & Marcus, J. (2012). *The Creation of Inequality: How Our Prehistoric Ancestors Set the Stage for Monarchy, Slavery, and Empire.* Cambridge: Harvard University Press.

Fonagy, P., Gergely, G., Jurist, E. L., & Target, M. (2002). *Affect Regulation, Mentalization and the Development of the Self.* New York: Other Press.

Foucault, M. (1980). *Power/Knowledge: Selected Interviews and Other Writings, 1972–1977.* New York: Pantheon.

Francesco, C. (1976). *A Brief History of Education.* Totowa: Littlefield.

Freire, P. (1973). *Extension or Communication.* New York: The Seabury Press.

Freud, S. (1910). The Psychoanalytic View of Psychogenic Disturbance of Vision. *SE, 11,* 209–218.

Freud, S. (1915). Instincts and Their Vicissitudes. *SE, 14,* 109–140.

Freud, A. (1942). *The Ego and the Mechanisms of Defence.* London: Hogarth Press.

Fricker, M. (1998). Rational Authority and Social Power. *Proceedings of the Aristotelian Society, 98,* 159–177.

Fricker, M. (1999). Epistemic Oppression and Epistemic Privilege. *Canadian Journal of Philosophy, 29*(sup1), 191–210.

Fromm, E. (1973). *The Anatomy of Human Destructiveness.* London: Pimlico.

Fromm, E. (2013). *Escape from Freedom.* New York: Open Road Media.

Furth, H. G. (1987). *Knowledge as Desire: An Essay on Freud and Piaget.* New York: Columbia University Press.

Goldstein, K. (1939). *The Organism: A Holistic Approach to Biology Derived from Pathological Data in Man.* New York: American Book Company.

Graeber, D. (2011). *Revolutions in Reverse: Essays on Politics, Violence, Art, and Imagination.* London: Minor Compositions.

Graham, G., Horgan, T., & Tiensen, J. (2007). Consciousness and Intentionality. In M. Velmans & S. Schneider (Eds.), *The Blackwell Companion to Consciousness* (pp. 468–484). Oxford: Blackwell.

Gruenewald, T. L., Kemeny, M. E., Aziz, N., & Fahey, J. L. (2004). Acute Threat to the Social Self: Shame, Social Self-Esteem, and Cortisol Activity. *Psychosomatic Medicine, 66,* 915–924.

Heidegger, M. (1962). *Being and Time.* New York: Harper & Row.

Hobbes, T. (1996). *Leviathan.* Cambridge: Cambridge University Press.

Hofer, B. K. (2002). *Personal Epistemology: The Psychology of Beliefs About Knowledge and Knowing.* London: Lawrence Erlbaum Associates.

Hoffman, A. M. (1996). *Schools, Violence and Society.* London: Praeger.

Horkheimer, M., & Adorno, T. W. (2002). *Dialectic of Enlightenment.* Stanford: Stanford University Press.

Horta, P. (2007). *Educom.Rádio: Uma Política Pública em Educomunicação.* São Paulo: University of São Paulo.

Husserl, E. (1973). *Experience and Judgement.* London: Routledge.

Illeris, K. (2007). *How We Learn: Learning and Non-learning in School and Beyond.* London: Routledge.

Illeris, K. (2009). A Comprehensive Understanding of Human Learning. In K. Illeris (Ed.), *Contemporary Theories of Learning: Learning Theorists… In Their Own Words* (pp. 7–20). London: Routledge.

James, W. (1918). *The Principles of Psychology* (Vol. 1). New York: Dover.

Jarvis, P. (1987). *Adult Learning in the Social Context.* London: Croom Helm.

Jarvis, P. (2009). Learning to Be a Person in Society: Learning to Be Me. In K. Illeris (Ed.), *Contemporary Theories of Learning: Learning Theorists… In Their Own Words* (pp. 21–32). London: Routledge.

Kant, I. (1953). *Critique of Pure Reason.* New York: Macmillan.

Kegan, R. (2009). What "Form" Transforms? A Constructive-Developmental Approach to Transformative Learning. In K. Illeris (Ed.), *Contemporary Theories of Learning: Learning Theorists… In Their Own Words* (pp. 35–52). London: Routledge.

Kierkegaard, S. (1989). *The Concept of Irony.* New Jersey: Princeton University Press.

Kitchner, K. S. (1983). Cognition, Metacognition, and Epistemic Cognition: A Three-Level Model of Cognitive Processing. *Human Development, 26*(4), 222–232.

Leithäuser, T. (1976). *Formen des Alltagsbewusstseins*. Frankfurt: Campus.

Locke, J. (1990). *An Essay Concerning Human Understanding*. Oxford: Oxford University Press.

Lowe, R. (2007). *The Death of Progressive Education: How Teachers Lost Control of the Classroom*. London: Routledge.

Maslow, A. (1943). A Theory of Human Motivation. *Psychological Review, 50*, 370–396.

Maslow, A. (1954). *Motivation and Personality*. New York: Longman.

McCann, I. L., & Pearlman, L. A. (1990). Vicarious Traumatization: A Framework for Understanding the Psychological Effects of Working with Victims. *Journal of Traumatic Stress, 3*(1), 131–149.

McConkey, J. (2004). Knowledge and Acknowledgement: 'Epistemic Injustice' as a Problem of Recognition. *Politics, 24*(3), 198–205.

Meadors, P., et al. (2008). Compassion Fatigue and Secondary Traumatization: Provider Self Care on the Intensive Care Units for Children. *Journal of Paediatric Health, 22*(1), 24–34.

Merleau-Ponty, M. (2012). *Phenomenology of Perception*. New York: Routledge.

Oxford English Dictionary. (2014). *Epistemology*. Retrieved April 10, 2014, from http://www.oxforddictionaries.com/definition/english/epistemology.

Pearlman, L. A., & Saakvitne, K. W. (1995). Treating Therapists with Vicarious Traumatization and Secondary Traumatic Stress. In R. Figley (Ed.), *Compassion Fatigue: Coping with Secondary Traumatic Stress Disorder in Those Who Treat the Traumatized* (pp. 150–177). London: Routledge.

Piaget, J. (1953). *The Origin of Intelligence in the Child*. New York: Routledge & Kegan Paul.

Piaget, J. (1977). *The Development of Thought: Equilibration of Cognitive Structures*. New York: Viking Press.

Polanyi, M. (1969). Sense-Giving and Sense-Reading. In M. Green (Ed.), *Knowing and Being: Essays by Michael Polanyi* (pp. 181–207). London: Routledge & Kegan Paul.

Posner, M. I. (1978). *Chronometric Explorations of Mind*. Oxford: Lawrence Erlbaum.

Praetorius, N. (2000). *Principle of Cognition, Language and Action: Essays on the Foundations of a Science of Psychology*. New York: Kluwer Academic Press.

Ralph, S. (2013). *An Archaeology of Violence: Interdisciplinary Approaches*. New York: SUNY Press.

Reich, W. (1972). *Character Analysis*. New York: Farrar, Strauss and Giroux.

Rogers, C. R. (1959). A Theory of Therapy, Personality and Interpersonal Relationships as Developed in the Client-Centered Framework. In S. Koch (Ed.), *Psychology: A Study of a Science Vol. 3 – Formulations of the Person and the Social Context* (pp. 184–256). New York: McGraw Hill.

Rogers, C. R. (1961). *On Becoming a Person*. London: Constable.

Rogers, C. R. (1980). *A Way of Being*. Boston: Houghton Mifflin.

Rothschild, B. (2006). *Help for the Helper: The Psychophysiology of Compassion Fatigue and Vicarious Trauma*. New York: Norton.

Rousseau, J. J. (1984). *A Discourse on Inequality*. London: Penguin Books.

Sartre, J. P. (1956). *Being and Nothingness: An Essay in Phenomenological Ontology*. New York: Washington Square Press.

Scheff, T. J., & Retzinger, S. M. (2001). *Emotions and Violence: Shame and Rage in Destructive Conflicts*. Indianapolis: Lexington Books.

Schostak, J. F. (1986). *Schooling the Violent Imagination*. London and New York: Routledge & Kegan Paul.

Searle, J. (2007). Biological Naturalism. In M. Velmans & S. Schneider (Eds.), *The Blackwell Companion to Consciousness* (pp. 325–334). Oxford: Blackwell Publishing.

Shanon, B. (2002). Cognition, Epistemology, Ontology: Book Review of Praetorius on Cognition-Action. *Psycoloquy, 13*(7). Art.2.

Sherman, D. (2007). *Sartre and Adorno: The Dialectics of Subjectivity*. Albany: SUNY Press.

Siewert, C. (2003). *Consciousness and Intentionality*. Retrieved April 25, 2014, from http://plato.stanford.edu/archives/fall2003/entries/consciousness-intentionality/.

Smith, A. (1761). *Theory of Moral Sentiments*. London: A. Millar.

Smith, R. C. (2011). *Consciousness and Revolt: An Exploration Toward Reconciliation*. Holt: Heathwood Press.

Spinoza, B. (1985). *The Collected Works of Spinoza* (Vol. 1). Princeton: Princeton University Press.

Spivak, G. C. (1988). Can the Subaltern Speak? In C. Nelson & L. Grossberg (Eds.), *Marxism and the Interpretation of Culture* (pp. 271–313). Chicago: University of Illinois Press.

Sully, J. (1890). The Psychophysical Process in Attention. *Brain, 13*(2), 145–164.

Taube, M. (2012). *Evolution of Matter and Energy on a Cosmic and Planetary Scale*. New York: Springer-Verlag.

Thompson, E. (2001). Empathy and Consciousness. *Journal of Consciousness Studies, 8*(5–7), 1–32.

Treisman, A. (1964). Selective Attention in Man. *British Medical Bulletin, 20*, 12–16.

Trevarthen, C. (1998). The Concept and Foundations of Infant Intersubjectivity. In S. Braten (Ed.), *Intersubjective Communication and Emotion in Early Ontogeny* (pp. 15–46). Cambridge: Cambridge University Press.

Trevarthen, C. (2004). Brain Development. In R. L. Gregory (Ed.), *Oxford Companion to the Mind* (2nd ed., pp. 116–127). Oxford: Oxford University Press.

Trevarthen, C., & Reddy, V. (2007). Consciousness in Infants. In M. Velmans & S. Schneider (Eds.), *The Blackwell Companion to Consciousness* (pp. 41–57). Oxford: Blackwell Publishing.

Tye, M. (2007). Philosophical Problems of Consciousness. In M. Velmans & S. Schneider (Eds.), *The Blackwell Companion to Consciousness* (pp. 23–36). Oxford: Blackwell Publishing.

Van Hook, M. P., & Rothenberg, M. (2009). Quality of Life and Compassion Satisfaction/Fatigue and Burnout in Child Welfare Workers: A Study of the Child Welfare Workers in Community Based Care Organizations in Central Florida. *Social Work & Christianity, 36*(1), 36–54.

Velmans, M., & Schneider, S. (2007). *The Blackwell Companion to Consciousness*. Oxford: Blackwell Publishing.

Vygotsky, L. S. (1978). *Mind in Society: The Development of Higher Psychological Processes*. Cambridge: Harvard University Press.

Waismann, F. (1945). Verifiability. *Proceedings of the Aristotelian Society, Supplementary Volumes, 19*, 119–150.

Wider, K. (1997). *The Bodily Nature of Consciousness: Sartre and Contemporary Philosophy of Mind*. Ithaca: Cornell University Press.

Wu, X. J., Schepartz, L. A., Liu, W., & Trinkaus, E. (2011). Antemortem Trauma and Survival in the Late Middle Pleistocene Human Cranium from Maba, South China. *Proceedings of the National Academy of Sciences of the United States of America, 108*(49), 19558–19562.

Young, R. J. C. (2001). *Postcolonialism: An Historical Introduction*. Oxford: Blackwell.

CHAPTER 4

Conceptualising Violence in Relation to Social Circumstances and Subject Development

4.1   From the Individual to the Social

In the previous chapter, I conceptualised a specific type of cognitive behaviour that I propose we call 'violent epistemology'. I discussed what makes us capable of enacting violent epistemology, and some of the things that might motivate us to do so. This was all discussed on the level of the individual. As we know, individuals do not live in isolation, but live in a social world which comprises a large part of their 'facticity'—the conditions in which they exist (Sartre 1956). It is important, therefore, that any attempt to understand violence holistically also examines the relationship between the individual and the social.

The model of violent epistemic cognition presented thus far can help us understand individual responses to situations. However, it does not help us to clearly understand how violence becomes engrained in our societies, cultures, and institutions (including schools). As discussed in Chap. 1, violence is perpetrated not only by individuals but also by societies and institutions (Ross Epp 1996; Galtung 1996). In today's world, violence seems to be perpetuated as much by individuals who find themselves in difficult situations to which they struggle to respond non-violently, as it is by social circumstances marked by ideology, coercion, or even outright control and domination, and which limit the scope of individual choices (Hegel 1977; Sartre 1963; Adorno 1973; Sherman 2007; Smith 2011; Harber 2002; Ross Epp 1996; Galtung 1996). We are born and raised in a social world. The previous chapter illustrated how the enactment of

© The Author(s) 2019   81
B. M. Titchiner, *The Epistemology of Violence*, Critical Political Theory
and Radical Practice, https://doi.org/10.1007/978-3-030-12911-8_4

violence epistemology can be seen as a response to experiences that we have in this world, and as Social Constructivists[1] have highlighted, we often learn our ways of responding through social interactions and relationships with others, and through formative social institutions such as schools (Collins 2009), which are shaped by complex social, economic, and political histories. The relationship between the individual and their surrounding context is therefore not simple but plays a key role in the cycles of perpetuating violent epistemology, and for this reason, it must be examined.

If we consider the proposal that one motivation for enacting violent epistemology can be fear or anxiety felt in the face of the 'non-conceptual moreness' of experience (Smith 2011), we can discern that this anxiety relates to an existential facticity which will not change regardless of the type of society that we live in. While we can learn to manage our anxieties better and to respond to them without violence, there will always be an 'unknowable' dimension to experience. However, other motivations for enacting violent epistemology such as frustration felt at having one's self-actualisation thwarted, or overwhelming sadness felt at witnessing the destitution and suffering of others, might not be so commonplace if social circumstances were more conducive to human flourishing. Therefore, it is important to develop an understanding of how 'non-conducive social circumstances'[2] arise, and of the role these circumstances can play in thwarting self-actualisation and fostering the enactment of violent epistemology.

4.2   Defining Ideology as a Form of Violent Epistemology

A term which comes up repeatedly when researching social circumstances that are not conducive to human flourishing is 'ideology' (Morgan 2013; Adorno 1973, 2005; Aiyer 2001; Amann and Baer 2002; Benjamin 1977; Clarke 2004; Gillespie 2006; Harris 2000; Marcuse 1964). A number of authors' formulations of the concept of ideology also bear remarkable

---

[1] Note that this book supports neither a purely constructivist and individualist, nor a purely social constructivist perspective, but rather recognises the contribution that both constructivism (e.g. Piaget) and social constructivism (e.g. Vygostky) make to our understanding of human learning, development, and epistemology.

[2] The term 'non-conducive social circumstances' is used in this book to mean circumstances that foster the thwarting of self-actualisation and the enactment of violent epistemology.

similarities, analogies even, to the formulation of violent epistemology that I have proposed (Horkheimer 1947; Smith 2011; Morgan 2013; Sherman 2007). In light of this, I propose that if we examine the relationship between ideology and violent epistemology, we can better understand how the collective enactment of violent epistemology can result in the establishment of social circumstances which are not conducive to self-actualisation or the enactment of non-violent epistemology.

'Ideology' is commonly defined in such terms as 'a system of ideas and ideals' or 'the set of beliefs characteristic of a social group or individual' (Oxford English Dictionary 2016). These definitions present ideology as something rather relativistic and ethically neutral, and do not indicate any explicit relation between ideology and violent epistemology.[3] However, the work of some authors does present some analogies. Smith (2011) argues that ideological thought possesses an epistemic structure that differentiates it from non-ideological thought. Ideological thought, he argues, can be identified by one basic marker: the cognitive act of separating out one or a small number of dimensions from our experience with a phenomenon, and holding that/those dimension(s) up to be of superior importance in relation to all other dimensions. In the process, other dimensions are suppressed, pushed to the margins of awareness, or attributed little import. This conceptualisation is supported by Morgan (2013), who writes that ideology 'privileges a certain reading of reality, elevating certain elements of human existence, while ignoring and repressing others' (no page).

These formulations share characteristics with Adorno's 'identity thinking', in which a certain particularity of experience is generalised into a universal concept, and all particularities that challenge the validity and universality of that concept are subsumed or suppressed. Characteristics are also shared with Piaget's 'type α behaviour', and Rogers' 'Stage One behaviour' in which phenomena that do not fit well into a rigidified scheme are rejected. In the selecting of one or a few dimensions of experience and holding them to be of superior importance to all other dimensions, Smith and Morgan's conceptualisations of ideological thought also share the epistemic characteristics of violent epistemology because, in holding one or a few dimensions of experience to be superior to other dimensions, the fluid relationship between the generalities and particularities of experience is severed, and other particularities that may also hold importance become neglected or subsumed.

[3] See Horkheimer (1947, pp. 3–57) for a critique of subjectivist and relativist epistemology and its relation to the neutralisation of ideology.

Sherman (2007) explains how, in ideological thought, 'phenomena, which are levelled to conform to [an] ontological project, cannot be grasped in their full facticity: what conforms is abstracted from and transposed directly into ontology, in which it is absolutized, while what does not conform is set aside' (pp. 49–50). In this statement, Sherman also appears to be expressing the characteristics of violent epistemology, in which particularities that do not conform to a pre-existing scheme that the subject is 'protecting', are not fully acknowledged by the subject. Particularities that do conform to the pre-existing scheme are severed from their relationship with the remaining particularities, and assimilated into the scheme in an abstract manner (abstract because their relation with the remaining particularities is now severed). As long as the scheme, comprised of a select particularity or small number of particularities is held to be a general truth, absolutised and held as being 'identical' to the phenomena it purports to represent, then the subject will 'set aside' by pushing to the margins of awareness or subsuming under that scheme, all particularities that do not conform with it.

Like schema, ideologies are formed by humans to help us make sense of and respond to situations in the world. As Morgan (2013) writes, 'ideologies […] seek to present themselves as a unified body of thought, which provides a perspective on how the world functions and a method for action within this framework' (no page). As we have established, schema are a necessary dimension of cognition because they enable us to orientate ourselves and function in the world, and we can think of them as only becoming epistemically violent when we utilise identity thinking, type α/Stage One behaviour, and the severance of the general from the particular in forming and maintaining them. Assuming that they possess the epistemic structure outlined by Smith, Morgan, and Sherman, and since this structure appears to be formed and maintained through violent epistemology, I propose that ideologies can be seen as analogous to violent epistemic schema.

4.3   COLLECTIVE AFFIRMATION OF IDEOLOGY

So, how does the formation and maintenance of ideological schema on the part of the individual translate into the construction and maintenance of social circumstances that are not conducive to self-actualisation, and which foster ongoing enactment of violent epistemology? Adorno (2005) proposed that the individual subject who has created their own ideological schema or 'delusions' also experiences loneliness and craves community, and in search of community such individuals come together and, collectively affirming the ideological schema, form collectives based on their shared acceptance of such schema as valid representations of reality:

> The bottomless solitude of the deluded has a tendency to collectivisation and so quotes the delusion into existence. This pathic mechanism harmonizes with the social one prevalent today, whereby those socialised into desperate isolation hunger for community and flock together in cold mobs. So folly becomes an epidemic: insane sects grow with the same rhythm as big organisations. (Adorno 2005, p. 163)

Fromm (2013) also discusses a similar mechanism:

> In most cases the destructive impulses […] are rationalised in such a way that at least a few other people or a whole social group share in the rationalisation, and thus make it appear to be "realistic" to the member of such a group.[4] (p. 212)

Adorno (2005) suggests that as more and more people collectively affirm the validity of the ideological scheme, the more it is perceived and accepted as a true representation of reality, thus 'quoting delusion into existence'. He proposed that via this process, human civilisation has been built on violence. And as a result, individual subjects are born into a world that does not foster self-actualisation or non-violent epistemic relating with self, the phenomenal world, or others. In our societies, 'narrowing down the world, shutting off experience, developing an obliviousness both to the terrors of the world and [our] own anxieties' (Becker 1973, p. 178) has become almost necessary and very much normalised. As Becker writes, 'in order to function normally, man has to achieve from the beginning a serious constriction of the world and of himself. We can say that the essence of normality is the *refusal of reality*' (ibid.).

Adorno (2005) and Sherman (2007) argue that as a result of this we grow up with unmet needs and 'stunted' subjectivity, resulting in a sense of isolation from self, the phenomenal world, and others. In trying to ameliorate this isolation as well as our existential anxieties, they suggest that we have a tendency to look for a sense of security and belonging in

---

[4] This is precisely why purely social constructivist and relativistic epistemologies do not protect against violence (and may even unwittingly support its manifestation).

collectives that provide and affirm ideological schema, which can provide guidance and affirmation for action in the world.

One motivation behind violent epistemic cognition has not yet been discussed—that is, a desire for control and domination over ourselves, the phenomenal world, and others. As mentioned previously, the act of forming rigid conceptualisations of phenomena that sever the universal from the particular can be seen as an attempt to tie that phenomenon down and hold it in a 'safe' place within a rigidified world view (Becker 1973). In this sense, violent epistemology can be seen as an attempt to order the world and maintain a sense of control, eliminating the threat of not knowing and the vulnerability of disequilibrium that comes with being challenged by new and deviant information. A desire for control can also be seen in attempts to intentionally 'not know', when the full reality of one's experience is too uncomfortable, overwhelming, and perceived as threatening (ibid.). When the ideological schema of individuals become collectively affirmed, the desire for domination over phenomena is not eliminated, but rather 'the question of insecurity turns into a question of power and domination on behalf of a collective frame of reference' (Smith 2011, p. 88). In other words:

> The history of society largely represents projections of [our destructive responses to] the basic epistemic conditions of human experience via the endless historical re-emergence of models of (social) thought and action driven towards domination (i.e. totalitarianism, barbarism, political dictatorship, colonialism, economic and social monopoly, and so on). (ibid., p. 24)

Inherent to the epistemic structure of ideology is also the phenomenon of hierarchical thinking. By selecting and separating out one dimension or particularity of experience and holding it up to be of superior importance compared to all other dimensions, the subject is allocating hierarchies of value to dimensions of phenomena. When collectively affirmed, hierarchies inherent to an ideological scheme can translate into social hierarchies:

> Ideology, in the simplest sense, is the process of hypostatisation [...] it is represented by certain fundamental epistemological features, which [...] often [...] take the form of certain specific recurring phenomena in the formation and practice of social collectivity (i.e., hierarchical organisation). (ibid., pp. 32–33)

Some examples of this could include the historical tendency of societies to categorise people into hierarchies of social class (Sidanius and Pratto 2001).

One effect of hierarchical societies, Young (2001) argues, is the maintenance of 'in-groups' and 'out-groups' marked by 'the repression of the difference of those who do not conform to the dominant norms' (p. 59). People who are different 'become viewed as in some way deviant or inferior. Lacking the normality of the dominant group, they become marked out as Other' (ibid.). Maintaining such rigid social structures has historically often involved rituals of violence. As Ralph (2013) writes, such rituals serve as a means to maintain social relations, reinforce cultural messages, and maintain the power of the collectively affirmed ideology. In such an ideological social atmosphere, 'sanctified violence and ritual can offer justification to an individual, or a group, that their victims are morally and spiritually inferior, or antithetical to society, thereby making the violence more acceptable' (ibid., p. 8).

The result of the collective affirmation of ideological schema (which contain inherently controlling, dominating, and hierarchical characteristics) is that, according to Adorno (2005), our modern societies are constantly being shaped by hierarchies and 'delusions' (ideologies) which become embodied in the sects, big organisations, and entire structure of a society, forming what he called a 'bad totality'. Adorno's reference to collectivity as central to the construction of a 'bad totality' recognises the importance of collectives in determining the influence of ideologies within society, but also the participation of individuals as central to this. As Smith (2011) writes:

> If the concrete phenomenon of self-deceptive thought implies anything for us here, it is the *initial choice* [of the individual] to suppress or emphasise some qualities of experience over other qualities of experience, and how this becomes the groundwork for a systemic enterprise. (p. 74)

Smith is referring to the fact that violent epistemology occurs in individual cognition, and relies on the *choice* of the individual subject to create and maintain ideological schema by suppressing and emphasising certain particularities or dimensions of experience.

However, Smith is also arguing that this individual choice lies at the heart of the embedding of ideologies into our social systems. He illustrates this further:

> [W]hen an ideological group is formed around the belief in racial supremacy and is found to express significant discrimination toward other groups of people, it's the inner prejudice of the individuals (of the subject) to blame. The group in this case only represents the instrument for the prejudice;

it symbolises a form of mutual recognition of belief in the abstract. While this [may] seem like an obvious observation, the problematic status of the subject in an ideological collective tends to be commonly overlooked. (ibid., p. 81)

Therefore, while on the one hand, as Adorno argues, it is the collective affirmation of ideology that 'quotes it into existence' on a social level, on the other hand this would not be possible without individual subjects choosing to enact and seek affirmation for their violent epistemic cognition.

This view is also affirmed by Gramsci (2011), who argued that the ideology of one group cannot be simply imposed upon others. Rather, the alliance of others must be won through their consent. Without such consent, an ideology cannot grow from being perceived as the delusion of a small number of individuals to a hegemonic social ideology that is accepted by a significant proportion of a society as 'common sense'. As Smith (2011) writes:

> A totalized worldview is not dominantly secure without achieving unceasing affirmation of itself on a social level. This affirmation is found in the mutual recognition of others, as it is the collectivising moment of any ideological development which is integral to the birth of a functional totality. (p. 86)

However, as with a violent epistemic scheme that the subject can only maintain by constantly guarding it against the onslaught of particularities that present themselves to challenge the scheme's integrity, the collective development and maintenance of an ideological totality

> is a constant struggle against a multitude of resistances to ideological domination, and any balance of forces that it achieves is always precarious, always in need of re-achievement. Hegemony's 'victories' are never final, and any society will evidence numerous points where subordinate groups have resisted the total domination that is hegemony's aim, and have withheld their consent to the system. (Fiske 1987, p. 41)

In sum, we can consider that individual acts of violent epistemology can be collectively affirmed through mutual affirmation. While ideological hegemony is never absolute, if a significant proportion of society consents to an ideological scheme and its hierarchical, controlling, and dominating attributes, a degree of ideological hegemony can result which is not only built upon but also officially sanctions hierarchical social organisation, in-groups and out-groups, violence against social 'deviants', and the narrowing of (and desensitisation towards) one's experience. The outcome, McConkey (2004) argues, is a 'society [that] is less just through its exclusion of uncomfortable truths' (p. 6).

4.4 Non-conducive Social Circumstances

It is easy to imagine how such circumstances might not be conducive to healthy self-actualisation and non-violent epistemic thought. When discussing the hierarchical, controlling, and dominating attributes of ideological thought, Horkheimer and Adorno (2002) proposed that three key aspects leading to the 'bad totality' of modern societies are the historical human behaviours of dominating over 'external' nature (the phenomenal world), repressing 'internal' nature (ourselves), and dominating over each other. A fourth factor inherent in all of the above and which is heavily implied in *Dialectic of Enlightenment* (though the term is not explicitly used) is what Horkhiemer (1947) called 'instrumental reason'. In *Dialectic of Enlightenment*, Horkheimer and Adorno propose that in a 'bad social totality' 'The control of internal and external nature has been made the absolute purpose of life' (p. 25). Below I outline how these ideas can contribute to an overall concept of 'non-conducive' social circumstances.

4.5 Domination over External Nature (the Phenomenal World)

Horkheimer and Adorno (2002) famously presented the argument that in effort to secure our own self-preservation, humans have employed reason (and with it technology) as an instrument to dominate over nature:

> Enlightenment, understood in the widest sense as the advancement of thought, has always aimed at liberating human beings from fear and installing them as masters. [...] Enlightenment's program was the disenchantment of the world. It wanted to dispel myths, to overthrow fantasy with knowledge. (Horkheimer and Adorno 2002, p. 1)

They tell of how Enlightenment thinkers proposed a systematic enquiry into nature, and how 'knowledge obtained through such enquiry would not only be exempt from the influence of wealth and power but would establish man as the master of nature' (ibid.).

While the Enlightenment was fuelled by ideals of freedom and liberation from dependence on superstitions, magical rituals, and mythology through the establishment of 'objective facts', Horkheimer and Adorno argued that the rationalistic, positivistic thinking that emerged from this period actually reverted to an instrumental subjectivism because it subjugated nature to humanity's subjective motivations and ends (self-preservation) and thus could not be exempt from the influence of subjective interests, including those of people in positions of wealth and power. In this way, Enlightenment thinking was unaware of its own internal contradictions:

> What human beings seek to learn from nature is how to use it to dominate wholly both it and human beings. Nothing else counts. Ruthless toward itself, the Enlightenment has eradicated the last remnant of its own self-awareness. Only thought which does violence to itself is hard enough to shatter myths. (Horkheimer and Adorno 2002, p. 2)

As Horkheimer (1947) explained, being instrumentalised as a means to advance human knowledge of nature, reason began to be utilised in the manner perceived as most efficient for achieving this task. Only those aspects of phenomena which could be severed from their relationships with other particularities in order to classify and organise them (thus reducing them to a mass of data to be computed) were perceived as worth acknowledging. Particularities and concepts (such as emotions, desires, happiness, and justice) which did not submit so easily to this process began to be seen as 'scientifically unverifiable and useless' (p. 24) and to be attributed to a type of thought that is 'uncertain, superstitious, nonsensical, in short more "metaphysical", than their own isolated assumptions that are simply taken for granted and made the basis of their intellectual relation with the world' (p. 85). As a result, a reductionistic kind of thinking emerged:

> Concepts have been reduced to summaries of the characteristics that several specimens have in common. By denoting a similarity, concepts eliminate the bother of enumerating qualities and thus serve better to organize the material of knowledge. [...] Any use transcending auxiliary, technical summarisation of factual data has been eliminated as a last trace of superstition. Concepts have become 'streamlined,' rationalized, labour-saving devices. (ibid., p. 21)

This 'streamlined' thought which acknowledges only the particularities that make phenomena alike, whilst relegating those which demonstrate the diverse, varying, and changeable qualities of experience, is seen by

Horkheimer to have been instrumental in the expansion of industry, which as we now know has had such a destructive impact on the natural world:

> The advantage of mathematics—the model of all neo-positivistic thinking— lies in just this 'intellectual economy'. Complicated logical operations are carried out without the actual performance of all the intellectual acts upon which the mathematical and logical symbols are based. Such mechanization is indeed essential to the expansion of industry; but if it becomes the characteristic feature of minds, if reason itself is instrumentalized, it takes on a kind of materiality and blindness, becomes a fetish, a magic entity that is accepted rather than intellectually experienced. (ibid., p. 23)

This type of instrumental rationality has resulted, according to Horkheimer and Adorno (2002), in an increasing distancing between human subjectivity and the phenomenal world, which better enables us to dominate, control, and manipulate it:

> Human beings purchase the increase in their power with estrangement from that over which it is exerted. Enlightenment stands in the same relationship to things as the dictator to human beings. He knows them to the extent that he can manipulate them. [...] In their mastery of nature, the creative God and the ordering mind are alike. Man's likeness to God consists in sovereignty over existence, in the lordly gaze, in the command. (ibid., p. 6)

This 'estrangement' could also be seen to be exacerbated by the division between subject and object that exists in Enlightenment thought, and also in the vast majority of philosophical thought that came both before and after the Enlightenment era (including that of Horkheimer and Adorno). However, as Zuidervaart (2007) highlights, missing from such thought is 'any indication that the object can also be a subject' (p. 119). Historically, the object has primarily been defined as 'what human beings can know and, by extension, what they can (try to) make, control, or influence' (ibid.). However, as Zuidervaart argues, 'this leaves out of account an entire range of relations within which human beings and their "objects" are mutual subjects' (ibid.):

> Animals, for example, perceive us just as much as we perceive them, and they have needs and emotions that no mere "object" could have. So too, humans share biospheres with plants and animals. Although dramatically shaped by

human activity, for better and for worse, biospheres are co-constituted by nonhuman life. In that sense plants and animals have an "agency," or at least a subjectivity, that exceeds mere "objecthood," and on which human "subjects" depend. (ibid., p. 120)

Zuidervaart argues that there is a need for recognition of the 'mutual intersubjectivity of human beings with other creatures [, of] the mutual interdependency of all organisms in the biospheres they inhabit' (p. 122). He argues that human control over other organisms becomes illegitimate and destructive when it promotes human flourishing at the expense of the interconnected flourishing of all organisms in the biosphere. As he puts it, 'Freedom is not a freedom to dominate but a freedom to flourish' (ibid.). In light of this, he agrees with Horkheimer and Adorno's argument that violence based on freedom conceived as 'freedom to dominate' has permeated human civilisation from its inception, and that this pursuit of freedom (essentially from fear) has been based on a misrecognition of the subjectivity of other creatures, which has violated the very meaning and pursuit of freedom.

4.6   Repression of Internal Nature (Ourselves)

Not only has the instrumental reason of Enlightenment thought come to deny the subjectivity of other beings, as Horkheimer and Adorno (2002) argue, it has also come to deny its own subjectivity, creating a distance not only from the phenomena of experience but also from the self and the multidimensional particularities of our emotions, desires, bodily sensations, and so on, which have come to be seen as separate from, and unnecessary for, the functioning of reason:

> Not only is domination paid for with the estrangement of human beings from the dominated objects, but the relationships of human beings, including the relationship of individuals to themselves, have themselves been bewitched by the objectification of mind. Individuals shrink to the nodal points of conventional reactions and the modes of operation objectively expected of them. (ibid., p. 21)

Rather than being successful in the pursuit of objectivity, Horkheimer and Adorno argue that humans have instead developed a shrunken, narrowed, form of subjectivity:

The self which, after the methodical extirpation of all natural traces as myth-ological, was no longer supposed to be either a body or blood or a soul or even a natural ego but was sublimated into a transcendental or logical sub-ject, [which] formed the reference point of reason, the legislating authority of action. (Horkheimer and Adorno 2002, p. 22)

This creation of a self-identity as 'rational' being necessitated, as Sherman (2007) argues, a 'domination over the self' (p. 241).

Through the repression of all aspects of the self which did not match this rigid self-schema, Sherman argues, that in striving to absolutely 'know' the phenomenal world through this one-dimensional self-identity of 'rational' being, humans have created a normalised neurosis which

is simply this boring imprisonment of the self in itself, crippled by its terror of the new and unexpected, carrying its sameness with it wherever it goes, so that it has the protection of feeling, whatever it might stretch out its hand to touch, that it never meets anything but what it knows already. (ibid., p. 241)

This repression of so many dimensions of our being has resulted, accord-ing to Horkheimer and Adorno (2002), in a 'sacrifice of the self':

Paid for by a denial of nature in the human being for the sake of mastery over extrahuman nature and over other human beings [...] the human being's mastery of itself [...] which is dominated, suppressed, and dissolved by virtue of self-preservation [...] practically always involved the annihila-tion of the subject in whose service that mastery is maintained. (pp. 42–43)

As I explain a little later, this domination over the self contributes to what Sherman (2007) calls the de-formation of the subject—a de-formation that operates in co-constitutive relation with 'non-conducive' circumstances, in a vicious cycle of individual and 'social pathology' (Smith 2016).

4.7   Domination over Others

Horkheimer and Adorno (2002) purport that domination over nature and ourselves has also translated, by way of the same instrumental reason, into domination by some human beings over others. Just as with nature and our own selves, the violent epistemology of instrumental reason enables the reduction of other human beings to objects that can be utilised in the service of ideological schema. Fuelled by self-preserving aims, the 'rational being' thus manages to justify the exploitation of the other, whether in the form of direct control or indirect coercion. This phenomenon, as Zuidervaart (2007) argues, can be identified throughout the 'various societal formations that have characterised Western civilization, from Homeric times to the twentieth century' (p. 124). Based on the analysis of Brazil's social history presented in the following chapter, I propose that this pattern has also been present in non-Western societies and continues into the twenty-first century.

Ideological schema used to justify the exploitation of humans have taken many forms throughout history, from mythologies and religions to social, scientific, and political doctrines. The most predominant and all-encompassing of these has taken the form of economic ideology (Horkheimer and Adorno 2002; Sherman 2007; Smith 2011). Regardless of ideological justifications, Zuidervaart (2007) argues that, 'exploitation is always illegitimate and destructive, directly destructive for the exploited and indirectly destructive for the exploiters' (p. 124). Horkheimer and Adorno (2002) argued that exploitation is directly destructive for the exploited because it forces the suppression and appropriation of the physical, emotional, psychological, and intellectual needs and desires of the exploited for the benefit of the exploiter(s), and is indirectly destructive for the exploiter(s) because it requires the same reduction and sacrifice of one's own subjectivity in order to formulate and maintain the necessary schema to justify such exploitation. As Horkheimer and Adorno illustrate:

> [The exploited] cannot enjoy their work because it is performed under compulsion, in despair, with their senses forcibly stopped. The servant is subjugated in body and soul, the master regresses. No system of domination has so far been able to escape this price, and the circularity of history in its progress is explained in part by this debilitation. (ibid., p. 27)

They go on to argue that instrumental reason (which in the name of ideology suppresses the particularities, needs, and desires of individual human beings) fosters social circumstances in which:

> Not merely are qualities dissolved in thought, but human beings are forced into real conformity. [...] Each human being has been endowed with a self of his or her own, different from all others, so that it could all the more surely be made the same. [B]ecause that self never quite fitted the mold [of the predominant collectivised ideology], enlightenment throughout the liberalistic period has always sympathized with social coercion. The unity of the manipulated collective consists in the negation of each individual. (ibid., p. 9)

Horkheimer (1947) argues that:

> This explains the tendency of liberalism to tilt over into fascism and of the intellectual and political representatives of liberalism to make their peace with its opposites. This tendency, so often demonstrated in recent European history, can be derived, apart from its economic causes, from the inner contradiction between the subjectivistic principle of self-interest and the idea of reason that it is alleged to express. (p. 20)

This 'tilting' between a liberalistic (and more recently neo-liberalistic) state and fascist, authoritarian, or dictatorial political tendencies can be seen not only in European history but also in Brazil, as we will see in the following chapter.

While the most common form of domination over other human beings can be seen in the economic exploitation of the various stages of capitalism, this phenomenon is also evident in other forms, including racism and prejudice. As Horkheimer and Adorno (2002) state:

> The self which learned about order and subordination through the subjugation of the world soon equated truth in general with classifying thought, without whose fixed distinctions it cannot exist. (p. 10)

The classifying behaviour inherent in the positivism of Enlightenment thought can also be seen in the classification of human beings into different classes or categories based on the isolation of one dimension of being (wealth, bloodline, religion, skin colour, gender, age, etc.) which becomes violent epistemology when that dimension is held up as more important than all other dimensions.

Such categorisations, which entail a severing of the relationship between generalities and particularities of individual human beings, can be formed as rigidified schema in which the fearful, anxious, or threatened subject seeks security. In this sense, it is not so much the dimension of being that is isolated, as the fact that it is isolated and used in this way that matters when it comes to violent epistemology being expressed as prejudice. As Sartre (1944) stated, 'if the Jew did not exist, the anti-Semite would invent him' (p. 13). For both Adorno and Sartre it was the epistemology behind the 'anti' rather than the selection of the dimension of 'Semite' (as opposed to other possible dimensions that could be selected to create a category) that mattered. As Sherman (2007) explains:

> To sustain his object of hate, and thus solidify his own (reactive) self-understanding, the anti-Semite must close himself off to the richness of experience since the truths of experience tend to undermine the stereotypes that provide the very stuff of the anti-Semite's identity. (p. 220)

This reading reflects Adorno's argument that:

> The less anti-Jewish imagery is related to actual experience and the more it is kept 'pure' from contamination by reality, the less it seems to be exposed to disturbance by the dialectics of experience, which it keeps away through its own rigidity. (p. 311)

The above descriptions contain clear analogies to the model of violent epistemology presented in the previous chapter, especially with regard to Piaget's type α behaviour. While the example used here is anti-Semitism, we can imagine how the same epistemic behaviour can apply to other forms of prejudice. As I highlight in the next chapter, one form that is particularly prevalent in Brazil is that of racism based on the classification of people by skin colour.

4.8   A Vicious Cycle: Non-conducive Circumstances and the De-formation of Subjectivity

As mentioned above, Horkeimer and Adorno use the term 'bad totality' to refer to the entirety of a society built on instrumental reason, and the various forms of domination it entails. However, Holloway (2010) criticises Horkheimer and Adorno for presenting a 'totalizing theory' which does not adequately acknowledge the presence and potential for 'cracks' in the social totality where other forms of relating with the world, ourselves, and each other can emerge. However, one thing that is prevalent in Horkheimer and Adorno's argument regarding the collectivisation of ideology is that it fosters social circumstances which, while not 'total' and absolute, are generally not conducive to the enactment of non-violent epistemic behaviour. For this reason, I have chosen to introduce the term 'non-conducive circumstances' as an alternative to 'bad totality'.

As illustrated in some of the examples given above, in a society built on violent epistemology (enacted in the name of self-preservation), 'self-preservation succeeds only to the extent that, as a result of self-imposed regression, self-development fails' (Adorno 1967, pp. 85–86). This 'failure of self-development' is what Sherman (2007) terms the de-formation of the subject. Sherman writes of how Sartre spoke of selfhood as 'being formed within the dynamic interaction between consciousness, other persons, and the natural world' (ibid., p. 8), meaning that our developing subjectivity, which operates in mediation with our self-concept, is shaped by the interactions that we have with others and our environment. Bronfenbrenner (1979, 2005) and Kegan (2009) also support this view. For the vast majority of humans who are born and raised in ideological social circumstances, the ideological aspect will have played a role in shaping these interactions to a greater or lesser degree. As Sherman (2007) writes, 'the formation of the subject is inextricably intertwined with the contemporary dynamics of domination and subordination' (p. 190).

Given that, according to Sherman, subjectivity 'is the result of experience', he proposes that 'to the extent that we misconceive our relation to the [phenomena] of our experience, we deform our experiences, and, therefore, ultimately our selves' (ibid., p. 273). Reflecting Horkheimer and Adorno's argument, Sherman indicates that when we enact violent epistemology, we simultaneously deform not only our experiences of phenomena but also our own developing subjectivity. When we consider this process occurring 'inextricably' with the contemporary social dynamic, we can imagine the development and maintenance of a widespread, normalised social pathology (Smith 2016), which is more conducive to the de-formation of subjectivity than it is to healthy self-actualisation, as Fromm (2013) illustrates:

> A society could be called neurotic in the sense that its members are crippled in the growth of their personality. Since the term *neurotic* is so often used to denote a lack of social functioning, we would prefer not to speak of a society in terms of its being neurotic, but rather in terms of its being adverse to human happiness and self-realisation. (p. 165)

Likewise, considering the entwinement of subject de-formation with social dynamics also sheds light on why Benjamin (1977) states that 'the ego creates an increasingly hostile world through its exercise of domination and control' (p. 46).

As noted earlier, the formation of ideology and its development into functional hegemony begins with the acts of individual subjects which over time become collectively affirmed by other subjects. Indeed, as Smith (2011) reminds us, 'ideology [...] is a product of the subject [...] not a mystical force; it is created by human beings' (p. 81). If we remember that ideology can be seen as analogous to violent epistemology because it isolates and 'holds up' certain particulars of experience whilst suppressing others, then we can also consider the collective affirmation of ideology as a collective de-formation of subjectivity.

For Horkheimer and Adorno (2002), identity thinking and the 'bad totality' (or non-conducive circumstances) are just different expressions of the same underlying epistemic behaviour. They write of how, in the collectivisation of ideology into social structures (with the instrumental reason it entails), 'the control of internal and external nature has been made the absolute purpose of life [and] self-preservation has been finally automated' (p. 24). Rather than fostering the flourishing and free development of human subjectivity in all its diversity, as it relates openly to the multidimensional particularities of experience, Horkheimer and Adorno argued that society based on collectivised ideology fosters conformity and a closing down of the subject, in order to fit the 'mould':

> Through the mediation of total society, which encompasses all relationships and impulses, human beings are being turned back into precisely what the developmental law of society, the principle of the self, had opposed: mere examples of the species, identical to one another through isolation within the compulsively controlled collectivity. (p. 29)

As already stated, in contemporary society this is most clearly expressed through economic ideology. Bronner (2004) explains how underpinning capitalist social relations is an instrumental reason which subjects everything to the calculation of costs and benefits. Under this reason, he argues, 'knowledge' has become 'freed from any commitment to liberation', transforming 'itself into a whore employed by the highest bidder' and '[internal and external] nature into an object of domination' (p. 3). Horkheimer and Adorno (2002) go on to speak of the 'violence' of economic ideology which 'amputates the incommensurable', dissolves the diverse qualities of humans and phenomena in thought, and forces human beings into 'real conformity'. In the 'exchange society', they write, 'the possibilities conferred by birth are moulded to fit the production of goods that can be bought on the market (p. 9). In these comments, Horkheimer and Adorno are referring to the reduction of human beings to their economic value by instrumental reason employed in the name of economic ideology.

This example begins to illustrate how, aside from the de-formation of the subject that is inherent to the establishment of ideology, once established, ideology can in turn foster the de-formation of the subject in a continual 'feedback loop'. As Horkheimer and Adorno highlight, we are born into pre-established, ideological, social circumstances. We develop with ideological epistemology as a significant frame of reference during our formative years, and under the 'possibilities conferred by birth' into such society, we begin our young lives already being coerced to relate with ourselves, others, and the phenomenal world in violent epistemic ways. Thus, society built on ideology fosters the de-formation of subjectivity from birth. As it mediates 'all relationships and impulses', the violent epistemology of ideological society is fostered through media, parenting, culture, social policy, schooling, and through all kinds of daily experiences.

One particularly problematic aspect of ideological social circumstances is that they assign 'conditions of worth' (Rogers 1959) to individuals. Those individuals who align most accurately with the dimensions of experience that are held up above all others are perceived to be of most value (e.g. in capitalist society, those individuals who are most economically productive and who accumulate the most wealth). Likewise, those dimensions of the self that are perceived to be most instrumental to economic productivity are held to be of superior value than those which are seen as superfluous. The problem with living in such an environment is that (as Rogers found in his research) being subject to such conditionality can have an incredibly destructive impact on the formation of the subject.

In order to meet such conditions, individuals must suppress certain dimensions of themselves which, as Horkheimer and Adorno (2002) argued (especially in relation to labour in late capitalist societies), 'enforces the self-alienation of individuals' (p. 23). As Sherman (2007) describes, motivated by the desire for self-preservation, identity thinking applied to the self (the development of a rigid self-concept to which one tries to conform such as in Sartre's (1956) concept of 'bad faith') is fostered and perpetuated by capitalism. While the diverse and multidimensional particularities of phenomena are reduced to their 'exchange value', the diverse, multidimensional particularities of individuals are reduced to the identity of 'worker'.

This employment of violent epistemology as instrumental reason functions to make both phenomena and human beings 'fungible', which, as Sherman (2007) states, 'progressively tends to alienate human beings from themselves (p. 241). Horkheimer and Adorno (2002) also explain how, as an attempt to overcome fear and preserve the self, the contradictory outcome of the Enlightenment is that it has resulted in societies which reduce, deform, and alienate the self, resulting in isolated individuals who remain ever more fearful for their self-preservation. In capitalism this manifests as the experience of society being largely indifferent to anything beyond one's economic role:

> The self, entirely encompassed by civilization, is dissolved in an element composed of the very inhumanity which civilization has sought from the first to escape. The oldest fear, that of losing one's own name, is being fulfilled. For civilization, purely natural existence, both animal and vegetative, was the absolute danger. Mimetic, mythical, and metaphysical forms of behaviour were successively regarded as stages of world history which had been left behind, and the idea of reverting to them held the terror that the self would be changed back into the mere nature from which it had extricated itself with unspeakable exertions and which for that reason filled it with unspeakable dread. (ibid., p. 24)

The reduction of the self to its economic value extends to the body, which as a dimension of self is sublimated, suppressed, and appropriated in the name of the prevailing social ideology, and as Honneth (1995) states, is often subject to 'silent acts of […] enslavement and mutilation' (p. 121). In contemporary society, this process can be overt (such as in prisons, certain workplaces, and schools) but also complex and subtle, making it harder for subjects to understand and resist:

> The more complex and sensitive the social, economic, and scientific mechanism, to the operation of which the [capitalist] system […] has attuned the body, the more impoverished are the experiences of which the body is capable. The elimination of qualities, their conversion into functions, is transferred by rationalised modes of work to the human capacity for experience. (Horkheimer and Adorno 2002, p. 28)

According to Rogers (1959) and Fromm (2013), a common response to the isolation, alienation, and fear for self-preservation that results from being subject and reduced to such conditions of worth is to adapt in whatever way seems possible. Rogers argued, based on his studies, that all humans experience a need for positive regard (both in the eyes of others and in the form of self-regard). He found that when individuals are subjected to conditions of worth (rather than unconditional positive regard), they exhibit a tendency to selectively deny and distort experiences which did not fit with such conditionality. As Rogers (1959) writes, 'he cannot regard himself positively, as having worth, unless he lives in terms of these conditions' (p. 225). Horkheimer and Adorno present an analogous argument:

> The countless agencies of mass production and its culture impress standardized behaviour on the individual as the only natural, decent, and rational one. Individuals define themselves now only as things, statistical elements, successes or failures. Their criterion is self-preservation, successful or unsuccessful adaptation to the objectivity of their function and the schemata assigned to it. (pp. 21–22)

Rogers (1959) explains how this process of adaptation occurs:

> Because of the need for self-regard, the individual perceives his experience selectively, in terms of the conditions of worth which have come to exist in him. [...] Experiences which are in accord with his conditions of worth are perceived and symbolized accurately in awareness. [...] Experiences which run contrary to the conditions of worth are perceived selectively and distortedly as if in accord with the conditions of worth, or are in part or whole, denied to awareness. [...] Consequently some experiences now occur in the organism which are not recognized as self-experiences, are not accurately symbolized, and are not organized into the self-structure in accurately symbolized form. [...] Thus from the time of the first, selective perception in terms of conditions of worth, the states of incongruence between self and experience, of psychological maladjustment and of vulnerability, exist to some degree. (p. 226)

We see here how the attempt to adjust psychologically to a society which places conditions of worth on us can result in psychological 'maladjustment' and the de-formation of subjectivity. As Rogers writes, such conditions of worth can become introjected to the extent that the individual internalises them, making it very difficult for the individual to integrate experiences which might challenge these conditions. We see in this a violent epistemology that is analogous to Piaget's type α behaviour. From this point on, Rogers states:

> [The subject's] concept of self includes distorted perceptions which do not accurately represent his experience, and his experience includes elements which are not included in the picture he has of himself. Thus he can no longer live as a unified whole person [...]. Certain experiences tend to

threaten the self. To maintain the self-structure defensive reactions are necessary. [...] This, as we see it, is the basic estrangement in man. He has not been true to himself, to his own natural organismic valuing of experience, but for the sake of preserving the positive regard of others he has now come to falsify some of the values he experiences and to perceive them only in terms based upon their value to others'. (ibid., p. 226)

This threatenedness manifests, as Fromm (2013) argues, as a 'kind of constant anxiety [which] results from the position of the isolated and powerless individual' (p. 213). Fromm details 'mechanisms of escape' through which individuals attempt to overcome this feeling of insignificance by either renouncing their integrity 'or by destroying others so that the world ceases to be threatening'. One such mechanism, he claims, is the solution found by the majority of individuals in modern society:

> The individual ceases to be himself; he adopts entirely the kind of personality offered to him by cultural patterns; and he therefore becomes exactly as all others are and as they expect him to be. The discrepancy between "I" and the world disappears, and with it the conscious fear of aloneness and powerlessness. (ibid., p. 218)

An important outcome of this, however, is what Fromm calls 'the thwarting of life', in which:

> The isolated and powerless individual is blocked in realising his sensuous, emotional and intellectual potentialities. He is lacking the inner security and spontaneity that are the conditions of such realisation. This inner blockage is increased by cultural taboos. (ibid., pp. 213–214)

To put it briefly, 'external social repression', as Adorno et al. (1950) says, 'is concomitant with the internal repression of impulses' (p. 759). That is, social circumstances built on violent epistemology and the de-formation of subjectivity foster the perpetuation and furtherance of both. The outcome of such (mal)adaptation to the conditions of worth of ideological society, as we have seen above, is the further destruction of the self, and potentially also, others, and the phenomenal world. Fromm (2013) writes that the more the drive towards life (or self-actualisation to use Rogers' terms) is thwarted, the more the individual is likely to feel driven towards destruction in a distorted attempt to self-actualise. Destructiveness, as Fromm says, 'is the outcome of unlived life' (ibid., p. 216).

Those individual and social conditions that make for suppression of life produce the passion for destruction that forms, so to speak, the reservoir from which the particular hostile tendencies—either against others or against oneself—are nourished. (ibid.)

This discussion of hostile tendencies is reminiscent of Horkheimer and Adorno's (2002) illustration of the 'hardened subject'. They write of how blocked attempts to self-actualise can leave a 'scar' on the developing subject:

Mental life in its earliest stages is infinitely delicate. [Just as] the body is crippled by physical injury, the mind [is crippled] by fear. (p. 213)

'At the point where [the child's] impulse has been blocked', they say, especially 'if the thwarting has been too brutal', 'a scar can easily be left behind, a slight callous where the surface is numb' (p. 214). As examples of such 'blocking', they mention how 'not only the forbidden question but the suppressed imitation, the forbidden weeping or the forbidden reckless game, can give rise to such scars' which in their turn can

lead to deformations [and] produce 'characters' hard and capable; [...] produce stupidity, in the form of deficiency symptoms, blindness, or impotence, if they merely stagnate, or in the form of malice, spite and fanaticism, if they turn cancerous within. Goodwill is turned to ill will by the violence it suffers. (ibid.)

This metaphorical blindness and impotence, which Horkheimer and Adorno describe, appears to refer to the development of 'blindness' manifest as the suppression and negation of particularities of experience, and 'impotence' manifest as the type of powerlessness described by Fromm, characterised by an inability to respond to the world sensitively and non-violently as an autonomous subject. The problem, as Fromm (2013) highlights eloquently, is that adaptation to a society built on ideological epistemology that ascribes conditions of worth to individuals, while often perceived as healthy and 'normal', is actually not healthy at all because it is not conducive to the healthy development of the subject:

From the standpoint of a functioning society, one can call a person normal or healthy if he is able to fulfil the social role he is to take [, if he is able to work in the fashion required [and] is able to participate in the reproduction of society [...] From the standpoint of the individual, we look upon health or normalcy as the optimum of growth and happiness of the individual. If the structure of a given society were such that it offered the optimum possibility for individual happiness, both viewpoints would coincide. However, this is not the case in most societies we know [...] there is a discrepancy between the aims of the smooth functioning of society and of the full development of the individual. [...] This differentiation is often neglected. Most psychiatrists take the structure of their own society so much for granted that to them the person who is not well adapted assumes the stigma of being less valuable. On the other hand, the well adapted person is supposed to be the more valuable person on a scale of human values. If we differentiate the two concepts of normal and neurotic, we come to the following conclusion: the person who is normal in terms of being well-adapted is often less healthy [...]. Often he is well adapted only at the expense of having given up his self in order to become more or less the person he believes he is expected to be. (pp. 162–164)

In this lengthy but eloquent quote, Fromm provides great insight into the functioning of a societal 'feedback loop' (Myrdal 1944), or a vicious cycle in which, as Marcuse (1969) states:

Repression disappears in the grand objective order of things which rewards more or less adequately complying individuals and, in doing so, reproduces more or less adequately society as a whole. (p. 51)

This social pathology, as Smith (2016) states, plays an active role in the reproduction of all or most facets of contemporary social life. 'Within modern capitalist society', he writes, 'with its dominant and coercive institutions and structures, as well as its deeply ingrained instrumental rationale and mode of cognition (Parton 2015a), the subject is both produced and reproduced. Within this process of reproduction [...] social norms, traditions [and], patterns, and structures of behaviour [are] reproduced' (no page).

To summarise, we can see ideological social circumstances as having developed via the collective affirmation of ideological structures of thought which include domination over nature, ourselves, and other human beings, and entail the de-formation of subjectivity and the sublimation of the body as an outcome of ideologically driven instrumental reason. In turn, ideological social circumstances can be seen as 'non-conducive' to the healthy development of human subjectivity, because they foster a further de-formation of the subject by encouraging conformity with conditions of worth. The result is alienation from ourselves, others, and the phenomenal world and a kind of (mal)adaptation to an already pathological society in which our self-actualisation is often thwarted. A further stunting of development can occur as a result of this thwarted self-actualisation, potentially resulting in destructive tendencies and a 'hardening' of subjectivity which interferes with our ability to respond sensitively to our experiences. This de-formation of subjectivity contributes to a 'feedback loop' in which circumstances that are not conducive to healthy subject development, nor to the enactment of non-violent epistemic behaviour, are reproduced.

4.9   Overview and Potential Pathways of Response

Throughout the last two chapters I have presented many ideas, and I have attempted to explain clearly how they can all work together to form a coherent theoretical framework. However, it may be beneficial at this point to provide a visual illustration in the form of a diagram, accompanied by a brief recap, summarising how these core ideas relate to each other to form a broad and multidimensional conceptual model of violent epistemology and non-conducive circumstances.

From the start of Chap. 3, I have intentionally emphasised the existence of phenomenological freedom (or cognitive agency) because it is this, I propose, that enables us to choose whether or not to enact violent epistemology. To a certain degree, this also enables us to decide how to respond to the phenomena of our experience, including the circumstances (facticity) in which we find ourselves. Figure 4.1 outlines what I propose to be the potential pathways of response that a subject could follow during any given moment, in the process of interacting with the phenomena of experience. It also outlines a number of 'scenarios', illustrating some key ways in which chosen responses can either contribute to the further de-formation of subjectivity and perpetuation of ideology, or to a healthier form of subjectivity, and to behaviour that is less likely to be violent or reinforce ideology.

The diagram is not intended to be read as a linear, deterministic map of cause and effect. Certain dimensions are represented in a linear fashion for the sake of readability, but are probably more correctly thought of as operating cyclically—for example, it is likely more accurate to think of emotions and cognition as operating in constant mediation with one another, rather than as always occurring one before the other (Padesky and Greenberger 1995). Each dimension of the diagram is briefly summarised in the text that

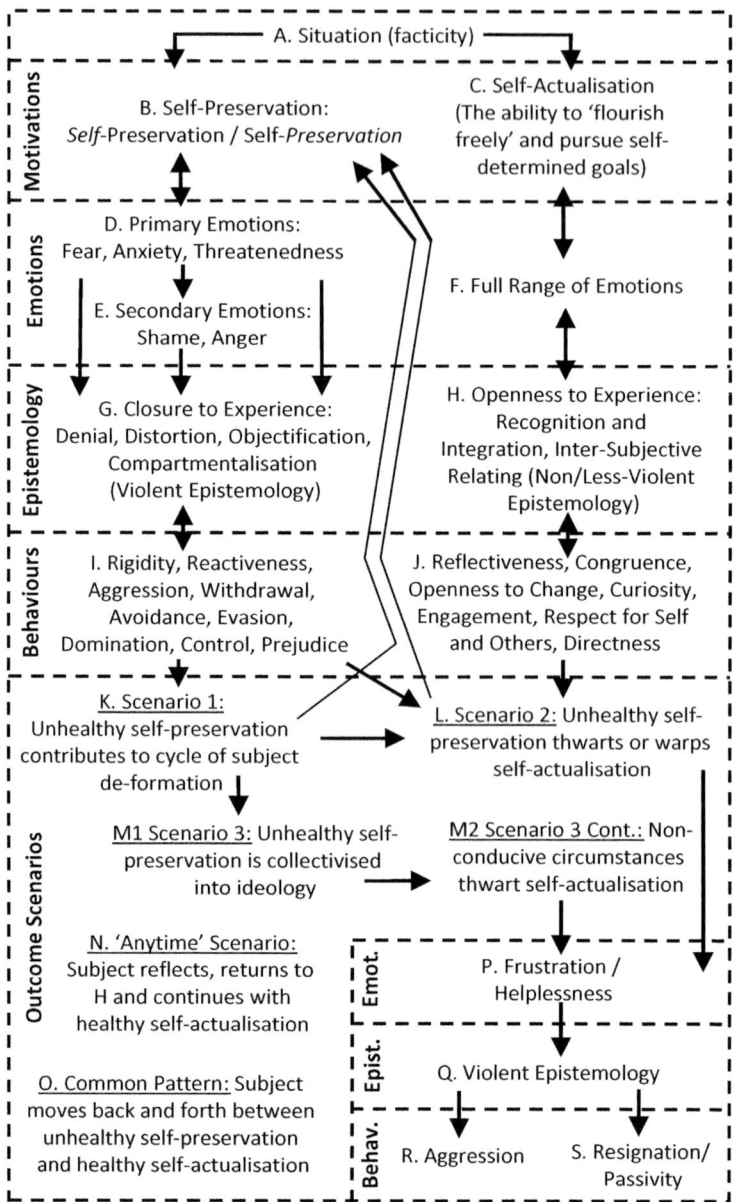

Fig. 4.1 Overview of a theory of violent epistemology and non-conducive circumstances, showing potential pathways of response

follows. The conceptual framework relating to dimensions C, F, H, J, N, and O are summarised here but discussed in more detail in Chap. 8. This diagram will also form a key point of reference for the school case-study analysis presented in Chap. 7, and may therefore be worth bookmarking.

A. The Situation (Facticity). This represents the 'situation' (Sherman 2007, pp. 7–8) (or 'facticity' in Sartrean terms) in which the subject is situated. This can be a momentary situation bound by time (i.e. an interaction) or the wider familial, institutional, and societal environment within which the subject lives (Horkheimer and Adorno 2002; Bronfenbrenner 2005). In today's world, many 'situations' constitute 'non-conducive social circumstances' which as Sherman (ibid.) writes, 'not only limit[...] the ways in which a person can act on his phenomenological freedom, but also fundamentally circumscribe[...] the very nature of his selfhood'. However, it is possible to have situations which are more conducive to self-actualisation, healthy subject-formation, and non-violent ways of relating with the world, ourselves, and others. I discuss what these may look like in Chap. 8.

B. Self-Preservation. As discussed in Chap. 3, self-preservation and self-actualisation appear to constitute two core motivations commonly experienced by humans for acting in daily life. The motivation of self-preservation can be comprised of *self*-preservation (the preservation of the social, psychological, and emotional self) and self-*preservation* (the preservation of the biological self).

C. Self-Actualisation. In Chap. 3, I discussed the core motivation of self-actualisation which is described as the 'tendency to actualize, as much as possible, [one's] individual capacities [...] in the world' (Goldstein 1939, p. 162), 'the desire for self-fulfilment' (Maslow 1943, p. 10), and a 'striving [...] to move toward growth' (Rogers 1980, p. 118). I also discussed how self-actualisation depends, according to Maslow (1943), on the satisfaction of basic physiological needs as well as the need for safety, love, and esteem. As described earlier in this chapter, the non-conducive social circumstances of late capitalist society do not tend to foster the satisfaction of all these needs and therefore, as Maslow stated, 'basically satisfied [self-actualised] people are the exception' (ibid., p. 11).

D. Primary Emotions. Next, we come to the emotional dimension of experience. The arrows connecting self-preservation to primary emotions represent the primary emotions (discussed in Chap. 3) commonly associated with self-preservation, that is, fear, anxiety, and threatenedness. Such emotions have been identified in relation to physical self-*preservation*, as well as to psychological, emotional, and social *self*-preservation.

E. Secondary Emotions. As discussed above, non-conducive social circumstances can foster situations in which, as Fromm (2013) states, 'the individual ceases to be himself' and adopts 'the kind of personality offered to him by cultural patterns' (p. 218). As Adorno et al. (1950) argued, this 'external social repression' fosters the 'internal repression of impulses' (p. 759), creating a situation in which, often as a result of cultural taboos 'the isolated individual is blocked in realising his sensuous, emotional and intellectual potentialities' (Fromm 2013, pp. 213–214). In such circumstances, certain primary emotions such as fear, anxiety, and threatenedness may be experienced by the subject as taboo and therefore 'unacceptable', resulting in the negation of these emotions. As Scheff and Retzinger (2001) found, subjects who behaved violently tended to negate and suppress emotions that they felt to be unacceptable, and instead redirect their emotional energy into expressions of anger and rage. These could be considered secondary emotions.

F. Full Range of Emotions. Connected to dimension C, this dimension relates to the idea that in social circumstances that are more conducive to fostering free and healthy self-actualisation, the subject's ability to fully experience and acknowledge the full range of their emotions would also be fostered. As Sherman (2007) states:

> Under the right state of affairs [...] the individual would feel free to open himself up to the world, which would mean that self-identity would become more fluid, the individual would be in a position, as Nietzsche states, to become who he is. Openness to a world in which the individual can actually afford to be open is therefore the very condition of the liberated subject. (p. 281)

We can imagine how in more conducive, non-ideological social circumstances, the individual would be better able to self-actualise. This is discussed in more detail in Chap. 8.

G. Closure to Experience. This is the basic epistemic characteristic of the cognitive behaviours discussed in Chap. 3, which are central to what I have termed 'violent epistemology'. These include Piaget's (1977) 'type α behaviour', Adorno's (1973) 'identity thinking', Jarvis' (2009) 'non-learning', Leithäuser's, (1976) 'everyday consciousness', Rogers' (1961) 'Stage One', Smith's (2011) 'ideology', Horkheimer and Adorno's (2002) 'domination over internal and external nature', and Horkheimer's (1947) 'instrumental reason'. All of the above entail cognitive behaviours characterised by the negation of certain particularities of experience; the suppression of particularities and their relegation to the margins of awareness; the over-focussing on certain dimensions of phenomena at the expense of all other dimensions; and the distortion or severing of the relationship between the generalities and particularities of phenomena. Inherent in all of the above is a closure to certain dimensions of experience. The arrows leading from dimensions D and E to dimension G illustrate how closure to experience can be motivated by certain emotions.

H. Openness to Experience. This dimension relates to an alternative attitude towards experience than that described in Chap. 3 and presented as dimension G. If we agree with Sartre that we maintain phenomenological freedom at all times, then we cannot assume that closure to experience will always follow from the experience of the emotions outlined in dimensions D and E. Phenomenological freedom theoretically enables the subject to, in any moment, open themselves to acknowledging, observing, and engaging with any particularities of experience. However, as discussed, the individual may only feel able to be open 'under the right state of affairs' (Sherman 2007, p. 281). I discuss this further in Chap. 8.

I and J. Self-Preserving and Self-Actualising Behaviours. Dimensions I and J represent a non-exhaustive list of the types of behaviours that we might expect to be fostered by violent and non-violent epistemologies. In dimension I we see types of behaviours that may be fostered by violent epistemology. If we consider deformed subjectivity as characterised by repression and closure to experience, which in turn thwarts self-actualisation, then we can formulate that a self-actualising subjectivity would stem from an openness to experience and an absence of repression. Here I suggest just a few ways in which such a subject might act in the world.

Outcome Scenarios. The bottom half of the diagram presents what I have called 'outcome scenarios'. These represent the possible outcomes of the motivational, emotional, epistemic, and behavioural 'pathways' described in the top half.

K. Scenario 1. As discussed earlier in this chapter, the enactment of violent epistemology through dimensions B, D, E, G, and I can be seen as contributing to cycles of subject de-formation (Sherman 2007).

L. Scenario 2. The arrow leading from scenario 1 to scenario 2 represents the notion that the enactment of violent epistemology and the continued de-formation of subjectivity 'thwarts or warps' self-actualisation (Rogers 1959) because through 'self-imposed regression, self-development fails' (Adorno 1967, pp. 85–86). The thwarting or warping of self-actualisation can also perpetuate the cycle of subject de-formation (Fromm 2013), represented by the arrow leading back from scenario 2 to dimension B.

M1. Scenario 3. This represents how violent epistemology can be seen as analogous to ideological thought, and how ideological thought, if collectivised into social ideology, can foster social circumstances which are not conducive to healthy self-actualisation and the enactment of non-violent epistemology.

M2. Scenario 3 Cont. This represents how non-conducive social circumstances often constitute the 'situation' or 'facticity' in which we find ourselves. In such circumstances not only are violent epistemic ways of relating with the world, self, and others fostered in developing subjects, but there are also many constraints on freedom which can prevent the self-actualisation of the developing subject.

P, Q, R, and S. Dimensions P, Q, R, and S represent how violent epistemology is not only motivated by the type of existential anxiety identified in the works of Horkheimer and Adorno (2002), Smith (2011), and Sherman (2007), but also by emotions which can arise in response to living in non-conducive circumstances that restrict, thwart, and warp self-actualisation and expose the subject to overwhelming amounts of social suffering. As discussed above, this can result in withdrawal and/or destructive behaviours. This was something that I witnessed particularly in DCX School, and which is demonstrated further in Chap. 7.

N. 'Anytime' Scenario. When it comes to considering the possibility of change, or of other, non-violent ways of relating, dimension N is of crucial importance. It represents the existence of 'phenomenological freedom', and therefore the subject's potential capacity to pause, reflect, and reopen themselves to experience, and to reintegrate neglected particularities into their schema. For a person who is deeply engrained in the de-formation cycle, 'opening up' can invite serious challenges to existing orientations and self-identity, and may therefore be highly unsettling (as discussed in Chap. 8). However, the existence of phenomenological freedom means that whatever stage we might be at in the cycle of de-formation, we are never pre-determined to enact violent epistemology.

O. Common Pattern. The diagram presents the cycle of violent epistemology and subject de-formation, and the cycle of non-violent epistemology and self-actualising subjectivity, as binary antitheses. This is largely for the purpose of presenting the complex conceptual framework presented in this book, in an easily digestible format. However, on the one hand, we have established that individuals are born into a social context, and in contemporary society, this is almost always marked by ideology. It is therefore hard to imagine a subject not marked by some degree of de-formation or 'scarring' (Horkheimer and Adorno 2002). On the other hand, as Holloway (2010) stated, ideology is never absolute, and there are always 'cracks' which make other ways possible. In contemporary societies, subjects are often bombarded with vast amounts of stimuli from multidimensional and diverse phenomena, and from a wide variety of conflicting cultural and political viewpoints. In light of this, the interrelation between subjects and the world has the potential to be incredibly diverse, varied, and complex. Therefore, it is probably more correct to think of subjects as moving back and forth between violent and non-violent epistemology, and between subject de-formation and self-actualisation. Based on the arguments presented in this chapter, we can propose that the amount of time spent by the subject in violent or non-violent epistemic pathways of response can be influenced by the degree of existing de-formation and scarring, the conduciveness (or non-conduciveness) of circumstances in which the subject is situated, and the subject's choices as an epistemic agent.

The theoretical framework presented in the last two chapters illustrates how a multidisciplinary, 'radical enquiry' approach can produce a much more detailed and comprehensive framework for understanding the root causes of violence than those currently existing within the field of education. Over the following chapters, I demonstrate the usefulness of this framework by applying it to the case-study of DCX School and its surrounding context.

References

Adorno, T. W. (1967). Sociology and Psychology. *New Left Review, I, 47,* 79–97.

Adorno, T. W. (1973). *Negative Dialectics.* London: Routledge.

Adorno, T. W. (2005). *Minima Moralia: Reflections from Damaged Life.* London: Verso.

Adorno, T. W., Frenkel-Bunswick, E., Levinson, D. J., & Sanford, R. N. (1950). *The Authoritarian Personality: Studies in Prejudice Series* (Vol. 1). New York: Harper and Brothers.

Aiyer, A. (2001). Hemispheric Solutions? Neoliberal Crisis, Criminality and "Democracy" in the Americas. *Urban Anthropology and Studies of Cultural Systems and Economic Development, 30*(2–3), 239–268.

Amann, E., & Baer, W. (2002). Neoliberalism and Its Consequences in Brazil. *Journal of Latin American Studies, 34*(3), 945–959.

Becker, E. (1973). *The Denial of Death*. London: Collier Macmillan.

Benjamin, J. (1977). The End of Internalization: Adorno's Social Psychology. *Telos, 32*, 42–64.

Bronfenbrenner, U. (1979). *The Ecology of Human Development: Experiments in Nature and Design*. London: Harvard University Press.

Bronfenbrenner, U. (2005). *Making Human Beings Human: Bioecological Perspectives on Human Development*. London: Sage.

Bronner, S. E. (2004). *Reclaiming the Enlightenment: Toward a Politics of Radical Engagement*. New York: Columbia University Press.

Clarke, S. (2004). The Neoliberal Theory of Society. In A. Saad-Filho & D. Johnston (Eds.), *Neoliberalism: A Critical Reader* (pp. 50–59). London: Pluto Press.

Collins, J. (2009). Social Reproduction in Classrooms and Schools. *Annual Review of Anthropology, 38*, 33–48.

Fiske, J. (1987). *Television Culture*. London: Methuen.

Fromm, E. (2013). *Escape from Freedom*. New York: Open Road Media.

Galtung, J. (1996). *Peace by Peaceful Means: Peace and Conflict, Development and Civilisation*. London: Sage.

Gillespie, W. (2006). Capitalist World-Economy, Globalization, and Violence: Implications for Criminology and Social Justice. *International Criminal Justice Review, 16*(1), 24–44.

Goldstein, K. (1939). *The Organism: A Holistic Approach to Biology Derived from Pathological Data in Man*. New York: American Book Company.

Gramsci, A. (2011). *Prison Notebooks*. New York: Columbia University Press.

Harber, C. (2002). Schooling as Violence: An Exploratory Overview. *Educational Review, 54*(1), 7–16.

Harris, R. L. (2000). The Effects of Globalization and Neoliberalism in Latin America at the Beginning of the Millennium. *Journal of Development Studies, 16*(1), 139–162.

Hegel, G. W. F. (1977). *Phenomenology of Spirit*. Oxford: Clarendon Press.

Holloway, J. (2010). *Crack Capitalism*. London: Pluto Press.

Honneth, A. (1995). *The Fragmented World of the Social: Essays in Social and Political Philosophy*. New York: SUNY Press.

Horkheimer, M. (1947). *Eclipse of Reason*. New York: Oxford University Press.

Horkheimer, M., & Adorno, T. W. (2002). *Dialectic of Enlightenment*. Stanford: Stanford University Press.

Jarvis, P. (2009). Learning to Be a Person in Society: Learning to Be Me. In K. Illeris (Ed.), *Contemporary Theories of Learning: Learning Theorists… In Their Own Words* (pp. 21–32). London: Routledge.

Kegan, R. (2009). What "Form" Transforms? A Constructive-Developmental Approach to Transformative Learning. In K. Illeris (Ed.), *Contemporary Theories of Learning: Learning Theorists… In Their Own Words* (pp. 35–52). London: Routledge.

Leithäuser, T. (1976). *Formen des Alltagsbewusstseins*. Frankfurt: Campus.

Marcuse, H. (1964). *One Dimensional Man: Studies in the Ideology of Advanced Industrial Society*. Boston: Beacon Press.

Marcuse, H. (1969). *Eros and Civilisation: A Philosophical Inquiry into Freud*. London: Sphere Books.

Maslow, A. (1943). A Theory of Human Motivation. *Psychological Review, 50*, 370–396.

McConkey, J. (2004). Knowledge and Acknowledgement: 'Epistemic Injustice' as a Problem of Recognition. *Politics, 24*(3), 198–205.

Morgan, M. (2013). *The Paradoxical Perpetuation of Neoliberalism: How Ideologies Are Formed and Dissolved*. Retrieved November 30, 2014, from http://www. heathwoodpress.com/the-paradoxical-perpetuation-of-neoliberalism-how-ideologies-are-formed-and-dissolved/.

Myrdal, G. (1944). *An American Dilemma: The Negro Problem and Modern Democracy*. New York: Harper & Bros.

Oxford English Dictionary. (2016). *Ideology*. Retrieved August 21, 2016, from http://www.oxforddictionaries.com/definition/english/ideology?q=ideology.

Padesky, C. A., & Greenberger, D. (1995). *Clinician's Guide to Mind Over Mood*. New York: Guilford Press.

Piaget, J. (1977). *The Development of Thought: Equilibration of Cognitive Structures*. New York: Viking Press.

Ralph, S. (2013). *An Archaeology of Violence: Interdisciplinary Approaches*. New York: SUNY Press.

Rogers, C. R. (1959). A Theory of Therapy, Personality and Interpersonal Relationships as Developed in the Client-Centered Framework. In S. Koch (Ed.), *Psychology: A Study of a Science Vol. 3 – Formulations of the Person and the Social Context*. New York: McGraw Hill.

Rogers, C. R. (1961). *On Becoming a Person*. London: Constable.

Rogers, C. R. (1980). *A Way of Being*. Boston: Houghton Mifflin.

Ross Epp, J. (1996). Schools, Complicity and Sources of Violence. In J. Ross Epp & A. M. Watkinson (Eds.), *Systemic Violence: How Schools Hurt Children* (pp. 1–24). London: Falmer Press.

Sartre, J. P. (1944). *Anti-Semite and Jew*. New York: Schocken Books.

Sartre, J. P. (1956). *Being and Nothingness: An Essay in Phenomenological Ontology*. New York: Washington Square Press.

Sartre, J. P. (1963). Preface. In F. Fanon (Ed.), *The Wretched of the Earth* (pp. 7–34). New York: Grove Press.

Scheff, T. J., & Retzinger, S. M. (2001). *Emotions and Violence: Shame and Rage in Destructive Conflicts*. Indianapolis: Lexington Books.

Sherman, D. (2007). *Sartre and Adorno: The Dialectics of Subjectivity*. Albany: SUNY Press.

Sidanius, J., & Pratto, F. (2001). *Social Dominance: An Intergroup Theory of Social Domination.* Cambridge: Cambridge University Press.

Smith, R. C. (2011). *Consciousness and Revolt: An Exploration Toward Reconciliation.* Holt: Heathwood Press.

Smith, R. C. (2016). *Society, Social Pathology and the (De)formation of the Subject: Toward a Radical Philosophy of Psychology (Part 1).* Retrieved February 15, 2016, from http://www.heathwoodpress.com/r-c-smith-society-social-pathology-and-the-deformation-of-the-subject-toward-a-radical-philosophy-of-psychology-part-1/.

Young, R. J. C. (2001). *Postcolonialism: An Historical Introduction.* Oxford: Blackwell.

Zuidervaart, L. (2007). *Social Philosophy After Adorno.* Cambridge: Cambridge University Press.

CHAPTER 5

How Violent Epistemology Shapes the Contexts Surrounding Schools: Brazil, São Paulo, and the Baixada

5.1   A Socio-ecological Approach to Analysis

This chapter takes the conceptual framework presented in the previous two chapters and begins to demonstrate how it applies in practice. It does this by analysing the role of violent epistemology in the creation of the non-conducive circumstances that comprise a case-study context: Brazil, São Paulo, and the 'Baixada' neighbourhood in which DCX School is situated. I dedicate an entire chapter to this analysis because, aside from illustrating how violent epistemology translates into non-conducive circumstances, as Schick (2009) writes, it is important to locate trauma and suffering within concrete sociohistorical context, in order to better understand the co-constitutive relation between the two. As Morrell (2002) states, 'context is important—[teachers and students] operate within schools which in turn are located within communities. They have histories' (p. 42). Understanding the community in which DCX School is situated demands an examination of its broader sociohistorical context from a multi-level perspective.

To provide structure for this examination, I have drawn on Bronfenbrenner's (1944, 1979, 2005) bioecological model of human development, which conceptualises a series of structural layers comprising the social 'ecology' (or facticity), within which developing subjects are located. In line with Adorno (1973), Bronfenbrenner asserts that 'piecemeal analysis, fixed in time and space, of isolated aspects and attributes is insufficient and even misleading' (1944, p. 67). Bronfenbrenner's model therefore enables us to imagine the complex interrelationships between historical and social forces at

© The Author(s) 2019   115
B. M. Titchiner, *The Epistemology of Violence*, Critical Political Theory
and Radical Practice, https://doi.org/10.1007/978-3-030-12911-8_5

different levels of society, and the impact these forces have on schools and the individuals within them, in a holistic manner.

Complementing the discussion presented in Chap. 4, Bronfenbrenner's model enables us to think in terms of the

> …progressive, mutual accommodation, throughout the life course, between an active, growing human being and the changing properties of the immediate settings in which the developing person lives, as this process is affected by the relations between these settings, and by the larger contexts in which the settings are embedded. (Bronfenbrenner 2005, p. 107)

Figure 5.1 draws on Bronfenbrenner's bioecological model to illustrate how both the school and individual subjects can be seen as situated within

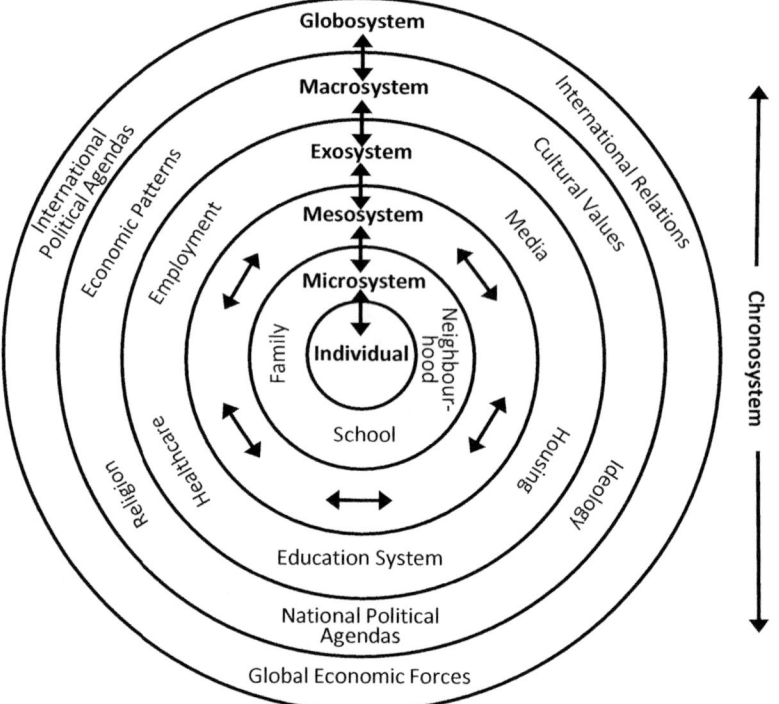

Fig. 5.1 Bioecological model of human development (developed from Bronfenbrenner 1979)

various levels of interconnected systems. Bronfenbrenner argued that the boundaries of these systems should be thought of as porous, shifting, and fluid—and the relationships between the different levels as complex, changeable, and not always clearly defined. The exact combination of elements within the system and their positioning in the diagram is therefore not intended to be read as absolute. Rather, this model is presented simply as a guide for structuring the case-study analysis.

The case-study analysis presented from here to the end of Chap. 7 is structured according to the nested levels presented in Fig. 5.1, which are defined as follows:

Globosystem. This entails factors exterior to, but encompassing or affecting the case-study country such as global economic forces and trends, international political agendas, and international relations. While this level is absent from Bronfenbrenner's formulations, I have included it because ignoring the impact of global and international forces would contradict the methodological intention to develop a holistic perspective on violence.

Macrosystem. Bronfenbrenner (2005) defined this as consisting 'of the overarching pattern of [sub]systems characteristic of a given culture, [...] or other broader social context, with particular reference to the developmentally instigative belief systems, resources, hazards, lifestyles, opportunity structures, life course options, and patterns of social interchange that are embedded in each of these systems' (pp. 149–150). I treat the macrosystem as analogous to the 'national' level of Brazil.

Exosystem. This 'encompasses the linkages and processes taking place between two or more settings, at least one of which does not ordinarily contain the developing person, but in which events occur that influence processes within the immediate setting that does contain that person' (Bronfenbrenner 2005, p. 148). While the city of São Paulo undoubtedly 'contains' the DCX students, they rarely venture out beyond the local neighbourhood. I treat the city as the exosystem because while students are largely excluded from the rest of the city, they are very much affected by events at the level of city planning as well as by broader city-wide issues such as rental prices, labour markets, social segregation, and municipal education policies.

Mesosystem. The mesosystem comprises 'the linkages and processes between two or more settings containing the developing person' (Bronfenbrenner 2005, p. 148), such as the relationship between home and school. The mesosystem is not discussed as a separate section within this chapter. However, Chap. 7 outlines the influence of experiences in the neighbourhood and home on teacher and student engagement with roles in DCX School.

Microsystem. 'A microsystem', Bronfenbrenner writes, 'is a pattern of activities, roles, and interpersonal relations experienced by a developing person in a given face-to-face setting with particular physical and material features and containing other persons with distinctive characteristics of temperament, personality and systems of belief' (2005, p. 148). The school therefore comprises a microsystem in itself, as do the family and neighbourhood. Because Chap. 7 is dedicated to a detailed analysis of the school microsystem, this chapter focusses on the primary microsystems experienced by DCX students outside of school—the neighbourhood and home life.

Chronosystem. The chronosystem cuts across all levels in the bioecological model. It represents Bronfenbrenner's assertion that human development is processual and situated within a historical, not just physical and social, context. The chronosystem can refer both to the ordering of events 'in their historical sequence and context' and to the impact of broader historical events, contexts, personal life events, and experiences on subsequent development (Bronfenbrenner 2005, p. 83). The concept of the chronosystem encourages consideration of the cumulative impact of violent epistemology and non-conducive circumstances over time. I incorporate the chronosystem throughout this chapter and the next, by analysing the impact of historical events at different levels of the nested systems.

Using the structure outlined above, the remainder of this chapter analyses how violent epistemology can be seen to have shaped the course of events at each nested level, and how these events have shaped the development and perpetuation of the 'non-conducive social circumstances' in which teachers and students at DCX School found themselves at the time of data collection.

5.2   The Globosystem: Violent Epistemology and the Globalisation of Economic Ideologies

This section focuses on what have arguably been the two main external forces to have shaped Brazil's development: colonialism and economic neoliberalism. The recorded history of Brazil begins in 1500, when the Portuguese nobleman Pedro Alvarez Cabral happened upon its northeast coast and claimed the land for Portugal (Levine 1999). This marked the beginning of colonial Brazil, the first significant manifestation of violent epistemic thought to shape Brazil's history. This happened in the context of the European 'age of discovery'—an age which has historically been attributed to the technological and intellectual 'superiority' and scientific curiosity of sixteenth century Europeans (Abulafia 2008). However, as Blaut (1993) argues, there is plenty of evidence to suggest neither technological nor intellectual superiority, but rather a simple geographical advantage over inhabitants of the African and Asian continents, who were also engaged in international travel, trade, and colonising endeavours at the time. The 'age of discovery', Blaut (ibid.) writes, began as feudalism was coming to an end and protocapitalist societies were beginning to form around the world. Mercantilism was on the rise in Europe, and in an environment of emerging capitalism, both citizens and rulers in Europe were looking to increase their wealth.

According to this account, rather than stemming from intellectual or technological superiority, the age of European 'discovery' and colonisation can be seen as closely associated with the growth of capitalism in Europe and its associated instrumental rationality of exploitation. Blaut explains how, as feudalism's ruling classes began to exhaust the potential of their own subjects to increase the production of material and economic surplus (exacerbated in Portugal by severe population reduction caused by the bubonic plague (Levine 1999)), 'they tried to conquer and exploit other communities of producers, to acquire external as well as internal fields of exploitation' (Blaut 1993, p. 271).

Rather than being motivated by scientific curiosity, the claiming of Brazil by Cabral in the pre-Enlightenment 1500s was motivated by the instrumental reason of early capitalist ideology. As the Portuguese crown faced problems of severe population and wealth reduction, the efforts to reach out, 'discover', and conquer new territories can be interpreted as motivated by self-preservation: the aim of the Portuguese crown was to amass as much wealth as possible in order to preserve and increase its power, status, and survival chances in a changing world. Considering the epistemic structure of ideology outlined in the Chap. 4, we can argue that at this time the economic dimension of life was isolated by the Portuguese crown and held up above all other dimensions in importance. Many atrocities would be carried out in the name of this economic ideology.

One of the greatest atrocities was the enslavement of indigenous and later African people in Brazil. This manifestation of violent epistemology has played a particularly significant role in shaping Brazil's history and development and has left an indelible mark on Brazilian society. Following

Cabral's arrival, Brazil's land was recognised as favourable for sugar production and claimed as an extension of Portugal with the sole purpose of becoming a sugar-producing territory to support Portuguese economic growth. After rather unsuccessful attempts to use indigenous people as a local labour force, the Portuguese plantation owners began importing people from the African continent to work as slaves on the plantations. Between 1550 and 1888, an estimated four million black Africans, mostly young males, were brought to Brazil as slaves. In the early nineteenth century, two-thirds of Brazil's population were African slaves or their descendants (Levine 1999).

Marcílio (2001) writes of how 'mobilizing slaves in great estates and plantations, Brazil entered into the global mercantilism at the time of the flourishing European renaissance' (p. 4). This history demonstrates how the Brazil we know today was founded on the violence and exploitation of slavery, carried out in the name of the economic ideology of emerging capitalism. This ideology is exemplary of violent epistemology: by holding up the economic dimension of life and repressing all other dimensions, slave traders and owners were able to perceive and treat indigenous and African peoples according to their usefulness for economic productivity, whilst attenuating other dimensions of their beings such as their humanity, pain, suffering, needs, and dignity. This is one of the most profound examples of instrumental reason being employed to justify the domination of some humans by others in the name of a collectively affirmed ideology. Brazilian society is still feeling the effects.

While it may have been the most influential, this was not the only manifestation of violent epistemology to come from outside Brazil and shape its early development. In the 1500s, the Portuguese state was officially Catholic, and colonial expansion was accompanied by a missionary zeal for spreading Catholicism to the 'infidels' of the new world (Hudson 1997). Not long after Cabral arrived in Brazil, the Jesuit order was founded and in 1540 the Portuguese king sent Jesuits to Brazil with the mission of pacifying and Christianising the native population (Levine 1999). Gathering native Brazilians into small towns and villages called 'Aldeias', the Jesuits endeavoured to instil in them the characteristics of 'good Christians'. These included, among other things, a European 'work ethic' which served to provide a pliable work force for the colony (Fausto 1999). While the intention to instil a 'work ethic' was arguably a manifestation of economic ideology, the missionary activities can also be attributed to religious ideology. By holding the notion of an all-powerful Christian God above all other dimensions of life and experience, the missionaries were able to reject the pre-existing lifestyle and beliefs of the indigenous population. On the face of things, the missionaries were more humane than the slave owners. However, their missionary activities can also be seen as acts of violent epistemology because they negated many of the indigenous population's particularities. Indigenous people in Brazil have struggled with economic and cultural appropriation, exploitation an extirpation ever since.

The economic ideology of mercantilism that fuelled Brazil's colonialisation, developed into full-blown industrial capitalism as industrialisation took hold in Europe and America in the mid-18th to early 19th centuries (Wood 2002). Brazil followed suit towards the end of the nineteenth century and throughout most of the twentieth century (Levine 1999). In Brazil, industrialisation was initially supported by the exploitation of newly freed slaves who had been made destitute and could be worked hard for very low pay since they had very little opportunity to make a living by other means. Freed slaves and their descendants, followed by European economic immigrants seeking a better life in the 'new world' (only to find a life of hardship and poverty as workers in industrial Brazil), together formed the foundations of an entrenched underclass[1] in Brazilian society that remains to this day (Kohara 2009).

The epistemic structure of thought behind industrial capitalism can be seen simply as a continuation of the instrumental reason of economic ideology. Slavery was formally abolished in the nineteenth century. However, domination over others in the form of economic exploitation continued as the notion of free labour became popular. By employing 'free' workers and paying a low wage, owners of the means of production were able to free themselves of the responsibility to provide for workers' basic needs (e.g. housing, clothing, sustenance, and medical care), placing this responsibility back on workers (Klein and Luna 2010). However, in Brazil, wages remained so low that workers often lived in squalor, barely able to provide for their basic needs (Kohara 2009). The violent epistemology of economic

---

[1] My use of the term 'underclass' in this book refers to the phenomenon of social stratification in Brazil, which can be seen as a symptom of ideology, and in which certain individuals and sectors of society are subject to stigmatising and exclusionary discourse and practices, and treated as belonging to a separate 'underclass'. This is not to be misinterpreted as an agreement with such discourse, or as an agreement with the reduction of diverse individuals to simple (e.g. class) categories. As already mentioned, the ideologies that foster this can be seen as global in nature, but this phenomenon is especially pronounced in Brazil due to the country's particular history.

ideology once again fostered a situation in which the economic dimension, along with the concepts of profit and economic growth, were held up above all other dimensions of life, allowing 'free' industrial workers to be perceived in narrow instrumental terms. Particularities such as workers' basic needs and quality of life were suppressed.

Between the 1970s and 1990s, popular support for the established model of industrial capitalism was waning in the 'developed' world, and global financial institutions and economic leaders showed increasing support for the ideas of economic neoliberalism. As Morgan (2013) writes, neoliberalism offered 'an attractive ideological framework because it presented itself as increasing individual freedom through limiting the extent that society could impinge upon individual action' (no page). However, as Bauman (2002) argues, this promise of freedom was false, because the collective adoption of neoliberalism simply made the universalisation of economic ideology all the more pervasive, as even more dimensions of life were assimilated into its schema.

One way in which neoliberalism sought freedom was through privatisation and deregulation, shifting elements that were formerly governed by society and the state, to the market. However, by positioning the market as the 'sole mechanism of governance', individual freedoms were actually reduced because (building on mercantilism and industrial capitalism's instrumentalisation of life under the economic dimension) neoliberalism simply furthered the constraint of individual action to the narrow framework of economic productivity, efficiency, and consumption (Morgan 2013). While neoliberalism purports that a deregulated market (rather than nationalised public services) offers more freedom to individuals through the ability to choose from a wider variety of market products, Marcuse (1964) argued that 'the range of choice available to individuals is not the decisive factor in determining the degree of human freedom, but [rather] what can be chosen and what is chosen by the individual' (p. 9). What the neoliberal free market has demonstrated in practice is increased economic competition. This puts companies under pressure to lower prices which increases pressure to reduce wages and make employees work harder and harder, leading to increased economic exploitation. For the majority of the working class whose 'freedom of choice' is dependent on their purchasing power and ability to compete in the job market, the result is actually a decrease in freedom. Employees have less free time, energy, and disposable income (if any), which hugely restricts their ability to choose what they want and need for a healthy and fulfilling life (Morgan 2013). In other words, the potential for self-actualisation is highly restricted.

Another criticism of neoliberalism is that, in a 'free' market where the 'free' individual is perceived as having limitless choice, responsibility for meeting basic needs and ensuring wellbeing is placed almost entirely on the individual. According to Clarke (2004), neoliberalism is based on unrealistic assumptions about economic and social relations, as well as about human needs and behaviour. The impact of this has been that since the 1990s, 'the whole world's population [has been subject] to the judgement and morality of capital' (ibid., p. 58). As a political project which has 'conquered the commanding heights of global intellectual, political and economic power', the neoliberal model 'does not purport to describe the world as it is, but the world as it should be' (ibid.). The point of neoliberalism, Clarke argues, 'is not to make a model that is more adequate to the real world, but to make the real world more adequate to its model' (ibid.). Strongly reminiscent of Piaget's type α behaviour, this manifestation of violent epistemology illustrates the 'doubly deleterious effects' (Harvey 2005, p. 76) of an ideology which refuses to accommodate phenomena that highlight its conceptual inaccuracies: as long as individuals who do not have many choices and opportunities available to them (e.g. due to lack of adequate housing and education, poverty, disability, prejudice, or any other reasons) are perceived as having access to limitless choice, 'personal failure is generally attributed to personal failings' (ibid.), with victims of non-conducive circumstance being blamed for their own destitution.

In Brazil, neoliberal economic policies began to take hold in the mid-1990s when the World Bank, International Monetary Fund (IMF), and US Treasury were heavily promoting such reforms for 'developing' countries. In 1994 a number of Latin American countries, Brazil included, agreed to a deal with the IMF in which some 60 billion dollars of external debt would be written off on the condition that they adopt neoliberal economic reforms (Harvey 2005). The common characteristics of economic policy supported by these Washington-based financial institutions were outlined in what Williamson (1989) called the 'Washington Consensus'. These included deregulation of the market, opening up to direct foreign investment, privatisation of state enterprise, and investment in 'pro-growth' and 'pro-poor' services like primary education, primary healthcare, and infrastructure. However, Harvey (op. cit.) questions whether a neoliberal state can simultaneously be 'pro-growth' and 'pro-poor' because 'the practices of the neoliberal and developmental state [which] is necessarily hostile to all forms of social solidarity that put restraints on capital accumulation [...] typically produce [...] legislation and regulatory frameworks that advantage corporations over human wellbeing' (p. 75). This illustrates yet again how ideological thought pushes phenomena (such as wellbeing) which do not serve the dimensions upheld in the core ideological scheme (capital accumulation), to the margins of awareness.

These neoliberal reforms came when Brazil was transitioning to democracy from a long period of military dictatorship. Rather than a civic overthrow of military rule, this transition was orchestrated by political and economic elites who understood that neoliberal democracy would better support their economic interests. There was no intention of redistributing wealth, but rather democracy paved the way for neoliberal economic policies and the perpetuation of social stratification (Saad-Filho 2012). Williamson (2002) illustrates how the ideas attributed to the Washington Consensus have taken on the power of collectively affirmed ideology, as they 'have continued to gain wider acceptance over the past decade, to the point where Lula [Brazil's 'pro-poor' Worker's Party president from 2003 to 2011] has had to endorse most of them in order to be electable. For the most part they are [taken for granted]' (no page) by both citizens and governments worldwide, meaning that even presidential candidates who may not fully agree with them, are under significant pressure to adopt them—as was the case for the 2003–2016 Brazilian Worker's Party presidencies.

Brazil's political and economic elites have always worked together to preserve their wealth and power. However as Harvey (2005) states, under neoliberalism representative democracy is often overwhelmed and corrupted by money power, to the extent that 'the coercive arm of the state is augmented to protect corporate interest and, if necessary, to repress dissent' (p. 77). The repression of dissent has been illustrated time and again in Brazil over the last five years, as people protesting against economic injustice have repeatedly been subject to physical violence at the hands of the military police.[2] This demonstrates the type α behaviour inherent to ideology, showing how when dimensions of life that do not serve the economic dimension attempt to push themselves into the foreground of awareness, the apparatus of structurally engrained ideology (such as Brazil's military police) does what it can to prevent these particularities from challenging the equilibrium of the schema. In Brazil, this

---

[2] This included the violent repression of school children at the end of 2015, who were sprayed with tear gas, beaten, shot at with rubber bullets, and arrested when protesting public school closures in São Paulo which were to be carried out in the name of efficiency savings (Attanasio 2015).

repression can be seen as motivated by the self-preservation motivation of the Brazilian elites.

In all the different forms it has taken since 1500, pervasive globalised economic ideology (whether mercantilism, industrial capitalism, or neoliberalism) has consistently resulted in exploitation, violence, injustice, and inequality in Brazil, as a result of the economic dimension of life being held over and above all other dimensions. Over the years, sensitivity to these injustices, on the part of some, has fostered discussion about the need for universal agreements on, and protections for, basic inalienable rights for all people. The horrendous events of the Holocaust and Second World War spurred the establishment of the United Nations (UN) and the Universal Declaration of Human Rights in the late 1940s. As attention turned to global economic development in the late 1980s, the spread of neoliberal ideology to 'developing' nations acted as a catalyst for the UN to push for the fulfilment of basic human rights, one of which was the right to education. In 1990, representatives from countries around the world met in Jomtien, Thailand and agreed on a World Declaration on Education for All. In 2000 international representatives met again at the World Education Forum in Dakar, Senegal, and agreed on the Dakar Framework for Action, which contained a set of six goals to be achieved by 2015 (UNESCO 2016):

1. Expand early childhood care and education.
2. Provide free and compulsory primary education for all.
3. Promote learning and life skills for young people and adults.
4. Increase adult literacy by 50%.
5. Achieve gender parity by 2005 and gender equality by 2015.
6. Improve the quality of education.

The Education for All goals have received widespread support from neoliberal governments for two reasons. Firstly, education has been heavily promoted by the World Bank as a worthwhile investment because it increases a nation's human capital and therefore potential for economic growth (Robeyns 2006). Secondly, even though it contains many internal contradictions, neoliberalism is grounded in liberal theory, which promotes ideas such as human rights, freedom, and education (Williamson 2002). While in practice neoliberalism places many restrictions on freedom and fails in many cases to fulfil basic human rights, these underlying liberal 'values', along with the economic argument for increasing human capital, indicates why many governments have supported Education for All.

The second Dakar goal (universal, free, and compulsory primary education) has spurred a huge effort over the past 20 years to enrol as close as possible to 100% of primary age children in schools across the world. However, massive increases in enrolment have generally not been met by proportional increase in resource allocation, resulting in over-crowded, under-resourced schools providing 'education' of questionable quality (Alexander 2008). While there is recognition in Goal 6 of the need to improve the quality of education, defining what 'quality' means is a highly contentious area of debate, and many schools in developing countries (Brazil included) have maintained a traditional nineteenth century European schooling model in practice, even if attempts to move away from this have been written into policy (ibid.). In Brazil, the increase in enrolment has caused many to argue that the overall quality of public education has decreased (Marcílio 2001). In response, an expanding private education market has arisen, creating a division between those who can afford to send their children to better-resourced private schools and those who have to make do with under-resourced public schools. This has further contributed to social stratification (ibid.).

5.3   THE MACROSYSTEM: VIOLENT EPISTEMOLOGY AND THE ESTABLISHMENT OF SOCIAL INEQUALITY IN BRAZIL

Brazil provides a valuable case-study on violence, because violence and exploitation have been core drivers of the country's development ever since Cabral set foot on its shores. From this point onwards, Brazilian history demonstrates clear examples of domination over external nature (the phenomenal world), repression of internal nature, and control/domination over others, all of which point towards an underlying violent epistemology. This section explores manifestations of this epistemology in more detail, focussing on the three main consecutive periods in Brazil's history: colonialism, industrialisation, and neoliberalism.

As mentioned previously, the first significant economic ideology to impact Brazil was the early capitalist mercantilism that fuelled Cabral's claiming of the land for Portugal. Often referred to as the 'discovery' and cited as the beginning of Brazilian history, this event already illustrates the violent epistemic thought which, viewing the land with an instrumental reason that saw only economic potential, pushed to the margins of awareness certain important particularities: namely that the land had been home to human populations for thousands of years with an established way of life in their own right (Levine 1999). Negating these factors (which if acknowledged could challenge the equilibrium of the colonial schema), the land was called 'Brazil', and the people who lived there assimilated into Portugal's economic project, seen as free for the taking (Fausto 1999).

The arrival of colonisers spelled disaster for the indigenous population. As the Portuguese tried to enslave them in service of their economic endeavours, those who resisted were only able to preserve themselves through self-isolation, moving to distant and poor regions. Others survived by siding with the Portuguese against rival tribes—a continuation of inter-tribal conflict that already existed. Those who were unable to resist suffered cultural violence, epidemics of diseases imported from Europe, and death. After three decades marked by efforts to occupy land and establish a colony and trading posts, Portugal provided incentives for commercial endeavours with massive land holdings, which tended to produce higher profits than those with less land (Fausto 1999). A significant legacy of this has been the establishment and preservation of a vocal oligarchic elite who do not shy away from exercising their political clout, as Freyre (1986) writes:

> What we had in our country was great landowning and autonomous fami-lies, lords of the plantation, with an altar and a chaplain in the house and Indians armed with bow and arrow or Negroes armed with muskets at their command; and from their seats in the municipal council chamber these mas-ters of the earth and of the slaves that tilled it always spoke up boldly to the representatives of the crown. (p. 4)

Fausto (1999) also describes how plantation owners 'wielded considerable economic, social, and political power in the life of the colony' and 'formed an aristocracy based on wealth and power' (p. 37). To this day, there has been no significant land reform in Brazil. Most of the land is still owned by a small minority of the population (in 1999, 1% of landowners owned 44% of the land in Brazil's northeast (Levine 1999)) and much of it is left unfarmed, while the majority have no access to land. This land ownership policy, which was established in the name of economic ideology, repre-sents one of the key contributing factors in the solidification of social inequality in Brazil.

As mentioned earlier, another significant factor in the establishment of social and economic inequality was domination over other human beings at a time when waged labour was not convenient for the interests of enter-prise. This began with the enslavement and catechisation of indigenous people. Because the indigenous population were in a good position to forcibly resist slavery in their native territory, and because they were also killed in huge numbers by European diseases, from the 1570s onwards, colonisers began to import Africans en-masse, providing the bulk of Brazil's workforce for the next 300 years. Slavery can be seen as one of the most explicit manifestations of violent epistemology in Brazilian history, simply by its reduction of human beings to their economic value (dimension) alone:

> Many slaves came from cultures which regularly worked with iron implements and in which cattle were raised. Because of this, their productive capacity was significantly higher than the Indians. It has been estimated that during the first half of the 17th century, during the peak years of the sugar economy, the purchase price of a black slave was recovered after 13 to 16 months of work. Even after a huge rise in slave purchase prices after 1700, slaves paid for themselves in 30 months. (Fausto 1999, p. 18)

This quote demonstrates how the same instrumental reason was applied to both Amerindians and Africans. Seen as economic instruments rather than people, slaves were afforded no rights whatsoever by law (Fausto 1999), and any action to promote their health and welfare was carried out in the name of economics rather than an acknowledgement of particularities which called for a more humane response, as Kerr (2014) writes:

> Everyone involved in this despicable trade had one aim and one aim only— to make as much profit as possible. In order to do that, they had to keep alive as many of their cargo as they could; and not just alive, they had to be in good condition when they arrived on the other side of the ocean so that they could be sold for the best possible price. (p. 38)

However, this did not mean dignified treatment. As Kerr (ibid.) describes, slaves were packed into ships like sardines, lying in spaces smaller than graves, and instruments such as the multi-tailed whip 'cat-o-nine-nails' were used to maintain subordination. Slave life was hard and conditions brutal, with almost 50% of children dying before age five (Klein and Luna 2010). However, the ideology of reducing people to their economic (and also racial) dimensions as a justification for domination and exploitation was collectively affirmed to the extent that slavery went largely unquestioned for centuries. As Johan Mauritas, a 1600s governor of Dutch Brazil once said, 'It is not possible to effect anything in Brazil without slaves... and they cannot be dispensed with upon any consideration whatsoever; if anyone feels that this is wrong, it is a futile scruple' (cited in Kerr 2014, p. 40).

Aside from severe exploitation in the name of profit, Brazil's social stratification was also born in colonial society where people were classified by 'purity of blood' (race and skin colour) and occupation, in a hierarchical system. People were classified as either 'Persons' (free people) or 'non-persons' (slaves), and slaves were categorised by skin colour. This impacted on life opportunities, as lighter-skinned slaves were preferred for work in the masters' houses, whilst the darker skinned slaves were set to hard labour in the plantations. For free people racial mix, religious background, and family ties also defined access to (or exclusion from) certain occupations and groups (Fausto 1999). While it seems absurd to discuss slavery and self-actualisation in the same sentence, these examples illustrate how the violent epistemology of racial, genetic, and religious 'identity thinking' also restricted life chances and therefore the self-actualisation of both slaves and free people.

Though Brazilian society is very different today, the social stratification established in colonial times remains. While in colonial times wealthy rural landowners and merchants engaged in foreign commerce were at the top of the social pyramid, and recently arrived black Africans were at the very bottom, in contemporary Brazil wealthy (mostly white) men fly to business meetings in helicopters while Angolan immigrants and Haitian refugees struggle to survive in the poorest neighbourhoods.[3] This social stratification is indicative of the collectivisation of identity thinking into social ideology: as a single dimension of a person (i.e. skin colour) is separated from all other dimensions and constructed as an identity category, certain particularities or characteristics can be ascribed to this category through the severance of generalities and particularities, achieved and maintained through type α behaviour, reducing the diversity of individuals to prescribed social roles and assumed characteristics.

The abolition of slavery came about late in Brazil because it was strongly resisted by the Brazilian elites, whose wealth was built on the back of slave labour. Brazil had become an empire after the Portuguese court and Prince Regent fled to Rio de Janeiro to escape Napoleon in 1808. The Prince Regent was later succeeded by his son Pedro I who declared independence for Brazil. It was Pedro I's granddaughter, Princess Isabel, who

---

[3] In 2001, the average income of whites was twice that of non-whites (Schwartzman 2003).

signed a law abolishing slavery in 1888. This act was very unpopular with the Brazilian elite who staged a military coup the following year and declared the country a republic, headed by a dictatorship (Schwartzman 2003; Fausto 1999).

At this stage, the sugar industry (which had concentrated most of Brazil's wealth and population in the rural northeast) had declined, and Brazil's latest cash crop was coffee, produced mostly in the south. After abolition, two-thirds of the population were newly freed slaves or their descendants. However, various policies ensured that neither the former slave owners nor the government would be responsible for the wellbeing of this segment of the population, nor for their integration into society. Such policies included anti-vagrancy laws which stopped freed slaves coming to the cities to look for work (Levine 1999). The neglect of former slaves amounted to 'one of the bleakest chapters in Brazil's long history of governmental insensitivity to the needs of its underclass, largely black and of mixed race' (ibid., p. 123). As freed slaves and their descendants (along with their suffering) were pushed to the margins of awareness, so too were they held firmly at the margins of society.

Rather than supporting freed slaves into paid employment, the majority were left to live in poverty in the northeast with no access to land or income. To populate the growing cities of Rio de Janeiro and São Paulo, and to replace slave labour in the southern coffee plantations, immigration was encouraged from Europe and Japan. This movement of the economic centre of the country from the previously sugar-rich northeast to the urbanising, modernising, and coffee-producing south solidified an uneven concentration of wealth which remains today. The monopoly over land-ownership remained, but the decline in cultivation left most of the rural population in deep-seated poverty with no work, and no land to develop even a subsistence living (Levine 1999).

After the Second World War, Brazil entered a period of rapid industrialisation, economic growth, and modernisation in an attempt to revive its economy which, until 1930, had been largely dependent on exportation. The external shocks of the two world wars and the great depression resulted in drastic reductions in export revenues and finance from abroad (much of state revenue came from import tariffs on non-agricultural products), leading to a large fiscal deficit (Saad-Filho 2012). To remedy this, the economic policy of Import Substituting Industrialisation (ISI) was adopted from 1930 to 1980. This 'system of accumulation based on the sequenced expansion of manufacturing industry, with the primary objective of replacing imports' (ibid., p. 119), led to a huge shift away from agriculture and into industry.

This caused mass migration from rural areas to the cities, especially São Paulo. Between 1970 and 1981 Brazil's population shifted from being more than 50% rural to almost 80% urban (Melamed 2011), and in 2003 only 15% of Brazil's population remained in rural areas (Câmara et al. 2007). Industrialisation led to significant economic growth, but also tendential deterioration in income distribution (Saad-Filho 2012), marked by further concentration of revenue in the hands of the elites and the lowering of workers' salaries (Kohara 2009). Between 1960 and 1970, the richest 10% of Brazilians saw their share of total income increase from 28% to 48%, and most sectors were dominated by 4–10% of the largest firms (Green 2003). Goods tended to be expensive and poor quality, and there were not enough jobs to accommodate the vast numbers migrating to the cities. The needs of the poorest rural population were also neglected (Melamed 2011). In 1964, another military coup led to a 21-year dictatorial regime focussed on repressing the majority while offering stability and growth to the minority elites, middle classes, and workers in successful companies (ibid.). By the 1980s, the ineffective macroeconomic management of the industrial period contributed, in sum, to 'political instability, insufficient infrastructure provision, the concentration of income and the reproduction of mass poverty' (Saad-Filho 2012).

The transition from slavery to 'free' labour and from an agricultural to industrial economy can be seen as marked by a continuation of structurally engrained economic and elitist ideology. The economic reforms of ISI were clearly focussed on increasing overall economic growth and the wealth of the already wealthy, while the needs of the majority population, especially the descendants of slaves, the rural, and the poor, were neglected. This ideology was reinforced by the military dictatorship, which served to repress the poor majority and award increasing power and stability to minority elites. We can see this as a continued expression of the self-preservation motivation on the part of the Brazilian economic and political elites, coupled with a negation and repression of the popular classes and their particular needs, characteristic of the type α behaviour inherent to ideological epistemology.

This long history has provided the foundation for modern Brazil, which has some of the highest rates of social inequality and urban violence in the world. Although Brazil is now known to be one of the world's largest emerging economies, and inequality has decreased a little since the

Worker's Party presidencies of 2013–2016, Brazil's social, political, and economic development has held fast to its legacy of social exclusion and extreme stratification. Since the move away from ISI, this has been perpetuated by the introduction of neoliberal economic policy and its associated ideology.

Introduced to Brazil in the 1990s, neoliberal economic policy assumes that with economic growth, poverty will be reduced by default through a 'trickle-down' effect (Saad-Filho 2012). In Brazil, neoliberal policies have been consolidated into a durable macroeconomic regime. However, while this regime has brought significant economic growth, it has not resulted in significant wealth redistribution (Amann and Baer 2002). As Kohara (2009) writes:

> The [social problems that exist] in Brazil [are] the result of a model of economic and political development, in which an interest in obtaining profits prevails above any other interest, a model that has always been imposed by the dominant elites. The concentration of wealth in the hands of a minority and, consequently, extreme poverty for the larger part of the population, has prevented Brazil from being an egalitarian nation. In the last few decades there has been an improvement in certain social indicators such as the index of literacy, the percentage of children registered in schools, the reduction of infant mortality and the increase in life expectancy at birth. But these advances have not impeded the worsening of many other problems, such as the lack of adequate habitation in the big cities, violence, environmental pollution, and difficulties in urban mobility. (p. 29)

The introduction of neoliberal economic policy was accompanied by a 'substantial increase in the openness of the economy to foreign trade, [and] a dramatic retreat of the state's participation in the economy' (Amann and Baer 2002, p. 957). This reopened the doors for foreign imports, and existing industries had to deal with a reduction in market share. The economy began to shift from industrial to service-based enterprise as newly privatised companies[4] were encouraged to install labour-saving technologies, and substantial numbers of workers were dismissed. Between 1990 and 1997 employment in manufacturing dropped by 40% (Saad-Filho 2012).

---

[4] Instead of offering out share ownership to the public, privatisation authorities chose to transfer the assets of public enterprises to a select group of long-established major domestic and foreign investors (Amann and Baer 2002).

This huge reduction of job opportunities in the industrial sector was, however, not compensated by a comparable increase of opportunities in the service sector (ibid.). What opportunities did exist were more poorly paid and less secure (Amann and Baer 2002), while the wages of the minority who remained in the industrial sector increased. Public utilities were also privatised, and as incentive to the new owners, regulators allowed price-hikes. For people living in Rio de Janeiro for example, the cost of public services rose by 90% between 1990 and 1994, massively increasing the cost of living (ibid.). These examples illustrate how rather than resulting in a 'trickle-down effect', neoliberal restructuring has perpetuated poverty and economic inequality in Brazil.

Gillespie (2006) argues that the structural deficits caused by neoliberal modernism (displacement from the land, joblessness, migration to urban areas, social dislocation and isolation, greater income inequality, and increased poverty) lead to social disorganisation and violence. According to Huggins (2000), at the time of writing, the richest 10% of Brazil's population earned 69.5 times more than the poorest 10%. This, along with the endurance of powerful political elites throughout Brazil's history, is a good indicator of structural violence which Galtung (1996), Galtung and Hivik (1971), Montiel and Wessells (2001), and Nagler (1997) argue results from an unequal distribution of economic and political power where one class benefits from this disparate system while another suffers.

This level of structural inequality, research has shown (cf. Bourguignon 2001; Fajnzylber et al. 2002; Wade 2004), can foster frustration, aggression, and interpersonal violence. Smith (2012) argues that this has contributed to the high levels of interpersonal violence in Brazil, which have increased since the introduction of neoliberalism. Andrade and Lisboa (2000) also found dramatic increases in homicide rates in Rio de Janeiro and São Paulo that coincide with the structural adjustments introduced in the 1990s: in Rio de Janeiro the rate of male homicides per 100,000 inhabitants aged 5–24 rose from 149 in 1981 to 275 in 1995, while in São Paulo the rates for the 5–14 and 24–44 age bracket more than doubled, rising from 54 to 128, and 49 to 106 respectively for the same period.

Violence disproportionately affects Brazil's poor, with homicide numbers being the highest in areas with the most poverty (Gillespie 2006) and socio-economic disparity (Gawryszewski and Lucianna 2005). Part of this has been attributed to the state, which Aiyer (2001) suggests acts in a disciplinary manner, working to enforce social control under the neoliberal regime. According to this view, neoliberal policies require states to relinquish control of their economies but maintain control in the maintenance of law and order. Huggins (1998) and Huggins et al. (2002) give examples of how violence was routinely used as a means of formal social control and state surveillance in Brazil throughout the transition to capitalist democracy, largely carried out by police, paramilitary, and military forces.

Of course, state violence was common in Brazil prior to the democratisation that accompanied neoliberalism—the practice of state-sponsored torture and assassinations during the military dictatorship of 1964–1985 is well-documented (Mezarobba 2006, 2008). However, this pales in comparison to the levels of state violence that accompanied the democratisation and neoliberalisation process. According to Huggins (2000), in 1992, in the greater metropolitan area of São Paulo alone, 1470 civilians were killed by police. This is almost four times more than the total amount of police killings throughout an entire 15 years of Brazil's 21-year dictatorship. While during the dictatorship state-sponsored violence was mostly perpetrated against politicians, academics, and students considered to be a threat to the regime, since the transition to neoliberal democracy it is most commonly directed at the 'undesirable' poor (Aiyer 2001). The privatisation that accompanies neoliberalism has also extended to security forces in Brazil, with growth of private security services, 'rent-a-cops', death squads, lone-wolf 'justice-maker' killers, and lynch mobs, some of which are employed by the rich in order to protect themselves from the poor (Huggins 2000; Gillespie 2006).

Between 2003 and 2016, when the Worker's Party presidents Luiz Inacio (Lula) da Silva and Dilma Rousseff were in power, more efforts were made to redistribute wealth. However, these were limited because both Lula and Dilma had to comply with neoliberal economic policy. As such, there has not been any redistributive economic or land reform. As Gillespie (2006) highlights, the globalisation of neoliberalism has not lived up to its promise of improving standards of living for the majority. Rather, it has contributed to rising poverty, escalating violence, and a whole host of derivative problems for the poor.

To summarise, violent epistemology has been particularly evident in two aspects of Brazil's development since 1990. Firstly, in the globally pervasive economic ideology of neoliberalism and its enforcement in Brazil by the Washington-based financial institutions, and secondly, in the self-preserving behaviour of the Brazilian elites which has continued from previous periods. These factors have combined to foster 'non-conducive social circumstances' characterised by extreme social inequality and prejudice between rich and poor. This more implicit, structurally engrained violence has been responded to by the state, the wealthy, and the poor with explicit interpersonal violence. Examples of this are presented in the next section.

The history outlined in this section illustrates how inequality, exploitation, poverty, social exclusion, and violence are historically engrained and deep-rooted characteristics of the 'facticity' or social circumstances of Brazil. These issues can be traced back to their roots in colonialism and slavery, and their perpetuation can be seen all the way through industrialisation and urbanisation, into contemporary Brazil in the grip of neoliberalism. Throughout the history of modern Brazil and every change of political regime, one thing has stood out: a type α behaviour evident in the 'extraordinary capacity of the Brazilian elites to defend the status quo and their own interests by controlling, co-opting, and, if necessary, repressing [...] forces in favour of radical social change' (Bethell 2000, p. 16).[5]

Such historical repression led to a long period of very little popular mobilisation for change, and Brazilians consequently developed a reputation for their 'extraordinary capacity [...] for tolerating poverty, exclusion, inequality, and injustice and thus collaborating in their own subordination' (ibid.). However, inspired by the 2011 'Arab Spring' and the spate of popular uprisings that followed around the world, and dissatisfied with government spending in the build up to the 2014 World Cup and 2016 Olympics, public protests have become much more common in Brazil over the last five years. However, true to form, the military police have consistently responded with violent repression.

5.4   THE EXOSYSTEM: SOCIAL STRATIFICATION IN SÃO PAULO

Of all Brazilian cities, São Paulo has experienced the highest levels of population growth since industrialisation. It is Brazil's largest urban area and is ranked among the most important global metropoles. In 2010 Brazil had the seventh largest GDP in the world (World Bank 2010), and in 2009 close to one quarter of the country's wealth was concentrated in São

---

[5] Indeed, following a recent resurgence of the Brazilian far-right, Worker's Party President Dilma Rousseff was impeached in August 2016 (Watts 2016), and former 'pro-poor' Worker's Party president Lula jailed on allegedly false corruption charges in April 2018, in an apparent attempt by the far-right to keep him from being re-elected (Treece et al. 2018).

Paulo (Kohara 2009), making it the second largest BRICS[6] economic region (Florida et al. 2009). However, as with the rest of Brazil, São Paulo is also marked by huge extremes of inequality. Unemployment levels are high, the statutory minimum salary is grossly inadequate compared to the cost of living, and in 2003, 28.9% of people in the municipality of São Paulo were recorded as living in poverty (IBGE 2003).

São Paulo is considered to be a vibrant cultural hub, but urban planning and infrastructure has been unable to keep up with the speed of population growth (more than 20 million people live in the São Paulo metropolitan area alone) (Levine 1999), meaning that habitation is a grave problem. While the city is home to some of the most extensive luxury housing complexes in the world, adequate accommodation is dependent on financial circumstances, which for the majority of the population are poor. As Kohara (2009) writes, 'come nightfall, thousands of people can be found in the entrance queues of overnight hostels, many others making beds on the pavement from cardboard, and millions more housing themselves in precarious slums and tenements' (p. 19).

São Paulo's population is heavily influenced by generations of economic migration and immigration (Levine 1999). The city's rapid urban growth began in the first two decades of the twentieth century when immigrant labourers were attracted to the area to fill the labour gap in the coffee industry after the abolition of slavery. Between 1880 and 1900 São Paulo's population increased from 64,000 to 239,000 inhabitants (Fausto 1999), and this growth continued as the city began to industrialise and immigrants came from Europe and Japan in the hope of achieving a better life. The majority of immigrant workers, however, found themselves unsupported, heavily exploited by industry, and suffering appalling living and working conditions (Canton 2007).

Around 1950 the influx of foreign immigration waned, and as the city was still in full industrial swing it began to attract more economic migrants from all over Brazil, especially the now poor, rural north-eastern regions. Between 1950 and 1980 over three million people (workers and their families) moved to São Paulo from other areas of Brazil (Municipal Prefecture of São Paulo 2012), and population growth continued at a rapid pace until the end of the twentieth century. This expansion was not matched by growth in the city's labour market however, and hundreds of thousands of people were forced into the underground economy, further solidifying the city's 'permanent underclass' unable to access stable

---

[6] BRICS refers to Brazil, Russia, India, China and South Africa—a group of countries considered to be major emerging national economies.

employment. Meanwhile, the elites maintained tight controls on society, suppressing any dissent (Levine 1999, pp. 21–22).

Since its early days, São Paulo has been characterised by extremes of wealth and poverty. Today it is a city of two worlds, in which the extremely wealthy live in high-security luxury condominiums offering enclosed 'life-style packages' (Landman and Schonteich 2002), travel by bullet-proof car from underground garage to underground garage or by helicopter from the top of one high-rise building to another. As a result, a certain type of socio-spatial segregation exists, in which different social classes are confined to specific geographical areas. This is exemplified by the geographical demarcation of favelas, tenement neighbourhoods, and the fortified enclaves of the elites. As Barker (2002) writes:

> Enclaves arise partly from a fear of crime. Although designed for collective use, they are private property—their walls and systems of surveillance enforce an internal social homogeneity by keeping the lower classes out. The most extreme examples of these enclaves are like city-states within the city, with tens of thousands of residents and hundreds of private guards. In this respect, enclaves mark the end of a particular type of modern public space. Enclaves embody a concept of urban space characterized by bounded zones of class homogeneity rather than a public space of […] heterogeneity, and a free circulation of differences. (p. 1032)

The children of these 'enclave' families attend international private schools and participate in a variety of extracurricular activities. On the other end of the social scale are the children who live on the streets, in hostels and tenements, and in favelas on the urban peripheries.

The elitist attitudes of the colonial and imperial oligarchies remain today in the plutocratic social groups of São Paulo, who live lives of luxury alongside extreme poverty as if it were an unpleasant truth that would rather be forgotten (Barker 2002). While middle and upper class children attend private fee-paying schools, public education is seen as being of terrible quality and only suitable for the poor. The wealthy visit shopping complexes, yacht clubs, and jockey clubs (all named after the North American and European institutions upon which they are modelled) at weekends. Spending the day at the shopping mall in São Paulo is something of a cultural event, an opportunity to get dressed up and show off one's social status (Lara 2008).

This world, in which social status is married with purchasing power, is reliant on social exclusion for its very survival. That is, as Marx famously asserted all those years ago, social status associated with high purchasing power, the consumption of 'luxury' items, and exclusive leisure pursuits (this 'ideal' of the modern, affluent lifestyle) depends on a permanent 'underclass' for its very existence, both in the form of cheap labour as well as by providing 'lesser' and 'outsider' groups from which to distinguish itself (Marx 1990). The Brazilian media has presented, over time, the upper and middle class lifestyle as the ideal of modernity, especially with regards to consumption, as words like 'paradise' and 'dream' are frequently associated with the consumer ambitions and collective lifestyles of these groups, presented as aspiration for the rest of the population (Lara 2008).

The media present the idea that social mobility and a lifestyle of luxury (associated with social status and inclusion) are open to all. However, this is entirely incongruent with the reality of social and economic exclusion experienced by a large portion of the population. While on the one hand television and magazines present the ideal of a modern, westernised lifestyle reminiscent of upper-middle class North American suburbia, on the other hand (aside from the fact that its integrity is rarely questioned), most of the population can never achieve this ideal because Brazil's social and economic system (while outwardly presenting itself as democratic and 'free' in line with the current phase of neoliberal capitalism) relies on social hierarchy, masks an underlying plutocracy, and produces social and economic exclusion. In this way São Paulo's sharp social divisions are insidious; there are no formal or legal barriers to social mobility and integration, but inequality and prejudice are deeply engrained in Brazil's history and economy.

The promotion of this 'ideal' way of life can be seen as a manifestation of the collective affirmation of economic ideology and an associated ideological identity concept. In the latter, the economic dimension of individuals is isolated and held up as superior to all other dimensions, meaning that desirable characteristics become those that reflect this dimension—namely expressions of material wealth and affluent lifestyle. This collectively affirmed identity concept can be experienced by individuals (especially the most excluded) as replete with conditions of worth (Rogers 1959) which represent gateways to social inclusion. The desire to conform to such conditions can manifest as explicit acts of violence. This is demonstrated in Bill and Athayde's (2006) interviews with adolescent boys in Brazil's urban drug-trafficking gangs:

> Imagine your mum worked in a family's home, that she was never able to give you any presents. When she did it was second-hand clothes or toys, left in her boss's rubbish, or toys offered out of charity after her boss's children didn't want them anymore, because they were really old (Boy's response to being asked why he entered a life of crime). (Bill and Athayde 2006, p. 94)

Turning to crime as a means to meet societal conditions of worth was not uncommon in young people in the neighbourhood in which the case-study school was situated, as this data excerpt illustrates:

> Teacher 1 gave me an example of a student of hers, who had just come out of prison. She asked him what he had done, and he told her he had stolen some money. She asked why, and he replied, 'spending Christmas without money, teacher, nobody wants that'. She said to him 'ah, I've also spent really miserable Christmases with almost nothing to eat'. 'No' he had replied, 'there's no problem with food teacher, even if there's not enough food there's always someone in the community who gives you some, or who invites you to eat at their house. The problem is not having money to take a girl to the cinema, or to a party, and not having good clothes and good trainers'. (Field notes 11/05/2011)

Aside from a desire to conform to conditions of worth associated with the 'ideal' identity concept promoted in the Brazilian media, Bill and Athayde's interviews also illustrate how 'destructive' and 'hostile tendencies' (Fromm 2013) can stem from isolation, powerlessness, and an 'unlived life' (ibid.), or 'thwarted self-actualisation' (Rogers 1959) and the 'scars' left by such thwarting (Horkheimer and Adorno 2002):

> Athayde: Why are you in this life, even knowing that it only has disadvantages?
> Boy: Out of revolt. Out of hate. Sadness. Pain. I hold all this in my chest. Suffering. Various things. I try to give good things to my family. Even today my family can't [have everything they want], but I try to do what I can (Bill and Athayde 2006, p. 79).
> That was where I started to enter a life of crime, the life I have now. It all started eight years ago, when my family was going through that suffocation, that tragedy, you know brother? The day to day, me seeing my mum go out to work, those conditions, she couldn't give the best to us, you know? What I wanted I couldn't have. The remote control car, a bike... couldn't have it. Until, we lived in a little wooden shack, it caught fire. Ten years old I took a punch in the face from a police man. I hold this in my chest, in my heart. It created a grievance against him, and so I began to enter this life that I'm in now, the life of crime, the right side in the wrong life. (ibid., p. 78)

These tales are reminiscent of Adorno's statement that 'wrong life cannot be lived rightly' (2005, p. 39), and illustrate dimensions P, Q, R, and S of the conceptual model presented in Chap. 4—that violent epistemology and action can be fostered by non-conducive social circumstances, which thwart self-actualisation and promote the de-formation of subjectivity.

However, even when an individual is not necessarily caught up in a cycle of subject de-formation and experiences a conscious desire not to engage in violence (whether epistemic or in action), the constraints on choice imposed by non-conducive social circumstances can appear to leave them with no other option:

> I'm here [working wrapping up drugs] because society out there doesn't provide any way of life for us to follow. If we want to look for work, it's hard. Even to find a school is hard, we don't have a school here. [...] I'm not a criminal, I'm here because I need to help out at home, because I don't want to see my mum suffering. [I'm] a person who wasn't meant to be here. But this is what the government wants, it's what the governor wants, to see us here. Because he doesn't pay attention to anything. He doesn't give us a right to defence, doesn't give us a job. Our mum went out to get a job and was humiliated. We have to have been to university. How are we going to get a job then? So, we are obliged to return to crime, but a lot of the time we don't want this. (Bill and Athayde 2006, p. 180)

The excerpts cited above illustrate the impact of social exclusion in a society shaped by neoliberal economic ideology as a form of violent epistemology. However, mainstream popular discourse on crime and violence in São Paulo tends (as with the similar types of discourse discussed in Chap. 3) to lean on the notion of an inherently violent human nature, with a minority of 'untamed' or 'pathological' individuals being seen as the perpetrators within an otherwise 'civilised' and healthy society. As Caldeira (2000) explains:

> Paulistanos from different social groups [...] share certain conceptions about crime and evil. They seem to think that the spaces of crime are marginal ones, such as favelas and tenements, and that their inhabitants, potential criminals, are people from the fringes of society, humanity, and the polity. They also see crime as a phenomenon related to evil, something that spreads and contaminates easily and requires strong institutions and authorities to control it. This control is seen as a labour of culture against the forces of nature. (p. 53)

This view, strengthened by neoliberal discourse, places the blame on individuals who are unable to achieve an unobtainable ideal, and who are erroneously seen to have excluded themselves from society. These individuals, commonly perceived as the main perpetrators of violence, are seen as social outcasts and labelled 'marginals'. When Bill and Athayde (2006) asked a so-called marginal what he thought about Brazil, he voiced a different perspective:

Unjust country. Unjust. An unjust country. All we have is this here [the life of the favela and drug trafficking]. But the real 'marginal' is in a suit and tie. In a suit and tie, and justice doesn't see this. (p. 81)

This boy's perspective reminds us of how, without a holistic model of violence that incorporates the epistemic and social dimensions, all of a society's ills can be blamed on a select group of individuals without recognition of the bigger picture or of our collective social and epistemic responsibilities.

The idealised lifestyle presented in the Brazilian media is a reflection of the elitist and idealised vision of North American and European cosmopolitanism upon which Brazil's (particularly São Paulo's) urban development has been modelled. This rather fantastical view aspires to mimic cities like Paris and Los Angeles, but is shaped by hygienist and neo-hygienist[7] thought, which imagines a city in which the poor do not exist (Kohara 2009). As industrialisation and mass migration/immigration into São Paulo caused rapid urban growth, in the late 19th and early 20th centuries elites looked to Europe for a model of urban expansion. An image of urban modernity emerged based in a positivist, liberal, republican discourse, and (perceived) European 'civility', cleanliness, 'order', and 'progress'. However, São Paulo's high numbers of poor freed slaves and their descendants, along with economic migrants and immigrants, did not conform to this ideal. This population was seen as dirty—their neighbourhoods as centres of contagious disease, their habitations unsanitary, and their dispositions as idle and prone to vices (ibid.).

Sobrinho (2013) describes how at this time 'an incipient liberal-capitalist culture flourished, fed by ideas of a way of life imported from Europe which identified the white, "civilised" subject as the ideal profile of man' (p. 233). The upper classes intended to diffuse a 'bourgeois aesthetic' based on idealised Parisian customs, whiteness, cleanliness, and Christian family morality. Plans were made to construct great avenues and

---

[7] My use of the term 'neo-hygienist' is based on analyses of how hygienist thought shaped São Paulo's development throughout the 19th and 20th centuries—a period in which 'hygiene' meant 'sanitising' the poor and 'cleaning' them from the city (Sobrinho 2013). Local researchers Kohara (2009), Canton (2007), and Frúgoli (2000) who have all spent significant time researching the neighbourhood in which the case-study school is located, discuss how recent initiatives to 'cleanse the [area] of street vendors, street children, beggars and the unemployed' (ibid., p. 102), and enforce the degradation of tenements so as to increase land value for property development (Kohara 2009), represent a resurgence of hygienist attitudes. Frúgoli (2000) has called this a 'new sanitation' of the city.

neighbourhoods, to demonstrate grandiosity and good taste (ibid.). As this conceptual blueprint was held up and began to dominate, anything perceived to be 'tropical' or 'backwards' was rejected.

While São Paulo's elites worked to foster this new modernised urban space, a certain 'disorder relating to the backwardness of the tropics' prevailed in the precarious living conditions of the poor, who were seen to oppose the goal of 'civilisation'. As Chalhoub (2006) explains:

> The poor [...] came to be seen as dangerous because they posed problems for the organisation of public works and the maintenance of public order. The[y] also represented danger of contagion. Th[is] appeared in the Brazilian political imaginary at the end of the 19th century via the metaphor of contagious illness: the dangerous classes continued to reproduce themselves as the[ir] children would remain exposed to the bad habits of their parents. Thus, in discussions about the repression of idleness, [...] the strategy to combat the problem was generally presented as consisting of two stages: more immediately, it was advisable to reprimand the supposed nonworking habits of the adults; in the longer term, it was necessary to provide for the education of minors. (p. 29)

To acknowledge particularities such as Brazil's long history of exploitation, lack of opportunity, prejudice, social exclusion, and low wages would have posed a threat to the liberal discourse of individual freedom and responsibility that allowed for inequality to go unchallenged. By negating these particularities, the elites instead saw the suffering of the poor as a threat to the stability of the ideological schema of the 'clean, healthy and disciplined city' (Sobrinho 2013). Rather than recognising the unsanitary living conditions and ill health of the poor as products of capitalist exploitation, and rather than acknowledging the inexistence of sufficient opportunities for work, such particularities were neglected from awareness, reinforcing discourses of deficiency that blamed the poor for their own degeneration (ibid.). As such, a process of 'hygiene and "social cleansing"' (ibid., p. 211) took place. In the name of 'order and progress',[8] men dressed in blue overalls went knocking on the doors of the poor with buckets full of acrid green disinfectant, forcing literal cleansing.

---

[8] The positivist thought of Aguste Comte had a strong influence in Brazil in the nineteenth century, so much so that the motto written on Brazil's flag 'order and progress' is directly inspired by his words.

The idealised image of 'European modernity' also promoted a 'whitening' of the population. European immigrants were given preference for employment in industry over the descendants of freed slaves, who tended to migrate from rural areas and had darker skin. Whiteness and urbanity were associated with modernity, while non-whiteness and rurality were associated with backwardness. Rather than acknowledging and integrating the poor, non-white, rural migrants into socially just urban planning, this population was largely rejected by being pushed wherever possible to the margins of the urban perimeter, and the margins of awareness (Kohara 2009). As Levine (1999) describes:

> The lower classes, residing on the periphery of the glittering symbols of progress, were as often as not victims of modernisation. Affluent Brazilians ignored the plight of the poor, whether urban—often living in shanty-towns and tenements in close proximity to their stately homes—or in the rural hinterland. (pp. 78–79)

These hygienist efforts to bring 'civilisation' to São Paulo have resulted in more cosmetic than structural change, and the attitudes which cling to an imaginary European or North American ideal remain to this day. This was exemplified during my stay in São Paulo when residents of the wealthy neighbourhood Higienópolis (from Greek, meaning 'city of hygiene') petitioned against the planned installation of a Metro station within the neighbourhood. They argued for the station's relocation as they feared that public transport would cause 'gente diferenciada' [differentiated people] (a 'callow euphemism' for people of low purchasing power) to 'invade' the area (Matias 2011). The petition gained 3500 signatures, and the planned location for the station was moved. This is just one example of how hygienist attitudes remain[9] among São Paulo's upper classes, how ideological thought works to exclude that which it cannot accommodate within its schema, and how Brazilian elites maintain the power to influence urban development to this day.

Although Brazil markets itself as a racial democracy, the legacy of slavery, colonialism, and hygienism has resulted in the persistence of racial inequality. State violence against the poor, and in particular (though not

---

[9]Another example is how these attitudes were found amongst administrative workers in the city's education system: when visiting schools, the workers from the Regional Directorate of Education who accompanied me would cry 'hold your noses and secure your handbags!' as we entered poor neighbourhoods.

exclusively) young black men is a particularly powerful illustration of this. In São Paulo 10% of all homicides are carried out by policemen. As Levine (1999) describes, 'state police forces have committed numerous human rights crimes, including playing self-appointed vigilante assassins of suspected miscreants' (p. 162). This violence is especially targeted towards the poor and marginalised. A recent UNESCO study found that non-white men aged between 12 and 29 face a 50% higher risk of death by homicide than other cohorts of the São Paulo population (UNESCO 2014), and a 2013 study found that non-white adolescents between the ages of 12 and 18 were 3.7 times more likely to be assassinated than their white peers (Junior and Lima 2013).

Another indicator of racial inequality is income distribution. Government statistics (see Fig. 5.2) counter the rhetoric of racial democracy by showing that in the last national census more people in São Paulo classified as being 'black', 'mixed race', or 'indigenous' had either no

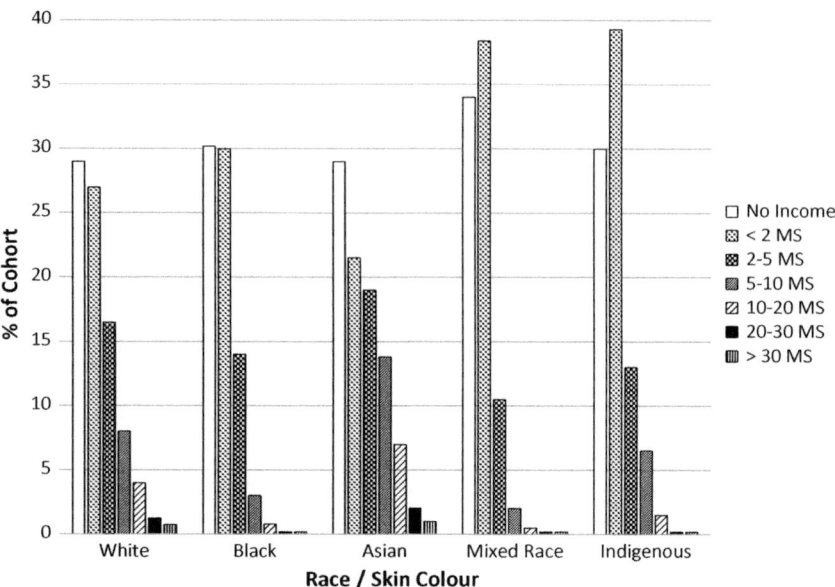

Fig. 5.2 Income distribution by race/skin colour in São Paulo. MS = Minimum Salaries (or equivalent) received per month. One minimum salary was equal to approximately US$271 at time of data collection

income or earned less than the equivalent of two minimum salaries per month, than people classified as being 'white' or 'Asian'. However, there was also significant stratification within the white and Asian populations, as by far the largest proportion of São Paulo's population, regardless of race or skin colour, had either no income or earned less than two minimum salaries (IBGE 2010).

Since the cost of living in São Paulo is comparable to that of major European and North American cities, these statistics highlight not only significant racial inequality, but also the real extent of poverty and social stratification regardless of skin colour.

This section has demonstrated how, by collectively affirming ideological schema that hold certain particularities to be of superior importance to others, Brazilian elites have shaped the development of São Paulo as a metropolis marked by extremes of wealth and poverty, lack of access to formal employment and dignified housing, socio-spatial segregation, high rates of violence, and racial inequality.

5.5   THE MICROSYSTEM: NON-CONDUCIVE CIRCUMSTANCES IN THE BAIXADA

The case-study school, DCX, is located in an inner-city neighbourhood of São Paulo known colloquially as the 'Baixada'. This research diary excerpt sets the scene:

> Arriving at the nearest metro station to the Baixada, I exit the train, and am shuffled up an escalator along with the crowd. Up ahead a woman, smiling and swaying, swings at two security guards, trying to hit them, and then leaps onto another escalator and rises up out of the station to the street, dancing and singing as she goes. As she reaches the top her shouts echo back down into the station, 'Bye Security! Ha Ha!' I dodge the incoming flow of people rushing towards the turnstiles, and climb out into the street. It is dark, the flashing lights of a police car greet me. A stream of people in office clothes strides in the direction from which I have just come, hurrying to make the train. A boy of around thirteen sells chocolate bars halfway up the station steps, his face pensive and serious, not paying attention to the box of bars in his arms.
>
> Lingering around the neatly dressed office workers, on the sidelines, their direction seemingly aimless in comparison, I see a woman, naked and wrapped in a grimy wool blanket and a man, alone, his trousers too long, dirty, ripped at the bottom where they catch under his sandals, his hair thick

with dirt from days and nights on the street. They seem to blend into the grime of the street itself, part of the architecture, almost invisible as they move in the shadows between the hustle and bustle of business-as-usual. A man holds out a pamphlet to me insistently, 'Hear the word of god, we want to save you!', his eyes gleaming. I shake my head and walk past, and as I wait at the traffic lights among more suited office workers, the naked blanketed woman streaks barefoot across the road in front of the oncoming traffic. Another woman, wearing clothes that she has evidently not chosen because they are much too big for her, holds out her hand and asks a man for some coins. The sound of an organ floats out of the cathedral behind me, and the flashing lights of another police van parked on the corner flicker across the crowd as a group of armed police sit and stand about the van, invigilating. There is a familiar tension in the night air.

I cross the street. A man pulls a broken fridge and some cardboard boxes in a cart through the surge of people, shouting and talking to the general night air, his dirty dog following faithfully behind him. A little further on a ragged, sweating, unkempt man preaches to the deaf ears of passers-by, bible in hands, 'I was imprisoned, I was interned, nobody came to visit me. This is what Jesus suffered'. Crossing the square I weave between groups of teenagers playing and joking, lawyers in sharp suits smoking cigarettes and talking on mobile phones, and mothers sitting on the pavement with their toddlers on their laps and their belongings in bin-liners on the cobbles next to them. A small boy runs across my path with a shoe-shine stool on his back, looking back to his friend who shouts down at him from his perch high atop a rubbish lorry. Past another police car. I stop by a man on his hands and knees in the road searching fervently for something. A hot sweet smell fills the air as I run across the street past a young man selling steamed corn on the corner, and a woman selling socks on the wall.

As I begin the decent into the Baixada I pass a sign reading 'security area'. High walls and barbed wire. I pass security men, more people in suits and dodge a bullet-proof car as it leaves the law courts. I see a young man leaning on a lamp post in an empty side street, his back to the main road, looking nervously over his shoulder to make sure nobody sees the joint he is smoking. A tired looking mother holds her two young children's hands as they cross the road. A man across the street sits on a pile of black bin-liners on the pavement. A tall man leans out of a gap between two buildings and tells me that Jesus loves me, and a young woman walks past and jokes with him, crying, 'Jesus loves you!' and they laugh. In a dark doorway, a middle-aged woman lies on her side, wrapped in a blanket, her things in a tattered shopping bag at her feet. She stares expressionless out at the street. She looks sad and terribly lonely.

   In the middle of the road, the Brazilian flag has been painted across the tarmac reading 'order and progress', and further down a huge white Nike football is branded into the asphalt. I pass many men and try not to look at their faces. A teacher told me that if the gang members know you recognise them, and you happen to see them assaulting somebody in the street one day, they will be obliged to kill you. I pace on down the hill, past a group of young men in the shadows, the smell of marijuana rising from their midst. A young woman is leaning on the wall, tears streaming down her face and a joint smoking in her hand. A man kisses her on the forehead as she clutches at her stomach and cries, 'how did he end up here?' A tiny girl grasps at the woman's leg, looking up at her mother, temporarily forgotten. One of the students that I know from the school runs up the opposite side of the street, shouting 'Hi Beth!' I wave back and smile. A girl of no more than ten shuffles up the middle of the street, alone, with a fed-up look on her face, dragging her school case unenthusiastically behind her, intentionally letting it bash into cars and against the pavement as she passes.

   I look up and see a man in front of me, wandering dazedly into the street. The back of his scalp is almost completely cut off, and the huge centre of the wound oozes red and damp, as he rubs it with his dirty hand. A man walks smiling past him, coming out of the gym where loud music blasts. Mothers sit in doorways while their toddlers potter about the pavement. A young boy rides his battered bike in the middle of the crossroads, nearly getting hit as a car rumbles by him. As I turn the corner I come up almost face-to-face with the leader of the local organized assault gang standing outside the bar. I recognize him already and smile tightly, walking past. Suddenly eight or so young men come running down the street, agitated, and my heart skips a beat as I am quickly put on alert. I pause and wait to see if anything danger-ous is about to happen. It seems not, and I dodge a flying plastic bottle that one of them kicks in my direction as he rounds the corner. I notice that the streets are particularly dirty, and particularly dark. I skip over an open man-hole cover, and finally arrive at the high metal gates of the school, which seems to sit in its own pool of shadow at the bottom of the hill, surrounded on all sides by high, deteriorating buildings. I nod my head and wish 'Good evening!' to the five armed police officers by the gate, the blue flashing lights of their car gracing my skin as I wait for the doorman to let me in.

As this excerpt illustrates, markers of social inequality, precarity, and depri-vation are clearly visible in the neighbourhood. With its colloquial name of the 'Baixada' meaning lowland, it lies in the centre of São Paulo, but in an area of extreme degradation. Representative of the city's extreme socio-spatial segregation, it is just streets away from the legal district and main cultural centres. However, as Souza (2010) writes, the Baixada 'is basically inhabited by families of migrants, northeasterners principally, who live in tenements or in buildings invaded by "Sem Tetos",[10] known as "vertical favelas", and by street dwellers who live in hostels' (p. 12). The Baixada has one of the highest densities of tenement housing in the city, and in 2008, 42% of students at DCX School resided in tenements (Kohara 2009).

Many of the Baixada's inhabitants survive on informal labour, especially ambulant commerce (the touting of wares from easily portable, makeshift 'pop-up' stalls which can be quickly folded away and concealed if a police presence is noted), and by collecting recyclable materials which are exchanged for small change at recycling centres, or for food and clothing at the local homelessness association. Drug trade and prostitution are also present. The Baixada is a key arrival point for economic migrants and refugees and is also occupied by homeless children and adolescents who populate the squares near the school. Aside from the School, the Police, some NGOs, and the 'São Paulo is a School' programme who provide a few socio-educational activities, public services are notably absent and the culture that prevails is that of the evangelical churches, drug trafficking, and the prostitution of minors at the school gate (Souza 2010, p. 22).

The main issues faced by the Baixada's residents are related to housing, employment, crime, violence, and a poor quality urban environment with lack of access to the usual benefits of city living. The Baixada was originally established as a residential area, but of low value due to flooding from the nearby river. In the early twentieth century, residents were evicted to make way for industry, but the area was later repopulated by Japanese and Italian immigrants who came seeking employment in the expanding industries. In the 1950s, large high-rise housing blocks were constructed containing small kitchenettes, then in the 1970s a highway system constructed to link other areas of the city resulted in the installation of a series of large motorway viaducts right in the centre of the neighbourhood, cutting it in two and contributing to the area's degradation (Kohara 2009).

São Paulo's industrialisation, and later collaboration between government policymakers and property developers under the neoliberal regime, have both contributed greatly to the Baixada's degraded state. The influx of migrant and immigrant workers in the late nineteenth century that followed the abolition of slavery, created a housing problem. In response

[10] The Movimento Sem Teto (roofless movement) aims to tackle Brazil's housing deficit by occupying empty buildings as group squats. When housed in high-rise apartment blocks the occupations are often called 'vertical favelas', due to the poverty of their inhabitants and their illegal nature.

to the demand for cheap accommodation in the area, large country properties that lay on the peripheries of the growing city were divided into plots for constructing cheap housing that could be rented to industrial workers. The property owners' main aim was to extract income from their land, and houses were built on the lowest lying and least valued land in the river valley that is now the Baixada, which happened to be in the vicinity of the textile and cigarette factories where many came for work. Inadequate legislation coupled with high demand for rental accommodation resulted in a lack of control over building standards, and the houses were constructed without adequate sewerage or protection from flood waters. Bonduki (1998) recounts a description from the time:

> Individuals who live in misery and are housed in pairs, in dark cubicles and breathing foul-smelling gases that exude from their own unclean bodies, have lost at once the principles of morality and throw themselves blindly at crime and robbery to either lose their freedom or gain in this way means to eat or to sleep better. (cited in Canton 2007, p. 23)

Of course, discussion of 'principles of morality' and people 'blindly throwing themselves at crime' reflects questionable assumptions grounded in the prevailing hygienist attitudes of the time. However, this description offers valuable insight into living conditions in the early days of the Baixada. Legislation was later introduced to protect tenants' rights and, driven by the hygienist movement, laws were introduced to regulate the conditions of hygiene, sanitation, and maintenance of the buildings. This included a drive to constrain the spread of tenements in the city centre by demolishing them and moving low-cost housing to the urban peripheries. However, these laws were rarely upheld in practice. As Canton (2007) explains:

> At the end of the 19th century, the gap between the legal standards and the construction of popular housing, undertaken almost always by individuals who sought to obtain revenues from them through rental charges, began to widen. The constructions had to be achieved as cheaply as possible, an intrinsic requirement in this business because the pay levels of workers could not permit high rental charges. The tenements and collective houses were, therefore, essential for the reproduction of the workforce at low cost and, as such, couldn't be restrained and demolished on the scale expected by the laws of the hygienists. This conflict between legislation and reality, which has never disappeared, stemmed from the inevitable necessity for habitation in the process of the exploitation of the work force and has permeated the production of popular housing in São Paulo. (p. 24)

Since the shift from ISI to neoliberalism, the Baixada has become dominated by small business and trade in specialist products rather than large industry. However, many of the original tenement houses still remain, in a state of deterioration, alongside the now crumbling 1950s high-rise apartment blocks. While infrastructure such as asphalt streets and drainage has been installed, due to poor maintenance it is common to see open drain covers, streets piled with waste, and flooding which at times leaves students and teachers trapped within the school building. Despite São Paulo's rapid economic development over the past century, the tenements still maintain most of their nineteenth century characteristics (Kohara 2009). The rental system remains, and following adaptation from single to multi-family living spaces, they are now densely overpopulated by families on very low incomes, with an average of between two and four families (10.73 people[11]) occupying each living space designed for single-family occupation (Canton 2007).

The Baixada tenements are largely occupied by those who cannot access formal employment, and as such are excluded from the formal (regulated) rental market. In exchange for living in the city centre where it is easier to access to the informal labour market, tenants are exploited by landlords who know that their tenants cannot access formal tenancies, and therefore get away with charging exorbitant prices for rooms in terrible condition. This degree of marginalisation and exploitation (exacerbated by neoliberal economic policy) results in an extremely high level of precarity for tenants and their children, with tenement fires and unregulated evictions commonly leading to homelessness.

Kohara (2009) tracked the housing situation of 27 fifth-year students (approximately the same number and demographic that took part in my research) across one year, and found that almost 50% moved address within this period. The reasons for six of these moves were unknown. Five moves involved either repossession, eviction, or fire/safety hazards in the tenement. One child from this group became street homeless and passed away. Kohara (ibid.) also found that 42% of 65 students that he assessed, shared tenement accommodation with between two and ninety-nine other families, and a number of these students lived in just one room which was shared by their entire family for eating, sleeping, and carrying out all domestic activities.

The extreme degradation and precarious living conditions of the tenements has been perpetuated by a combination of forces, including a long

---

[11] This data is from 1997. According to Canton (2007) this situation has since worsened.

history of conflicting private interests. On one side are the tenement owners who want to maintain the tenements' existence in order to protect their ability to profit from them. On the other side are real estate industry stakeholders who want tenement inhabitants to be expelled from the city centre, to promote the development value of the land:

> The real estate sector defends its point of view, based on the hygienist vision of tenement housing, because, according to this vision, the poor are unhygienic, are propagators of disease, possess bad customs and cause real estate devaluation. (ibid., p. 66)

Formally, the municipal government has always attended to the interests of the real estate industry through legislation and the development of urban intervention programmes. However, it has also informally supported the interests of tenement owners by neglecting to enforce regulations that relate to living conditions and the rights of tenants. In both instances, political power and profit are help up to be of primary importance, while other dimensions such as the rights and wellbeing of tenants are neglected.

The Baixada's degradation has been further exacerbated by the introduction of legislation by heritage institutions to 'protect' the historic tenement buildings by (contradictorily) restricting investment in their maintenance. This 'freezing' of investment has also been connected to the political and economic agendas behind a government initiative called Operação Urbana Centro [Operation Urban Centre] (OUC) which (as in São Paulo's earlier days) aims at 'revitalising and redeveloping the city centre' to model the cosmopolitan urban centres of major European cities. The initiative designates 'reserved territories' within the city centre, which 'are characterised as deteriorated spaces, maintained in waiting for investment, stimulating real estate capital in its speculative process, envisioning great profits' (Canton 2007, p. 46). In this way, the Baixada which has been designated a reserved territory, has received next to no investment, 'fortif[ying] the situation of degradation' (Canton 2007, pp. 40–41). By promoting the neighbourhood's deterioration, OUC can be seen as operating according to an instrumental reason which serves the ideologically elevated dimensions of profit and everything associated with 'order and progress', while neglecting the needs and interests of the neighbourhood's current residents.

Another factor contributing to the marginalisation of the Baixada's residents is the participation of private organisations in the 'requalification' of the city centre. One example is the Associação Viva o Centro [Long Live the Centre Association], created in 1991 and formed by various banks, commercial companies, and service providers. The group, which maintains close relationships with São Paulo's administrative bodies, advocates for the development of the city centre through increases in public security, the recuperation of abandoned/degraded areas, the elimination of informal commerce, and incentives for new construction (Canton 2007). Aside from prohibiting informal commerce (viz. street vendors) in the area, Viva o Centro and the Municipal and State governments have also introduced a mega operation to clean the areas streets of beggars and homeless people, with the support of the Military Police and the Metropolitan Civil Guard (Frúgoli 2000).

When I frequented the area during my research, the absence of street vendors in the city centre was evident, but most had moved to Rua 25 de Março, a street known for its concentration of informal commerce, or to the main street leading into the school neighbourhood, securing safety in numbers in areas with reduced police efficacy. While there was a high police presence in the local area, many homeless and destitute people remained, camped on the pavements and wandering the streets under strict police surveillance.

Kohara (2009) found that the criminalisation of informal commerce was directly affecting a large proportion of DCX students, whose parents were reliant on income from such activities. Crackdowns on 25 de Março were common, during which police sweep the area, closing down commerce and arresting some vendors as 'examples'. Students' parents often lost income or got in trouble with the law in this way, which at times resulted in students going hungry or being made homeless due to missed rent payments. While the plans of Viva o Centro may not have been entirely successful, what remains clear is the predominance of official attitudes based on controlling, criminalising, and evicting the poor and marginalised rather than providing appropriate support. Viva o Centro can be seen as an example of violent epistemology because it maintains the rigid ideological scheme of neo-hygienism through the type α behaviour of rejecting and suppressing particularities that challenge this scheme—namely the poor.

5.6   Conclusion

Returning to the concept of nested systems presented at the beginning of this chapter, we can now assess the key ways in which violent epistemology has manifest at the different levels of these systems, over time, to foster the non-conducive social circumstances of the Baixada neighbourhood in which the DCX School and the majority of its students are situated. The two core manifestations that run throughout Brazil's history and are present at all levels from the globosystem to the microsystem, are:

- Economic exploitation in the name of mercantilist, capitalist, and neoliberal economic ideology which holds profit above all other dimensions of life, motivated by the self-preserving desires of those who hold political power and wealth.
- Social and economic exclusion in the name of racist and neo-hygienist ideologies which hold whiteness, cleanliness, order, and an (imaginary) ideal of European/North American style 'progress' above diversity, social inclusion, and the wellbeing of all sectors of society.

In relation to the former, we have seen a long history of economic exploitation from slavery to the low pay of industrial workers, to the precarious labour market of the neoliberal era. This has resulted in the suffering of generations of slaves and their descendants; impoverishment in northeast and rural Brazil when industrialisation wasn't coupled with land reform (leading to mass migration into cities that lacked adequate infrastructure); horrendous living conditions for industrial workers; and the criminalisation and exploitation of those who cannot access formal employment in the neoliberal 'job market', through crackdowns on informal commerce and expensive, poor quality housing.

In relation to the latter, we have seen how social class (and access to opportunities) was organised by skin colour during colonial Brazil; how racist anti-vagrancy laws prevented freed slaves from accessing work in the cities; and how their descendants were excluded from industrial work as white Europeans or lighter-skinned Asians were encouraged to immigrate instead. We have also seen how in modern Brazil people with darker skin (who are often descended from slaves and/or indigenous groups) continue to face police violence and repression, and how these groups face exclusion from society through neo-hygienist policies which label them as 'dirty, unsightly, and dangerous', and push them to the peripheries of cities where there is a lack of economic and educational opportunity, or into intentionally neglected neighbourhoods such as the Baixada where access to formal income is lacking, efforts to make an income informally are criminalised, and access to public services is scarce.

Influenced by the rhetoric of neoliberalism in contemporary Brazil, we see a situation in which the poor and marginalised (such as the Baixada residents) are perceived as being responsible for their own situation. At the same time, the long history of violent epistemology (manifest in the ways outlined above) that has fostered this situation is predominantly pushed to the margins of social and political awareness.

REFERENCES

Abulafia, D. (2008). *The Discovery of Mankind: Atlantic Encounters in the Age of Columbus.* New Haven: Yale University Press.

Adorno, T. W. (1973). *Negative Dialectics.* London: Routledge.

Adorno, T. W. (2005). *Minima Moralia: Reflections from Damaged Life.* London: Verso.

Aiyer, A. (2001). Hemispheric Solutions? Neoliberal Crisis, Criminality and "Democracy" in the Americas. *Urban Anthropology and Studies of Cultural Systems and Economic Development, 30*(2–3), 239–268.

Alexander, R. (2008). *Education for All, the Quality Imperative, and the Problem of Pedagogy.* London: University of London.

Amann, E., & Baer, W. (2002). Neoliberalism and Its Consequences in Brazil. *Journal of Latin American Studies, 34*(3), 945–959.

Andrade, M. V., & Lisboa, M. B. (2000). *Desesperanca de Vida: Homicidio em Minas Gerais, Rio de Janeiro e Sao Paulo: 1981 a 1997.* Rio de Janeiro: Mimeo.

Attanasio, C. (2015). Judge Halts São Paulo School Restructuring Following Student Protest Movement That Occupied Over 200 Institutions. *Latin Times,* December 2. Retrieved March 1, 2016, from http://www.latintimes.com/judge-halts-sao-paulo-school-restructuring-following-student-protest-movement-356585.

Barker, J. (2002). Review of City of Walls: Crime, Segregation, and Citizenship in São Paulo by Teresa P. R. Caldeira University of California Press 2000. *American Ethnologist, 29*(4), 1031–1032.

Bauman, Z. (2002). *Society Under Siege.* Cambridge: Polity.

Bethell, L. (2000). Politics in Brazil: From Elections Without Democracy to Democracy Without Citizenship. *Daedalus, 129*(2), 1–27.

Bill, M. V., & Athayde, C. (2006). *Falcão: Meninos do Tráfico.* Rio de Janeiro: Objetiva.

Blaut, J. M. (1993). *The Colonizer's Model of the World: Geographical Diffusionism and Eurocentric History.* New York: Guilford Press.

Bonduki, G. N. (1998). *Origens da Habitação Social no Brasil – Arquitetura Moderna, Lei do Inquilinato e Difusão da Casa Própria.* São Paulo: Estação Liberdade.

Bourguignon, F. (2001). Crime as a Social Cost of Poverty and Inequality: A Review Focusing on Developing Countries. In S. Yusuf, S. Evenett, & W. Wu (Eds.), *Facets of Globalization: International and Local Dimensions of Development* (pp. 171–191). Washington, DC: World Bank.

Bronfenbrenner, U. (1944). A Constant Frame of Reference for Sociometric Research: Part II. Experiment and Interference. *Sociometry, 7*, 40–75.

Bronfenbrenner, U. (1979). *The Ecology of Human Development: Experiments in Nature and Design*. London: Harvard University Press.

Bronfenbrenner, U. (2005). *Making Human Beings Human: Bioecological Perspectives on Human Development*. London: Sage.

Caldeira, T. P. R. (2000). *City of Walls: Crime, Segregation, and Citizenship in São Paulo*. Berkeley: University of California Press.

Câmara, J. H. C., Souza, F. D. C. S., Pinheiro, K. L. C. B., Barreto, S. L., & Alves, G. S. (2007). Crescimento econômico, urbanização e impactos socioambientais: o caso do município de Mossoró-RN. In *II Congresso de Pesquisa e Inovação da Rede Norte Nordeste de Educação Tecnológica, João Pessoa–PB*.

Canton, A. L. (2007). *Preservação Contraditória no Centro de São Paulo: Degradação da Vilas Preservadas na Baixada do Glicério no Contexto da Renovação Urbana (Operação Urbana Centro)*. São Paulo: University of São Paulo.

Chalhoub, S. (2006). *Cidade Febril: Cortiços e Epidemias na Corte Imperial*. São Paulo: Companhia das Letras.

Clarke, S. (2004). The Neoliberal Theory of Society. In A. Saad-Filho & D. Johnston (Eds.), *Neoliberalism: A Critical Reader* (pp. 50–59). London: Pluto Press.

Fajnzylber, P., Daniel, L., & Norman, L. (2002). Inequality and Violent Crime. *Journal of Law and Economics, 45*(1), 1–40.

Fausto, B. (1999). *A Concise History of Brazil*. Cambridge: Cambridge University Press.

Florida, R., Mellander, C., & Gulden, T. (2009). *Global Metropolis: The Role of Cities and Metropolitan Areas in the Global Economy*. Toronto: University of Toronto. Retrieved June 6, 2016, from http://www.creativeclass.com/rfcgdb/articles/Global%20metropolis.pdf.

Freyre, G. (1986). *The Masters and the Slaves*. Berkeley: University of California Press.

Fromm, E. (2013). *Escape from Freedom*. New York: Open Road Media.

Frúgoli, J. R. H. (2000). *Centralidade em São Paulo: trajetórias, conflitos, e negociações na metrópole*. São Paulo: EDUSP.

Galtung, J. (1996). *Peace by Peaceful Means: Peace and Conflict, Development and Civilisation*. London: Sage.

Galtung, J., & Hivik, T. (1971). Structural and Direct Violence: A Note on Operationalization. *Journal of Peace Studies, 8*(1), 73–76.

Gawryszewski, V. P., & Lucianna, S. C. (2005). Social Inequality and Homicide Rates in São Paulo City, Brazil. *Revista de Saúde Pública, 39*(2), 191–197.

Gillespie, W. (2006). Capitalist World-Economy, Globalization, and Violence: Implications for Criminology and Social Justice. *International Criminal Justice Review, 16*(1), 24–44.

Green, D. (2003). *Silent Revolution: The Rise and Crisis of Market Economics in Latin America.* New York: Monthly Review Press.

Harvey, D. (2005). *A Brief History of Neoliberalism.* New York: Oxford University Press.

Horkheimer, M., & Adorno, T. W. (2002). *Dialectic of Enlightenment.* Stanford: Stanford University Press.

Hudson, R. A. (1997). *Brazil: A Country Study.* Washington, DC: DA Pam.

Huggins, M. K. (1998). *Political Policing: The United States and Latin America.* Durham: Duke University Press.

Huggins, M. K. (2000). Urban Violence and Police Privatization in Brazil: Blended Invisibility. *Social Justice, 27*(2), 113–134.

Huggins, M. K., Haritos-Fatouros, M., & Zimbardo, P. (2002). *Violence Workers: Torturers and Murderers Reconstruct Brazilian Atrocities.* San Francisco and Los Angeles: University of California Press.

IBGE. (2003). *Pesquisa de Orçamentos Familiares 2002–2003.* Retrieved June 6, 2016, from http://www.ibge.gov.br/home/estatistica/populacao/condica-odevida/pof/2002/.

IBGE. (2010). *Pesquisa de Orçamentos Familiares 2008–2009.* Retrieved March 13, 2013, from https://ww2.ibge.gov.br/home/estatistica/populacao/condicaodevida/pof/2008_2009/default.shtm.

de Junior, A. O., & de Lima, V. C. A. (2013). Segurança Pública e Racismo Institucional. *Boletim de Analise Politico-Institucional, 4,* 21–26.

Kerr, G. (2014). *A Short History of Brazil: From Pre-Colonial Peoples to Modern Economic Miracle.* Harpenden: Pocket Essentials.

Klein, H. S., & Luna, F. V. (2010). *Slavery in Brazil.* Cambridge: Cambridge University Press.

Kohara, L. (2009). *Relação Entre as Condições de Moradia e Desempenho Escolar: Estudo com crianças residentes em cortiços.* São Paulo: University of São Paulo.

Landman, K., & Schonteich, M. (2002). Urban Fortresses: Gated Communities as a Reaction to Crime. *African Security Review, 11*(4), 71–85.

Lara, M. R. (2008). Jovens Urbanos e o Consumo das Grifes. In S. H. S. Borelli & J. F. Filho (Eds.), *Culturas Juvenis no Seculo XXI* (pp. 133–150). São Paulo: EDUC.

Levine, R. M. (1999). *The History of Brazil.* London: Greenwood Press.

Marcílio, M. L. (2001). O Atraso Histórico na Educação. *Braudel Papers, 30,* 3–11.

Marcuse, H. (1964). *One Dimensional Man: Studies in the Ideology of Advanced Industrial Society.* Boston: Beacon Press.

Marx, K. (1990). *Capital: A Critique of Political Economy* (Vol. 1). London: Penguin Books.

Matias, A. (2011, 15 May). Churrascão Diferenciado: Política, Internet e Brasil. *Jornal do Estado de São Paulo*, Caderno 2, D7.

Melamed, C. (2011). *Inequality: Why It Matters and What Can Be Done*. Retrieved August 26, 2016, from http://www.actionaid.org/sites/files/actionaid/inequality_why_it_matters_and_what_can_be_done.pdf.

Mezarobba, G. (2006). *Um Acerto de Contas com o Futuro: a anistia e suas conseqüências, um estudo do caso Brasileiro*. São Paulo: FAPESP/Humanitas.

Mezarobba, G. (2008). *O Preço do Esquecimento: as reparações pagas às vítimas do regime militar (uma comparação entre Brasil, Argentina e Chile)*. São Paulo: University of São Paulo.

Montiel, C. J., & Wessells, M. (2001). Democratization, Psychology, and the Construction of Cultures of Peace. *Peace and Conflict: Journal of Peace Psychology, 7*(2), 119–129.

Morgan, M. (2013). *The Paradoxical Perpetuation of Neoliberalism: How Ideologies Are Formed and Dissolved*. Retrieved November 30, 2014, from http://www.heathwoodpress.com/the-paradoxical-perpetuation-of-neoliberalism-how-ideologies-are-formed-and-dissolved/.

Morrell, R. (2002). A Calm After the Storm? Beyond Schooling as Violence. *Educational Review, 54*(1), 37–46.

Municipal Prefecture of São Paulo. (2012). *Historico Demográfico do Município de São Paulo*. Retrieved October 22, 2012, from http://smdu.prefeitura.sp.gov.br/historico_demografico/introducao.php.

Nagler, M. (1997). Nonviolence and Peacemaking Today. *ReVision, 20*(2), 12–17.

Robeyns, I. (2006). Three Models of Education: Rights, Capabilities and Human Capital. *Theory and Research in Education, 4*(1), 69–84.

Rogers, C. R. (1959). A Theory of Therapy, Personality and Interpersonal Relationships as Developed in the Client-Centered Framework. In S. Koch (Ed.), *Psychology: A Study of a Science Vol. 3 – Formulations of the Person and the Social Context*. New York: McGraw Hill.

Saad-Filho, A. (2012). Neoliberalism, Democracy and Development Policy in Brazil. In C. Kyung-Sup, B. Fine, & L. Weiss (Eds.), *Developmental Politics in Transition: The Neoliberal Era and Beyond* (pp. 117–139). London: Palgrave Macmillan.

Schick, K. (2009). To Lend a Voice to Suffering Is a Condition for All Truth: Adorno and International Political Thought. *Journal of International Political Theory, 5*(2), 138–160.

Schwartzman, S. (2003). *The Challenges of Education in Brazil*. Oxford: Oxford University. Retrieved August 26, 2016, from https://www.researchgate.net/profile/Simon_Schwartzman/publication/225088750_The_Challenges_of_Education_in_Brazil/links/0912f5064693c5c575000000.pdf.

Smith, C. (2012). *Neoliberalism and Inequality: A Recipe for Interpersonal Violence?* Retrieved January 24, 2015, from http://thesocietypages.org/sociologylens/2012/11/06/neoliberalism-and-inequality-a-recipe-for-interpersonal-violence/.

Sobrinho, A. S. O. (2013). São Paulo e a Ideologia Higienista entre os séculos XIX e XX: a utopia da civilidade. *Sociologias, 15*(32), 210–235.

Souza, E. S. (2010). *Escritura e Sucesso Escolar: Um diálogo entre psicanálise e educação.* São Paulo: PUC.

Treece, D., Saad, A., Macaulay, F., Dominguez, F. Evans, Y., & Carbonnier, S. (2018). *Brazil's Ex-President Lula Imprisoned to Keep Him Out of the Election.* Retrieved August 8, 2018, from https://www.theguardian.com/world/2018/jun/08/brazils-ex-president-lula-imprisoned-to-keep-him-out-of-the-election-letters.

UNESCO. (2014). *Índice de Vulnerabilidade Juvenil à Violência e Desigualdade 2014.* Brasilia: UNESCO.

UNESCO. (2016). *Education for All Movement.* Retrieved August 22, 2016, from http://www.unesco.org/new/en/education/themes/leading-the-international-agenda/education-for-all/.

Wade, R. H. (2004). Is Globalization Reducing Poverty and Inequality? *World Development, 32*(4), 567–589.

Watts, J. (2016). *Brazil's Dilma Rousseff Impeached by Senate in Crushing Defeat.* Retrieved August 8, 2018, from https://www.theguardian.com/world/2016/aug/31/dilma-rousseff-impeached-president-brazilian-senate-michel-temer.

Williamson, J. (1989). What Washington Means by Policy Reform. In J. Williamson (Ed.), *Latin American Readjustment: How Much Has Happened.* Washington, DC: Institute for International Economics.

Williamson, J. (2002). *Did the Washington Consensus Fail?* Retrieved December 20, 2014, from http://www.iie.com/publications/papers/paper.cfm?ResearchID=488.

Wood, E. M. (2002). *The Origin of Capitalism: A Longer View.* London: Verso.

World Bank. (2010). *Gross Domestic Product 2010.* Retrieved October 22, 2012, from http://siteresources.worldbank.org/DATASTATISTICS/Resources/GDP.pdf.

CHAPTER 6

How Violent Epistemology Shapes Schooling Systems: The Development of Public Schooling in Brazil and São Paulo

6.1   A Schooling System Built on Violence

The previous chapter illustrated how the sociohistorical context in which DCX School is located has been shaped by violent epistemology. Chapter 7 'zooms in' on DCX School itself to assess how the mesosystemic relationship between this context and the school impacts on subject development, interpersonal relations, and the ways in which teachers and students engage with their 'roles' within the school. However, these factors are not only affected by the non-conducive social circumstances surrounding the school, but also by violent epistemology embedded within the structures, pedagogies, ideology, and behavioural expectations that accompany the education system of which the School is a part. It is therefore necessary to first provide a brief history of Brazil's education system, and how its development has been shaped by violent epistemology.

A broad selection of literature discusses Brazil's 'long history of failure' when it comes to education, usually measured by matriculation rates and test scores in comparison to European and other BRICS countries (cf. Marcílio 2001; Kinzo and Dunkerley 2003; World Bank 2003, 2004; Schwartzman 2003; Luna and Klein 2006; Bruns et al. 2012). While these analyses cite some important contributing factors such as lack of investment and political complexities, seldom do they contextualise the perceived failures within Brazil's colonial past and postcolonial/neoliberal present. None of these studies consider the role of such things as violent epistemology or the violent epistemic aspects of their own frame of reference which

© The Author(s) 2019   159
B. M. Titchiner, *The Epistemology of Violence*, Critical Political Theory
and Radical Practice, https://doi.org/10.1007/978-3-030-12911-8_6

tends to be Eurocentric and rooted in the concept of human capital. Rather than repeating these analyses, I will explore the ways in which Brazil's schooling system has been built on and shaped by violent epistemology, demonstrating how such an analysis can provide a deeper understanding of the root causes of the problems experienced in Brazilian schools.

6.2   Colonisation

Collectivised ideology, with its violent epistemic structure and logic of instrumental reason, has shaped Brazilian schooling since the colonial era. For the first 250 years of colonisation, the only formal education in operation was that implanted by the Jesuits. The Jesuits brought European morals, customs, and religiosity, and a European model of education and pedagogy, overriding the indigenous populations' own educational practices (Rauber 2008). As Arrais do Nascimento et al. (2012) write:

> The model [of education] implanted by the Jesuits [...] was to be an instrument of domination for the Metropolis [Lisbon]. In this interim education assumed the role of colonising agent [...] configuring itself in a process of acculturation in which the natives had their culture and education depreciated. (p. 4891)

Jesuit schooling can be seen as shaped by violent epistemology in two ways: the adoption and universalisation of a rigid schema in which the teachings of Jesus were held above all other dimensions of life, and adherence to the economic ideology of the time which the schools served by instilling a 'work ethic'. By isolating and universalising European profit and religion, other dimensions of life were pushed to the margins of awareness, such as the pre-existing autonomy, ways of life, beliefs, and forms of education held by the indigenous populations. This negation can be seen as enabling the Jesuits to justify according to their own violent epistemic schema, the exploitation of these populations in the service of the prevailing European ideologies.

Despite its messianic ambitions, Jesuit schooling was only available to a small minority of the population, and it came to an end by the mid-eighteenth century when the Jesuits were expelled from Portugal and Brazil in efforts to conform to the European Enlightenment. In Brazil much of the catholic education was dismantled, and was not replaced by any other coordinated education provision for the time being (Schwartzman 2003). Until the late nineteenth century, public schools were virtually non-existent.

The plantation economy was fuelled by slave labour, and since slaves were already fulfilling their economic purpose, no other reason to provide education was considered. What formal education there was lacked coherence and resources (Marcílio 2001). Lack of education provision in the absence of economic need for it illustrates how dimensions of life (such as learning for personal interest and development) that do not serve the dimension that has been held up above all others in the prevalent ideology (in this period, profit from mercantile enterprise which was not dependent on an educated workforce) tend to be pushed to the margins of awareness and neglected.

6.3   LIGHTS OF THE REPUBLIC

Only at the beginning of the nineteenth century, with the arrival of the Portuguese court followed by independence, were attempts made to bring education provision in line with the developments of European nation-states. Education began again to be thought of as instrumental in progressing the ideological endeavours of the elite. Now that Brazil was its own nation, its sole purpose no longer to provide profits for the Portuguese State, Brazilian elites began striving to develop a national identity and prestige. Aspiring to the growing European trends towards rationalism, 'modernity', and bourgeois 'civilisation' (essentially Enlightenment), for which education was seen to be instrumental, the first higher education institutions and public secondary school were built. Elementary education was still sparse however, and no national system existed (Arrais do Nascimento et al. 2012).

Due to a lack of good quality public education, the number of private schools increased exponentially during this period in order to meet the demands of the influx of wealthier classes arriving from Portugal:

> The scenario [...] at the end of the imperial period, was one of an education divided between public schools of poor quality, and private schools that detained the best teachers and exclusively served the dominant classes. (ibid., p. 4895)

Although great changes were implemented during this time, all of the measures to improve education were taken with the objective of forming a Brazilian ruling class, and in this way served only the elites (Schwartzman 2003).

Despite the growing number of private schools, by the 1890s the concept of a public education *system* began to take root, in line with European Enlightenment ideals. In São Paulo, previously disjointed teaching units were brought together into 'school groups' and began to organise students according to age and proficiency—the beginning of the sequential, multi-serial-style education that is central to Brazilian public schooling today (Souza 1998). Unlike today however, these schools were housed in bespoke buildings constructed according to the most advanced architecture of the time (Schwartzman 2003). This coincided with the population expansion that accompanied immigration, as well as the elite's desires for an education system that mimicked those of modern European nation-states and could incorporate the diverse population into a coherent and integrated 'nation' (Schwartzman 2003). At this time, the ultimate nineteenth-century education model of graded schools built as 'veritable temples of knowledge' was introduced first in São Paulo, then in the rest of Brazil:

> Presented as the way in which the republicans could break free from the imperial past, the graded schools looked forward, projected a future in which, under the Republic, the people, reconciled with the nation, would beget an orderly and progressive country. (Faria Filho and Vidal 2007, p. 589)

With the aim of 'civilising the nation' in the aftermath of slavery (ibid.) for the first time the elites placed significant value and hope in education (Marcílio 2001) and a hegemonic schooling model was established, its characteristics described thus:

> The materials of intuitive teaching, the desks affixed to the floor, the central position of the teacher, all seemed to indicate predefined places for pupils and teachers in the classroom. [...] The rigid division of the sexes, the precise definition of individual places inside the classroom, and the control of body movements during class breaks gave shape to a dispositional and motor economy that distinguished the school pupil from the one not attending school.
>
> On the other hand, contact with the monumental architecture, the wide corridors, the tall ceilings, the grand dimensions of windows and doors, the rationalization and cleanliness of spaces, and the way the school building stuck out among the other city buildings were designed to impress upon the students the appreciation for rational and scientific education, valuing a cultural and aesthetic symbolism constituted by the lights of the republic. (Faria Filho and Vidal 2007, p. 589)

The influence of Auguste Comte's positivist ideas in Brazil at this time resulted in education policy dominated by rationalism and efficiency, and scientific tendencies in teaching. Along with the rigid control of space and movement in these new 'Enlightenment' schools, came the rigid control of time and activity within time, which fitted into the early industrial capitalist relations that were being established concurrently (Faria Filho and Vidal 2007). This period marked the beginnings of a Brazilian education system grounded in the instrumental reason of two interconnected spheres of ideology: a nationalism based in European positivist Enlightenment rationality; and the economic ideology of industrial capitalism.

In the service of these schemas, certain particularities were held up above all others: whiteness, hygiene, order, scientific rationality, urbanism, cultural homogeneity, and profit from industry. Aspects that did not fit this vision were marginalised, such as the pre-existing religious, cultural, and linguistic practices of the indigenous and majority black population as well as the physical, emotional, and psychological needs and interests of a diverse student population. As in other parts of the industrial world, by employing education in the service of the elevated dimension of profit, schools became institutions for preparing workers for industrial labour. The use of highly structured routines, control of physical movement, surveillance, and lack of space for students' personal interests and experience in the learning process was typical of nineteenth-century schooling, and illustrates how students were reduced to objects for exploitation, their subjectivity largely negated (Clovis de Azevedo 2007; Schwartzman 2003).

While the concept of public education had become popular and efforts were made to extend public elementary schooling to the children of workers, the poor, immigrants, and ex-slaves, administration of the school system was decentralised and its development lacked coherence throughout Brazil. Only the wealthiest regions managed to significantly strengthen their schooling provision, and it remained that only a minority of the population had access to schooling. In 1900 only 25% of children attended public primary education in the capital city of Rio de Janeiro, and the same proportion of the population at most were literate (Schwartzman 2003).

6.4   Dictatorship

The period of 1930–1945 was marked by the political dictatorship of Getulio Vargas. The beginning of the Vargas era coincided with the start of Import Substituting Industrialisation (ISI) and the concurrent increase in demand for specialist labour hands, for which it was necessary to invest in education (Arrais do Nascimento et al. 2012). Education became even more of a national priority and with a move towards political centralisation a Ministry of Education and Culture (MEC) was established for the first time. Article 149 of the 1934 constitution set out ideals for education, stating that education was the right of all, the responsibility of the family and the state, and had the purpose of producing 'effective agents for the moral and economic life of the nation' (ibid.). This statement of purpose illustrates the continued development of education in the service of 'civilising' and economic ideologies.

The 1934 constitution also stated that education should promote 'human solidarity' (ibid.), but in practice, this meant the enforced fostering of cultural hegemony and patriotism rather than acknowledgement of and respect for the diversity and particularity that existed within the population at the time. Various social groups protested by calling for education reform, from Marxists to Pragmatists, to Authoritarian Fascists, and to ultramontane Catholics. However, in the end, bureaucratic and administrative trends, fused with the conservative nationalist values of the Vargas regime, prevailed. The National Institute for Pedagogic Studies (INEP) was created with the aim of making education more technical and scientific, and there were concerted efforts to infuse students with patriotic ideals through the teaching of national and patriotic hymns. Immigrants' schools were also closed, and those who taught immigrant children in their mother tongue were prosecuted (Schwartzman 2003).

During this era, a distaste for the lavish architecture of the neo-colonial school buildings also began to develop, largely because they were expensive and signified for many the restriction of education to the elite. This criticism, along with the movement to universalise and popularise education, paved the way for the construction of simple, inexpensive school buildings that refused the colonial style. The buildings could be huge but were designed to be functional and rational (Faria Filho and Vidal 2007).

While this shift from one ideological schema (neo-colonialism) to another (industrial modernism) may have been considered progress, it did not necessarily represent a move towards less violent epistemology. In the schooling of the Vargas era, the 'rational' dimension (with its rejection of anything 'soft' or 'subjective' such as emotions, along with its subjugation of body to mind) and the economic dimension (with its rejection of all that is not considered to serve it) persisted as isolated, elevated, and universalised particularities in the service of which not only school architecture but also core aspects of school activities (pedagogy, timetables, movement) were employed. In the cold, hard, concrete architecture (which Brazil's public schools retain to this day), students and teachers perceived as objects of education for the purposes of forwarding the 'moral' and economic agenda of the nation's elites were overlooked as diverse subjects. Questions such as whether the school space was comfortable or suitable to inspire learning, and whether the model of education promoted satisfied teachers' and students' particular needs and interests, were left aside.

While efforts were increased during the Vargas era to create a universal public school system, at the end of the 1940s less than 50% of school-age children were enrolled in school, and only 13% of schools were government owned (Faria Filho and Vidal 2007). Between around 1950 and the late 1980s, the state struggled to expand public education provision to meet the pace of economic and urban growth. Meanwhile, public schooling was still considered to be of poor quality and the private education sector continued to expand, catering to both the elites and the lower middle classes. During this period, schooling continued to be seen as an instrument for furthering both modernisation and the political ideologies of authoritarian regimes. Continuing trends from the Vargas era, schools were perceived more and more as places to teach basic skills quickly, cheaply, and to as many people as possible.

> The growing simplicity and economy of school construction [...] in the 1950's and 1960's [...] pointed to changes in conceptions about school spaces and, therefore, about the place of the school in the Brazilian social environment. [T]he struggle for the democratisation[1] of schooling made itself felt in the functionalist buildings, technically designed for a quick and efficient education. (Faria Filho and Vidal 2007, p. 596)

In 1964, Brazil faced a military coup which resulted in another 21 years of dictatorship. Supported by the US government, the regime carried out a series of educational reforms, whilst instilling strict mechanisms to repress dissent through the imposition of a series of 'Institutional Acts'. These took away rights to free expression, to collective manifestation, and to protest, and sanctioned punitive acts including the blacklisting of 'subversives', interrogation, and political imprisonment. Most significant for education was Institutional Act No. 5 (AI-5), promulgated simultaneously with Decree No. 477. AI-5 gave powers to the president to close congress,

---

[1] In Brazil, the term 'democratisation of schooling' refers to universal school matriculation, not to any form of democratic governance.

revoke mandates, and suspend political rights. By enabling the president to act as sole executive and legislative authority, AI-5 stripped citizens of 'all individual guarantees [of rights], whether public or private' (Romanelli 1978, p. 226).

Decree 477 extended governmental repression throughout the education system, and significantly restricted the rights of students, educational workers, and teachers. The first article defined 'infractions' by teachers, students, and school workers that would justify disciplinary action. These included incitement to strike; attacks on people, goods, and buildings; and acts destined towards the organisation of subversive movements or the sequestering and use of school establishments for 'subversive ends'. These infractions, by decree, would be punished in a variety of ways: if the individual was a member of the teaching body or an employee of an educational establishment, they would be dismissed and prohibited from being reappointed for five years. If a student, they would be excluded and prohibited from re-registering at any educational establishment for three years. If the individual received any government support (such as scholarships), they would lose this and remain ineligible for government support for three years (Piletti 1990).

To enforce these acts, a Department for Political and Social Order (DOPS) was created, and it kept 'blacklists' of teachers and students who were taken to be subversives. Excessive state and military violence was often used to repress dissent, whether real or imagined (Dockhorn 2002). Rosa (2006) describes the impact of this:

> In virtue of this policy and of the laws installed to its benefit, many musicians, teachers, artists, writers and students were persecuted, imprisoned, tortured and exiled. Naturally we can comprehend, therefore, that at this level [of repression] people lived their own private form of censorship, or what we can call 'self-censorship'. [...] Most of the population that lived through this time came to know specific forms of pain and silence that, in the context of the regime, had a connotation of coercion and fear. (pp. 37–41)

The dictatorship affected not only the freedoms of students and educators, but also the style and content of education itself. At the end of the 1960s, the military government solidified agreements between the Brazilian Ministry of Education and Culture (MEC) and the United States Agency for International Development (USAID), which included reforms to Brazil's education system. These possessed characteristics which, according to Rosa (2006), had to be authoritarian, domesticating, and technicistic in order to serve transnational capital. Brazilian minister Roberto Campos believed that education at the time was disconnected from the labour market and not demanding enough of students, which he argued was leaving 'vacuums of leisure' that students were filling with 'political adventures' (Ghiraldelli 2000, p. 169). In line with this view, the USAID-MEC reforms aimed to depoliticise students and train them for the labour market.

Philosophy and political education was replaced in the curriculum with 'moral and civic education' and teaching hours for history were decreased, to reduce the chances of students becoming politicised in opposition to the state. Promoted by American policy technicians, technocratic approaches were expanded, based in concepts of scientific neutrality, rationality, efficiency, and productivity (Ghiraldelli 2000). This was largely in the service of the developmentalist project to accelerate Brazil's socioeconomic growth, in which education was seen to be important for the preparation of adequate human resources (Veiga 1989).

This economistic model of education came with efficiency aims embodied in a greater division of labour between those who plan and those who execute those plans on the ground. The discouragement of critical thinking and dialogue fostered by the restriction of humanities subjects, coupled with technicistic approaches, resulted in an education restricted to professional training for working-class children and the promotion of 'exact science' as the only valid knowledge (Pellanda 1986). These reforms transformed educators into technicians supervised by other technicians via technical and objective instructions, reinforced the separation of theory from practice in curricular content, and reduced students to instruments expected only to fulfil instructional objectives (Ghiraldelli 2000) aimed at meeting the needs of the growing economy (Aranha 1996). This resulted in a continued perception of public schools as 'second class' educational establishments. While in 1971 mandatory education was increased from four to eight years in continued efforts to keep up with international trends, grade repetition and dropout rates remained high for reasons ranging from problems of access to lack of relevance to learners' interests and needs.

Violent epistemology can be seen to have shaped education during this period in a number of ways. The isolation of the economic dimension pervaded schooling even further through the technicistic and efficiency aims of the USAID-MEC reforms. Through this process, dimensions of the curriculum which did not serve or which threatened the stability of the developmentalist agenda (such as the humanities and their inherent historical and political aspects) were excluded, while dimensions of student and teacher subjectivity which did not serve the economic agenda were also neglected. The continued aspiration to model European and North American nation-states, perceived as 'developed' and 'civilised', continued through the collaboration with USAID, and with this came the perpetuation of the universalisation of a particular ideal of 'progress' which neglected the wishes and needs of a diverse and heterogeneous population. Finally, in a powerful illustration of type α behaviour, all subversion and dissent, whether real or imagined, was actively and consciously suppressed through acts of law, coercion, and physical violence.

6.5   NEOLIBERALISM

In 1985, the military dictatorship ended and Brazil began its transition to democracy, paving the way for neoliberal economic reforms. In 1988 a new constitution was drawn up, in which free education was once again enshrined as a right of every person, then in 1996 a new Law of Directives and Foundations for National Education (known as LDB 1996, short for Lei de Diretrizes e Bases da Educação Nacional) (Piletti 1999)[2] was approved by the neoliberal administration of President Fernando Henrique Cardoso, in line with the global movement for Education for All and International Monetary Fund (IMF) structural adjustment programmes. LDB 1996 (Ministério da Educação 1996) included directives to increase investment of federal and municipal resources in education, increase levels of training for teachers, and universalise matriculation in school whilst assuring access and attendance for all students at the 'correct' age. From the 1990s onwards, the scope of education changed rapidly and access to basic education became near-universal (Schwartzman 2003).

In line with previous decades, the LDB 1996 attributed great importance to techno-scientific education and capacitation for the world of work. Citizenship was connected to the accumulation of basic skills and competencies that would enable students to continually reform their knowledge in a world of constant technological change (Leodoro 2001; Clovis de Azevedo 2007). This type of education reflected what Postman (1992) called the 'technocrat's ideal—a person with no commitment and no point of view, but with plenty of marketable skills' (p. 186). Leodoro (2001) accuses this approach of fostering an education in which students

[2] Law no. 9 394, 20/12/1996 (LDB 1996).

feel unstimulated and do not comprehend the value of pursuing understanding in relation to history and human existence.

While the directive for universal matriculation spurred a rapid expansion of provision, Brazil's long history of low investment in education and teacher training meant that a strong, valued teaching profession and the necessary infrastructure to cope with such expansion did not exist. Lack of resources and teacher training led to overcrowded schools, poor-quality teaching with great inconsistencies in classroom practice, and high numbers of students being held back to repeat years of schooling and leaving education illiterate or only semi-literate (Crespo et al. 2000). This rapid expansion was problematic both for schools and for the poorest students. While the percentage of adolescents not in school dropped significantly, public schools were not prepared to meet the needs of rapidly increasing numbers of adolescent students from poor backgrounds who had not previously engaged consistently with education (Marcílio 2005). Racial inequalities also persisted, with the white population having attended on average 5.75 years of schooling in 2001, whereas the non-white population averaged 4.04 years. Years of schooling were also found to correlate with income—the average income of white Brazilians was twice that of non-whites in the same year (IBGE 2001).

Throughout the 2000s, President Lula introduced the Bolsa Escola and Bolsa Familia programmes which helped Brazil achieve near-universal matriculation by providing cash incentives to families who enrolled their children in school. The numbers of students being held back to repeat grades also reduced significantly with the introduction of automatic grade promotion regardless of learning outcomes. In 2010, compulsory elementary education was also expanded from eight to nine years in duration (Koppensteiner 2011), and plans to increase the length of the school day from a half to a full day were also made. This further expansion means that aside from more young people than ever attending school, they are now also expected by law to spend more time (both in years and on a daily basis) within the school environment, exerting an even greater strain on teachers and resources.

This situation has continued to feed the division between public and private schooling, and between public schools in poorer and wealthier areas. For reasons such as geographical inequalities in resource allocation and more qualified/experienced teachers being less inclined to work in more challenging schools, the quality of public schooling in poor states, municipalities, and neighbourhoods tends to be lower than in wealthier areas (Schwartzman 2003). Due to the poor quality of public schooling, middle- and upper-class families continue to send their children to private schools, which tend to prepare students better for admission to the free and prestigious public universities. Students from public schools are less prepared to access public universities and must find the means to pay for private, lower quality university courses—something not possible for many. This inequity of access to quality education impacts disproportionately on students from low-income families.

Until LDB 1996, public school teachers were only required to hold a secondary school qualification. The majority were therefore poorly qualified and knew little of pedagogy or philosophy of education. Now all teachers of infant and the first four years of basic education must obtain a degree in a school of education or pedagogy, and teachers in the second half of basic education must obtain a degree in a specialist subject, but not necessarily be trained in pedagogy and philosophy of education (Koppensteiner 2011). The implementation of these requirements has been slow; in 2004, just 25% of teachers had obtained degrees, most of which were of questionable quality granted through distance learning or evening programmes, by providers which had sprung up to profit from the increase in demand. The fact that teachers in the second half of basic education are not required to have any training in pedagogy means that they may be knowledgeable in their subject but unprepared for teaching and classroom management. The failure to develop a quality system of teacher education, coupled with low pay and lack of resources, has resulted in high levels of discontent among teachers, who often feel devalued, alienated, and dejected (Schwartzman 2003, p. 24).

During the neoliberal era, the perpetuation of violent epistemology in schooling can be identified in a number of ways. As the economic dimension has been held above all other dimensions of life, the continued promotion of a technocratic and market-based approach to curricula and teaching (the result of continued efforts to join the neoliberal Western world in its perceived state of modernity) with its focus on educating students for the needs of a rapidly changing labour market has meant that dimensions of learning which do not serve the instrumental aims of developing 'basic skills and competencies', as well as the needs, desires, interests, and autonomy of students, have been pushed to the margins and suppressed. As Clovis de Azevedo (2007) states, in neoliberal schooling 'the world of desires, of feelings, of social and biological needs, has been conditioned and contaminated by the economic dimension' (p. 94).

The adoption of neoliberal ideology continued the trend of transplanting education systems from 'advanced' countries, with the aim of overcoming the 'chaotic' situation in Brazil (Marcílio 2005). In this way, legal reforms have been used as a magic wand, seen as able to create change on their own (Clovis de Azevedo 2007). However, this has illustrated the epistemic problems of severing the general from the particular. By importing general policy schema from other contexts without paying attention to the particularities of the Brazilian context, various problems have arisen resulting in a general sense of alienation and disaffection amongst teachers, and an atmosphere of chaos in schools as staff and students struggle to cope with demands while facing inadequate training and resources (ibid.).

One of the most insidious ways in which the violent epistemology of the neoliberal era has acted in education has been the placing of most of the responsibility back onto students and teachers. This era has brought an increase in flexible contracting (Americano 2011), temporary employment, underemployment, and autonomous/informal labour. This has created high levels of precarity for individuals and families, increases in structural unemployment, and an aggravation of social problems (Amann and Baer 2002). Rather than acknowledging these particularities as products of its own system (doing so would threaten the stability of the overarching schema), as discussed previously, neoliberal ideology works to negate the socioeconomic context and instead promote the discourse that the individual can resolve their own problems and is solely responsible for doing so (ibid.). Individuals who are unable to 'succeed' in school and in the labour market are therefore posited as deficient, lazy, and so on (Clovis de Azevedo 2007).

This discourse, which focuses on the initiative and disposition of the individual to face up to free competition and make the most of the opportunities offered by the market (in which individual success will be reserved for the 'most apt'—those who try hard and are able to permanently renew their skills), has, according to Clovis de Azevedo (2007), invaded the field of education. Imported policies formulated by international agencies such as the World Bank recognise that large proportions of the population in developing countries such as Brazil cannot afford to purchase education on the free market, and have therefore included directives for the provision of free, 'basic' education to meet the needs of students from low-income families (ibid.). However, this has perpetuated the division between those who have access to 'basic services' and those who are able to 'obtain more ample services, of better quality, via the market' (Coraggio and Torres 1997, p. 16).

While neoliberal rhetoric purports that the provision of public 'basic' education creates a level playing field, this can be seen as a violent epistemic generalisation because it severs the individual from their socioeconomic background, from the real opportunities available to them, and from their particular ability (or inability) to access and engage with these opportunities. Individuals who do not 'succeed' in school are seen as not trying hard enough, while the variety of particular factors that often make engagement in schooling difficult (poor-quality teaching, lack of resources, inadequate housing, poor nutrition, lack of parental support, unstimulating curriculum, psychological and emotional difficulties, etc.) are ignored. As neoliberal economic ideology is collectively affirmed to such an extent that the subject is reduced to an instrument of the economy rather than an autonomous individual with particular interests, desires, and needs, and as the rhetoric of individual responsibility for succeeding in the prescribed role of economic instrument is fostered within both schools and society, those who choose not to or are unable to participate as expected are labelled as 'marginals' and both literally and figuratively pushed to the margins. As Horkheimer and Adorno (2002) write:

> Tyranny leaves the body free and directs its attack at the soul. The ruler no longer says: You must think as I do or die. He says: You are free not to think as I do; your life, your property, everything shall remain yours, but from this day on you are a stranger among us. (p. 125)

In this way, students who are unable to or do not wish to conform and participate in schooling as expected are often subject to stigmatisation and social exclusion.

6.6   Today

While the ideologies outlined thus far have predominated in Brazilian education throughout its history, this has not occurred without resistance. In the 1920s, the ideas of the 'Escola Nova' movement, based on equality, reflexive freedom, and student autonomy, began to emerge. Although they were suppressed by the authoritarian nationalism of the Vargas Era, some of the Escola Nova ideas are still popular with educators. Paulo Freire was considered a subversive in his time and forced to live in exile during the dictatorship of 1964–1985. However, his ideas of educating for critical consciousness and using participatory and anti-authoritarian pedagogical methods are now considered favourably by many Brazilian educators. These more progressive, libertarian ideas have shaped a number of projects and initiatives within Brazil's education system over the last few decades, some of which have been initiated by local government. Educommunication (as summarised in Chap. 1) is one example, and a small number of public schools in São Paulo operate, with the permission of the municipal secretariat, according to more participatory and democratic principles by allowing students to participate in planning their own timetable and curriculum.

However, while these more progressive ideas and practices exist, the overarching atmosphere in public schooling is one in which a continual process of reforms, coupled with difficulties for teachers and schools in translating policy reforms coherently into practice, has resulted not in a coherent singular approach but rather a combination of approaches inherited from the past, in which authoritarian and technicistic practices prevail (Garcia 1995). The ideals and initiatives of more progressive teachers have largely been neutralised by the conservative structure of the traditional school. As Clovis de Azevedo (2007) explains:

> The [traditional] school institution [...] is not capable of absorbing progressive theories and practices of learning. The organisation of teaching is almost impermeable, there is no capillarity even for minimally coherent practice based in progressive and transformative educational thought. Progressive thought, as a rule, succumbs to the traditional school, suffers a theoretical impoverishment and doesn't result in new practices. In many cases it transforms itself into a neotechnicistic glaze, that rearticulates conservative pedagogy in 'modern' form [...] It tends to transform itself into sterile pedagogism or didacticism, strengthening the social isolation of the school and its inability to respond to the real needs of its students. (ibid., pp. 246–247)

As I demonstrate in the next chapter, this was the situation faced by teachers and students at DCX School.

REFERENCES

Amann, E., & Baer, W. (2002). Neoliberalism and Its Consequences in Brazil. *Journal of Latin American Studies, 34*(3), 945–959.

Americano, V. R. (2011). *Os Professores em Completação de Jornada (CJ) na Rede Municipal de Educação de São Paulo (2011): Condições do trabalho e implicações no currículo.* Dissertation. Pontifícia Universidade Católica de São Paulo. Retrieved February 2, 2018, from https://sapientia.pucsp.br/bitstream/handle/9627/1/Vanessa%20Rossi%20Americano.pdf.

Aranha, M. L. A. (1996). *História da Educação.* São Paulo: Moderna.

Arrais do Nascimento, P. E., Rodrigues, D. F., Lima, R. D., & Oliveira, P. F. (2012). *Historia da Educação no Brasil e a Prática Docente Diante das Novas Tecnologias*. IX National Seminar of Studies and Research on History, Society and Education in Brazil, 31 July–3 August, João Pessoa. Retrieved May 3, 2015, from http://www.histedbr.fe.unicamp.br/acer_histedbr/seminario/seminario9/PDFs/8.19.pdf.

Bruns, B., Evans, D., & Luque, J. (2012). *Achieving World-Class Education in Brazil*. Washington, DC: World Bank.

Clovis de Azevedo, J. (2007). *Reconversão Cultural da Escola: Mercoescola e Escola Cidadã*. Porto Alegre: Suline.

Coraggio, J. L., & Torres, R. M. (1997). *La Educación Según el Banco Mundial: un análisis de sus propuestos y métodos*. Buenos Aires: Minõ e Dàvila Editores.

Crespo, M., Soares, J. F., & Mello e Souza, A. (2000). The Brazilian National Education System of Basic Education: Context, Process and Impact. *Studies in Educational Evaluation, 26*, 105–125.

Dockhorn, G. V. (2002). *Quando a Ordem é Segurança e o Progresso é Desenvolvimento (1964–1974)*. Porto Alegre: EDIPUCRS.

Faria Filho, L. M., & Vidal, D. G. (2007). History of Urban Education in Brazil: Time and Space in Primary Schools. In W. T. Pink & G. W. Noblit (Eds.), *International Handbook of Urban Education* (pp. 581–600). Dordrecht: Springer.

Garcia, W. E. (1995). *Inovação Educacional no Brasil: Problemas e Perspectivas*. Campinas: Autores Associados.

Ghiraldelli, P. (2000). *História da Educação*. São Paulo: Cortes.

Horkheimer, M., & Adorno, T. W. (2002). *Dialectic of Enlightenment*. Stanford: Stanford University Press.

IBGE. (2001). *Pesquisa Nacional Por Amostra de Domicílios – PNAD 2001*. Retrieved August 26, 2016, from http://www.ibge.gov.br/home/estatistica/populacao/trabalhoerendimento/pnad2001/coment2001.shtm.

Kinzo, M. D'Alva, & Dunkerley, J. (2003). *Brazil Since 1985: Economy, Polity and Society*. London: University of London.

Koppensteiner, M. F. (2011). *Automatic Grade Promotion and Student Performance: Evidence from Brazil*. Retrieved July 19, 2015, from http://www.le.ac.uk/ec/research/RePEc/lec/leecon/dp11-52.pdf.

Leodoro, M. P. (2001). *Educação Científica e Cultura Material: os artefatos lúdicos*. São Paulo: University of São Paulo.

Luna, F. V., & Klein, H. S. (2006). *Brazil Since 1980*. Cambridge: Cambridge University Press.

Marcílio, M. L. (2001). O Atraso Histórico na Educação. *Braudel Papers, 30*, 3–11.

Marcílio, M. L. (2005). História da Escola em São Paulo e no Brasil. *Revista FAEEBA, 14*(24), 103–112.

Ministério da Educação. (1996). *LEI No. 9.394 de 20 de dezembro de 1996*. Retrieved March 2, 2019, from http://portal.mec.gov.br/seesp/arquivos/pdf/lei9394_ldbn1.pdf.

Pellanda, N. C. (1986). *Ideologia e educação e Repressão no Brasil Pós 64*. Porto Alegre: Mercado Aberto.

Piletti, N. (1990). *História da Educação no Brasil*. São Paulo: Ática.

Piletti, N. (1999). *Estrutura e Funcionamento do Ensino Fundamental*. São Paulo: Ática.

Postman, N. (1992). *Technopoly: The Surrender of Culture to Technology*. New York: Vintage Books.

Rauber, P. A. (2008). *Metodologia do Ensino Superior*. Dourados: Unigran.

Romanelli, O. O. (1978). *História da Educação no Brasil*. Petrópolis: Vozes.

Rosa, J. M. (2006). *As vozes de um mesmo tempo: a educação física institucionalizada no período da Ditadura Militar em Cacequi*. Santa Maria: UFSM.

Schwartzman, S. (2003). *The Challenges of Education in Brazil*. Retrieved August 26, 2016, from https://www.researchgate.net/profile/Simon_Schwartzman/publication/225088750_The_Challenges_of_Education_in_Brazil/links/0912f5064693c5c575000000.pdf.

Souza, R. F. (1998). *Templos de Civilização: a implantação da escola primária graduada no estado de São Paulo, 1890–1910*. São Paulo: Editora UNESP.

Veiga, I. P. (1989). *Repensando a Didática*. Campinas: Papirus.

World Bank. (2003). *Brazil – Equitable, Competitive, Sustainable: Contributions for Debate*. Washington, DC: World Bank.

World Bank. (2004). *Inequality and Economic Development in Brazil*. Washington, DC: World Bank.

CHAPTER 7

How Violent Epistemology Manifests in Schools: The Case of DCX

7.1 Introduction to DCX: An Institution That Bears the Brunt of Non-conducive Circumstances

DCX School is situated in the centre of the Baixada neighbourhood at its lowest point, in what was once a river bed but is now a dark street surrounded by crumbling tenements and high-rise apartment blocks. The school had approximately 1000 students enrolled at the time of research, and offered three shifts of schooling per day, running almost back-to-back from 8 am to 10 pm. DCX caters for all nine years of basic education, as well as a 'fast track' evening course for young people and adults who have missed out on schooling at the appropriate age. As a school of Fundamental Education, DCX is part of the São Paulo Municipal Education Network which comprises a bureaucratically complex organisational structure, made up of 11 core 'directorship' groups headed by the Municipal Secretary of Education.

Each directorship coordinates a different area such as 'Administration, Infrastructure and Logistics', 'Planning and Finance', or 'Information and Communication Technology', and includes up to 13 subgroups such as the 'Division for Evaluation and Qualifications' or the 'Division for Learning Technologies'. These in turn are divided into further subgroups, such as the 'Nucleus for Educommunication' or 'Nucleus for Assessment'. The primary Regional Directorates of Education (DREs) group comprises 13 offices spread throughout the city, each responsible for overseeing the operations

B. M. Titchiner, *The Epistemology of Violence*, Critical Political Theory and Radical Practice, https://doi.org/10.1007/978-3-030-12911-8_7

of all municipal education units within their region. There are 11 types of municipal education units, ranging from Centres of Infant Education (CEIs), to Municipal Schools of Fundamental Education (EMEFs) like DCX, Integrated Centres for Youth and Adult Education (CIEJAs), and a variety of combinations in between (Prefeitura de São Paulo 2016a).

Surrounded by the degradation of the Baixada neighbourhood, the large concrete building housing the DCX School is representative of the functionalist ideology that pervades contemporary Brazilian school architecture. Concrete walls, floors, and long corridors; square bare-walled classrooms with metal doors and high vents in place of windows; rows of simple desks facing a single blackboard in each classroom; and interior spaces divided by metal bars and padlocked gates. Aside from this almost prison-like architecture, the atmosphere within the school was shaped by the impact of violent epistemology manifest in a variety of non-conducive circumstances. I will provide a detailed breakdown and analysis of these below. Due to the quantity of primary data collected, I quote only the most illustrative excerpts in this chapter. Further supporting data is presented in Titchiner (2017).

Throughout the analysis presented in this chapter, reference will be made to the corresponding dimensions of the theoretical model diagram presented at the end of Chap. 4. These references will be presented in brackets throughout the chapter, as letters corresponding to the relevant dimensions of the model, separated by arrows representing a pathway of scenario(s) and response(s). For example, (L→P→Q→R) refers to outcome scenario L followed by the pathway of response P→Q→R as illustrated in the diagram, and the corresponding conceptual framework as outlined in Chaps. 3 and 4 and summarised at the end of Chap. 4. For reasons of limited space, each scenario and piece of data presented below cannot be discussed in great detail with reference to the conceptual framework presented thus far. These coded references are therefore presented to aid the reader in drawing connections between the two.

7.2   How Non-conducive Circumstances in the Baixada Affect Student Subject Development and Engagement with Schooling

Living in the non-conducive circumstances of the Baixada impacted students' subject development and engagement with schooling in a number of ways. The exclusion of families from the formal labour and rental markets had a direct impact on students, many of whom lived in cramped, over-crowded tenement accommodation or tiny high-rise apartments without space to move around. Many children's parents feared letting them out to play in the street, and kept them inside where they were often confined to sitting on the bed due to lack of space (Kohara 2009). Restricting students' ability to self-actualise, especially in terms of the need/desire to run and play, this situation resulted in pent-up energy and frustration for the younger students (particularly those in year five—mostly aged 10–12), who would often arrive at school agitated. The school building with its large ground-floor patio and long corridors represented for many children one of the only places that offered a space to satisfy the need to run around, play, and release this pent-up energy and frustration.

This caused many difficulties for teachers who struggled to manage the hyperactive, agitated, and often aggressive behaviour of large numbers of students. Break times were particularly problematic as up to 350 students at a time would be released onto the patio (and enclosed open space on the ground floor of the building). While this offered an opportunity for the children to 'blow off steam', levels of agitation were often so high that they would return from break with injuries and torn clothing after being caught in the ruckus or having been involved in physical conflicts with other students:

> The teacher said that the little kids are fighting a lot during break. The other teacher said 'yes, the other day a little boy came to me with his head all fractured and bleeding, it was ugly, they are really hitting each other'. (Observation notes 10 June 2011)

> What leaves me despairing is that they come back [from play time] injured, afflicted; today—today one came upstairs [to class] with their t-shirt ripped, because they had a fight downstairs. They were a third year. When it's not the fifth years, eh? Or the first years—the first years are fighting! During break. [...] It's the fights that start downstairs [during break] and continue upstairs [in class], they're ... the anxiety ... my god. (Teacher comment 18 April 2011)

The more timid students were fearful of break times for this reason, and could be seen hovering on the stairs, too afraid to go down to the patio. The pent-up energy and frustration resultant from thwarted physical self-actualisation also made it difficult for many students to engage in class-room learning. Following the traditional nineteenth century model of schooling, students were expected to remain in the classroom, seated and quiet, at all times other than break. Many students, especially those in year five, struggled to comply with this expectation which resulted in a difficulty engaging with the content of lessons, and also in tensions between students and the teachers who were expected to keep students calm, quiet, and in the classroom. Children would often become very agitated during lessons, and classes regularly broke into mayhem with students running around, crawling on the floor, throwing chalk and balls of paper, knocking over desks, and running out into the corridors shouting. Unable to manage the situation, teachers would often let the children go early, cutting lessons short. This level of agitation and disruption to lessons often prevented students from learning:

> Everyone is messing around in Teacher AR's math's classes and you can't learn the lesson. (Student comment 28 June 2011)

> Can there really be a class so out of control as this? Because every time I pass by, whoever is teaching them, I see the whole class on their feet, causing a riot. I've only not seen that in your class [to teacher 2]. Even in MRL's class, everyone's class. When I pass by they're not doing anything. They're on their feet, making a mockery, running around, and another thing, they're not full classes! They're not full classes! Today there were what, 24 students here in my classroom. Imagine. I've already taught classes of 42 5th year students in other schools. We teach, you know, they're not full classes. And thank god! Because if they were full we really wouldn't be able to stand this school anymore. But they're not. We can't complain about overcrowding. And we can't manage, and this isn't just today, it's been like this since 2006 when I came here. It's really typical, typical of this school, this clientele, these kids that only un-learn the whole time, there are some that have only regressed since the start of the year. (Teacher comment 23 May 2011)

These examples can be seen as manifestations of the outcome scenario/pathway of response M2→P→Q→R (and for some students, →S), as illustrated in the theoretical model presented in Chap. 4.

Because many of the Baixada residents are excluded from the formal labour market, the area attracts those who make their living by elicit means, including the drug trade, street muggings, and organised crime. One side-effect of this is that children are often witnesses to acts of violence either between those involved in these activities, or on the part of the police entering the neighbourhood to pursue them. Such incidents are not uncommon. For example, in 2015 a young man was pursued into a tenement building on the same street as DCX School and fatally shot by police officers in front of his pregnant partner, mother, and daughter (Globo 2015). DCX students are often direct witnesses to these incidents, or know somebody involved, or hear the stories.

> Walking home with a teacher, we saw a fight in the street. She said it reminded her of when the police tried to kill a young man in front of the school gates last year, right when the children were arriving for class, and she had asked them to take him somewhere else. A girl student had told her later that the police had taken him somewhere else and killed him. (Conversation with teacher 27 April 2011)

Many children are also exposed to domestic violence in the tenements, and some witness violence and aggression being espoused or modelled by their parents:

> There were some mothers complaining in the parents' meeting, really angry because their children had been beaten up at school. One mother wanted to beat up the boy who had hit her son, and the teacher had to try to calm her down, telling her that she couldn't do this because she will get in trouble for having hit someone else's child. (Observation notes 11 May 2011)

Another source of exposure to violence is through music, particularly some in the '*baile funk*' genre which is very popular in neighbourhoods with an organised crime presence in the community:

> I suggested that we could do some work around the rap group 'Racionais MCs' with the project students. The teacher agreed, and said that it's better than most of the baile funk music that the students suggested to her, which were 'totally full' of derogatory sexual lyrics. She said even the little kids are listening to it, it's just sexual derogation and lyrics which talk about crime in a way that makes her feel sick. 'They sing about crime as if it were a thing of honour, you know? They only sing about this and branded clothing'. (Conversation with teacher 18 May 2011)

If we consider the concept of phenomenological freedom then we cannot argue that students exposed to violence will automatically behave violently. However, it is possible that the emotional impact of witnessing, hearing about, and being subject to violence and aggression may have been a contributing factor in the students' agitated and aggressive behaviour, due to the impact of primary, secondary, and/or vicarious traumatisation (Rothschild 2006) (A→B→D→E→G→I), and/or the impact of learnt violent epistemology, where students prescribe to the belief that violence is an acceptable way of dealing with situations, when this is modelled by those around them (M1→G→I). Some aspects of student behaviour could be exemplary of learnt violent epistemology from such exposure:

> Do you know what they did today? Him and the other one, they made a gun … out of plastic bags … it was so well made … and they were in break time, terrorizing the other kids! It was them that had a big wooden weapon on Friday that I took from their hands. The same kids. They had a HUGE long piece of wood in their hands. (Teacher comment 9 May 2011)

Learnt violent epistemology could also be seen in the behaviour of students who prescribed to, or complied with, violent epistemic aspects of social discourse such as racism, homophobia, and concepts of beauty based on the stereotyped (often white) idealised body images presented in the Brazilian media (M1→G→I):

> Teacher 1: But why do think the students do this with [Teacher AR]?
> G5: I know teacher, because the student are preju … preju…
> Other student: Prejudiced.
> G5: Yeah. Because he's Japanese and they like to harass him, today they wrote on the board 'Little Jap'.
> PL: AR, little Jap, DJ AR little Jap faggot.
> Students giggle.
> Teacher 1: They wrote that on the board?
> G5: I know because they've written even worse things. (Conversation between teachers and students 28 June 2011)

> JSC [a boy of Angolan heritage] tried to log on to Think Quest.[1] 'Teacher, I can't get into my Think Quest!' he complained.
> 'Because you typed something wrong' said the teacher.
> 'Do you know what he wrote?' Said AP, 'He wrote JSC black cock'. AP started laughing. (Observation notes 17 June 2011)

> A new girl in class 5B was beaten up by other girls on her first day, because she was 'prettier than them'. (Observation notes 11 April 2011)

---

[1] Think Quest is a piece of software that the DRE has made compulsory for all schools to use in information technology (IT) lessons.

Other issues that stem from the social and economic exclusion of the Baixada neighbourhood are economic and sexual exploitation, and this could be seen in the behaviour of some of the students ($A{\rightarrow}B{\rightarrow}D{\rightarrow}E{\rightarrow}G{\rightarrow}I{\rightarrow}K$):

> One day V [age 13] climbed up on top of the school wall and started calling to the men in the bar next door 'trying to sell herself to them' said the first teacher. (Field notes 16 April 2011)

> AP and P stained EV's t-shirt. EV asked them for R$100 [Approx. £37.00] to keep quiet about it. 'They are influenced by something out there [in the neighbourhood]' said the teacher. (Teacher's meeting 15 June 11)

Another issue faced by some students is parental neglect or inability to provide adequate care and supervision for their children ($M2{\rightarrow}P{\rightarrow}Q{\rightarrow}R/S$):

> One teacher said that she asked a student if he was still living with his uncle, and he replied 'no, I live with my dad but my dad doesn't sleep at home' 'in other words he's alone at home, his dad doesn't look after him' she concluded. (Field diary 19 May 2011)

> They discussed a girl in the 2nd year who is twelve years old. Last year not one teacher could stand to have her in their class for more than a day. Her mother had left the family and the children stayed with the father, but he drank and neglected the children, and they didn't go to school. The girl and her mother ended up living on the streets. 'She has a great rancour, and even her mother is afraid of her because she already pulled a knife on her mother. It was her who swore at and kicked a teacher yesterday', the school director said. (Observation notes 12 April 2011)

Parents struggled to meet the needs of their children for a variety of reasons caused by social and economic exclusion, including family breakdown and death, incarceration, having to work long or antisocial hours, and attending night school:

> K, J, and the others that I can't remember their names in 5C. I think it's like this: Those who are in a degree of marginality,[2] are J ... K I don't know, if he smells I don't smell him, and R. R from 5C. His mum died. It was him whose mum died last year. R was RG's brother, from those four boys. I don't know how R's life has been, but it's R that is leading ALL the disruptions in 5A. (Teacher 9 May 2011)

---

[2] In this context, 'marginality' is used to mean involved in criminal activities.

Student's problems are not with the teachers, but come from outside [the school]. 'You threaten the boy but what does he have? Both parents in prison... (Pedagogical Coordinator 19 May 2011)

We returned to the classroom and the students were given invitations for a meeting with their parents, next Tuesday. PL said that his dad couldn't come, because he's doing night school, and that his mum works at night too. (Classroom observations 22 March 2011)

Absent fathers was a particular issue for many children. Mothers tended to be the primary or only caregivers. The students whose parents were most 'absent' tended to behave most disruptively in the classroom, were more aggressive, and struggled the most to engage in learning $(M2{\rightarrow}P{\rightarrow}Q{\rightarrow}R/S)$. Parental absence also meant that many students had to take on extra responsibilities at home and struggled to maintain a regular sleep pattern, often causing them to miss school activities and to struggle to engage at school due to exhaustion $(M2)$:

Another teacher said that there are students who she can tell that their parents clearly leave them on their own, because she hears the students saying 'ah, I wake up in the morning and lie there thinking about whether to get up or not'. (Field diary 19 May 2011)

[The teacher said] the girls won't arrive to help in the mornings because they go to sleep at 4 am and sleep for the whole morning—they don't even come to school. M said that one girl had told her she feels anaesthetised the whole time, and the teachers said that this is a serious problem but what could they do, right? They talked about how most of the students arrive late. (Observation notes 01 April 2011)

'I'm tired, I woke up at 5am today', said T.
    'Really?' I answered, 'why did you have to wake up so early'?
    'Tidy up the house before coming to school' she replied. (Conversation with student 26 May 2011)

N said that it's difficult for her to come to the project because she has to clean the house, and look after her little sister until her mum gets home. She's tired and sleepy. She wasn't going to come today, but just managed to at the last minute. (Conversation with a student 12 April 2011)

Another impact of high levels of parental absence was that parents struggled to engage with their children's school life. The awareness of parental struggles to meet their children's physical and emotional needs, as well as a perceived lack of 'education',[3] often resulted in teachers trying to take on a parenting role with students:

> J was telling the school director how a mother had complained because J had shouted at her children, in an attempt to break up a fight between them and another child. J said that she had asked the mother 'How many sons and daughters do you have at home?' The mother had replied that she had four. 'My god in heaven!' the school director exclaimed, then said 'well, here we have more than a thousand sons and daughters'. Then she went on to say that many of the children don't have care, warmth and 'education' at home, and that 'it's us [the school] who have to do this work'. (Conversation with teachers and school director 12 April 2011)

Due to the socio-spatial segregation of the Baixada, poverty, and parental absence, students lacked access to the wide range of 'cultural' products available in São Paulo, from radio and television to cinema, arts, theatre, and music. What access they did have was often limited to a few television programmes and a limited range of music. As a result, students struggled to engage with curriculum content due to the unfamiliarity of cultural references (M2):

> The teacher said the students don't have the habit of listening to the radio, at least not content-based radio. There is the same problem with the audio visual group. They like to use the recording and editing software but they lack repertoire. She said she asked the group to come up with ideas for a programme but nothing came out because they lack the repertoire. (Conversation with teachers 18 April 2011)

Due to the only very recent near-universalisation of public basic education, unequal access to quality education, and generational poverty which has impacted on parental engagement with schooling, many of the children's parents were illiterate or semi-literate. Coming from homes where reading and writing were not common practices, parental absence and low levels of parental literacy also meant that most students did not receive support with literacy or school work at home. As a result, many struggled to keep up with classroom activities, and this experience could be seen in expressions of low confidence and self-esteem in relation to learning,

---

[3] In Brazilian Portuguese, the use of the term 'educating' in this context refers to the instilling of manners, social skills, and discipline rather than to any other form of education.

especially (but not exclusively) in relation to reading and writing (M2→P→Q→R/S):

> Teacher 1: I get tired. They don't understand ANYTHING. You tell them to copy, understand? COPY, COPY, COPY ... a username and a password. They don't copy it right, they don't understand what is happening, you know?
>
> Teacher 2: On Friday I taught three lessons in a row for the 5th years because I was the only teacher there at the beginning, and I told the students to write a text during the three lessons. ONE text. LTC wrote two lines, during three lessons. [...] At the end I looked at their work and gave it back to them, and signed it. Obviously I didn't sign LTC's. As soon as she walked out the door she threw hers on the floor. I'll talk to her parents tomorrow.
>
> Teacher 1: Yeah. We really have to keep on their backs. (Conversation between teachers 23 May 2011)

> Today JF was incredibly agitated and messing around a lot—pretending to hit people, hitting G5, speaking to himself very loudly, messing about with equipment in the room, grabbing the microphone at random and making noises into it, kicking things, etc. As soon as my back was turned I heard a crash behind me. JF had pulled G5's chair from underneath him and G5 was lying on the floor. IN suggested that JF talk on the microphone. I agreed and we all tried to encourage him. He lifted his shirt over his head and hid under it, saying 'no, I don't want to, I'm really bad'. We encouraged him to try. He sat in front of the microphone and IN gave him the script. He held it in his hands and did nothing. IN said 'don't you want to read through it first?' He held his head down and whispered 'I don't know how to read'. IN said 'don't you know how to read?' and he said, counting off on his fingers 'I'm good aren't I? I don't know how to draw, I don't know how to count, I don't know how to read...'. (Observation notes 2 June 2011)

Students also demonstrated signs of lacking confidence when it came to reading out loud and verbalising their knowledge:

> MY arrived, and the teacher greeted her ... 'Hi MY! How good to see you! Pull up a chair!' MY came in and sat a little away from the group. The teacher called her to come closer and she resisted a bit, then came. [...] The teacher said we were going to continue our learning about the beginnings of cinema. She asked MY to tell FLP what she had learnt in the research that she'd done last week. MY said nothing. 'Go, tell us!' Said the teacher. But MY remained silent. The teacher encouraged her a number of times but she

said nothing. The teacher picked up the notes that MY had made last week and gave them to her, saying 'You can consult your notes if you like'. MY looked at the notes but still said nothing. [After some talk from the teacher about silent movies] MY said that film began with photographs and tried to explain the process of joining still images to create movement. She mumbled and didn't finish her sentence, looking at her hands while she spoke. (Observation notes 1 April 2011)

Other signs of low self-esteem that I witnessed included difficulty dealing with setbacks or challenges in the learning process (expressed as a tendency to become upset easily and/or to give up when faced with a problem or challenge), difficulty accepting praise, criticising or putting others down, and low expectations of self (A→B→D→E→G→I→K):

At one point JSU took the mouse to add effects to the animation. It went wrong and he got the slides in a mess. He got embarrassed and angry, and said 'this junk is no good for anything'. He sat down heavily in his chair and didn't try to use the computer again. 'Delete everything and start everything again!' he said to the other group members. He stayed in a bit of a bad mood for the rest of the session. (Observation notes 8 April 2011)

When B said what she thought about the video, BR (who was sitting away from the group at the back) laughed, and B (looking upset) said 'hey BR, why are you laughing? (Observation notes 27 May 2011)

On the first day of the project, student G introduced himself. 'My name is G and I'm lazy'. (Field notes 16 June 2011)

As these excerpts illustrate, lack of confidence and low self-esteem (caused by lack of parental support and difficulties engaging with schooling), contributed to a cycle of subject de-formation. In this cycle, students' self-schema of being 'bad' or 'lazy' thwarted further self-actualisation, resulting in agitation, aggression, and further disengagement from learning opportunities.

While the teachers tried to encourage the children towards a future in further and higher education, students demonstrated an awareness of their 'underclass' status. This was reflected in their knowledge of the fact that they were receiving a so-called second class education (representative of the longstanding division between 'quality' private education and 'basic' public education), and living in a neighbourhood neglected by the government. During discussions on these topics, they demonstrated an awareness of the impact of these factors on their life chances, perceived value, and voice in society.

Teacher 3: I'm going to bring to you all a piece of information that another teacher told me. You know that when you finish basic education, you'll go to college, to high school?

Students: Hmmm.

Teacher 3: I think this is an important piece of information to bring you. When they go to high school, most of the students from DCX, are dropping out. Why? Because they're not learning enough because of all the messing around [in class]. They get there and they can't keep up with high school. So this is very serious, because not finishing high school means not getting to university. (Conversation between teacher and students 16 June 2011)

Teacher: So, more or less half way down Avenida Angelica, there crossing Rua Sergipe, a new metro line was going to open, the orange line. And this is the Angelica line. And what happened? What happened? The RESIDENTS of that NEIGHBOURHOOD, which is called Higienopolis ... does anyone know what HI-GI-en-OPolis means?

RF: Hygiene?

Teacher: [Loudly] It's city of HYGIENE. From the Greek right? From the Greek city of hygiene. And the residents, what did they do, do you think? They made a PETITION, AGAINST the metro line in their neighbourhood.

G5: Why?

Teacher: Why? Ah, now that's the question. Why could it be, that they didn't want it? Could it be that the neighbourhood of Higienopolis—what do you all think? Is it a neighbourhood like the Baixada? What is the neighbourhood of Higienopolis like? Does anyone here know it?

RF: Rich.

Teacher: What?

RF: Rich.

Teacher: Did you all hear what he said?

Voices: Uhmmm ... a rich neighbourhood.

Teacher: A Neigbourhood of rich people. And, why could it be that they didn't want ... what was it that they didn't want there then?

Low voices: Opposed to poor people.

Teacher: Opposed to...?

Voices louder, in unison: Poor people.

Teacher: Poor people. But they didn't use this word, they gave the name [indignant tone] 'different people'. [...Reading own writing from screen] 'The Brazilian bourgeoisie wants to enjoy...'—what do I mean by enjoy?

JS: Make use of.

Teacher: Make use of. Very good. Use. '...the work of the 'different people'. What makes them different?

G5: The poor.

Teacher: The workers, right? Maids, doormen.

JS: Security guards.

Teacher: Security guards, rubbish collectors ... who else?

G5: All the people who...

JS: Shopkeepers.

Teacher: Shopkeepers, exactly. All the people who?

G5: Don't earn much.

JS: Police, teachers...

G5: My mum [...] Teacher?

Teacher: Yes?

G5: What are people, other than being 'different people'?

Teacher: AhhhhAHAHAHA ... like, the people there with their tiny dogs, right? To live there and not here is to not be 'different people'

IG: And what if people from other neighbourhoods signed petitions, without being rich people?

Teacher: That's what P said, and what JS always brings up, I mean, there was that Girl in Boi Mirim, right? In the extreme Eastern Zone, there are lots of problems with transport there, and in the extreme South Zone, right? There in my own periphery there are transport problems.

G5: Are there not problems with transport here in the centre?

Teacher: Well, here, principally in our region here—remember when we talked last year JS, about how not many lines, not many options of buses pass here in the area of the Baixada?

LC: You have to walk really far to be able to catch a bus.

Teacher: Right. And are these people heard, guys?

P: Not a bit!

LC: No.

Teacher: Do you know what would be great? We could...

G5: Pay three thousand in cash and get heard straight away.

Teacher: What lesson can we learn from this?

JS: That it's like, I can have an idea, I can have a project, I can have everything organised, but five guys with money come along, throw everything in the trash.

Teacher: That's right, it's true.

G5: And those who have money...

Teacher: Does everyone here think they are 'different people' or not? What do you think?

G5: I think so.

JS: I am.

Teacher: Are we 'different people'?

Voices: Yes, yes.

[...]

LC: What is 'different people', is it some type of race that was given to us? (Dialogue between teacher and students 18 May 2011)

The impact of this awareness, developed through living in a situation of social and economic exclusion, was visible in some students' expressions of frustration or resignation (M2→P→Q→R/S).

As illustrated above, the non-conducive circumstances of the Baixada neighbourhood and the family and home lives of students impacted on students' ability to self-actualise; on their behaviour at school and engagement with schooling; and on their subject development. The connections between these factors are complex. However, I have indicated some of the different ways in which these situations, circumstances, and student behaviours can be seen as manifestations of the outcome scenarios and pathways of response proposed in the theoretical model presented in Chaps. 3 and 4, in which violent epistemology can be seen to play a pivotal role.

7.3   How Non-conducive Employment Conditions Affect Teacher Subject Development and Engagement with Their Roles at School

While the majority of teachers did not live in the Baixada, the experience of entering and spending time in the neighbourhood impacted on teacher subjectivity. Bearing witness to such extreme social neglect affected teachers deeply:

> Teacher 3: I saw a video on YouTube, showing the neighbourhood, [...] I took the part coming down the hill. Which is something that many people, teachers, [...] we come down the hill, and the impact it has on us, [...] you know? [...] It's a thing that is kind of personal to us, nobody will understand this descent very well. The suffering and such, it has a very important relevance for us. [...] I think that everyone remembers the first time they arrived in the Baixada [...].
> Teacher 1: Yeah. Going down the hill, I always think, God and the Devil in the Land of the Sun,[4] right? This descent down the street, that I say is Justice, God, and the Devil,[5] understand? They live side by side. (Conversation between teachers 23 May 2011)

---

[4] This is a cultural reference to the film '*Deus e o Diabo na Terra do Sol*' by Brazilian film maker Glauber Rocha, which critiqued the social problems of 1960s' Brazil just prior to the commencement of the military dictatorship.

[5] Here the teacher is referring to the street leading down into the neighbourhood that begins with the law courts surrounded by high walls and barbed wire fencing, is flanked

There was a clip that she had filmed, which showed the front of the school building and, looking up, the tower blocks surrounding it. She said that with this image she wanted to show the feeling that she has of the school being swallowed by its surroundings. I said 'as if it was in the middle of a hole?' Yes! She replied. (Conversation with teacher 19 May 2011)

Witnessing visible suffering in the Baixada, teachers are regularly exposed to experiences that can cause secondary and vicarious traumatisation (Rothschild 2006). Another risk factor for secondary and vicarious traumatisation was the experience of losing students to preventable accidents such as tenement fires and violent crime. Most teachers at DCX School had experienced the death of at least one (often more) of their students in such ways. As a result, teachers expressed a keen awareness of the precarity of the children's lives. As discussed in Chap. 3, the emotional overwhelm associated with this can be a motivation for the response pathway $A \rightarrow B \rightarrow D \rightarrow E \rightarrow G \rightarrow I$.

Another factor which affected teachers was the threat to their own lives, particularly in relation to the organised crime gangs in the local area:

The [cartel leaders] went there … in the school. There were some kids provoking, and the big bosses came, they beat the boys up IN FRONT OF THE SCHOOL DIRECTOR, in the director's office, the director sitting there. They beat them up, hit the boys in there, and said to the director that, firstly, they didn't want the police there […]. And secondly, if the boys played up again it was THEM that the director had to call. Not the police […]. Can you imagine? […] If something happens here … people I don't even want to come [to work]… (Teacher 9 May 2011)

This constant feeling of insecurity was often mentioned by teachers, and as described in Chap. 3 can be one of the primary motivating emotions when it comes to enacting violent epistemology. DCX School was marked by high rates of attrition and teacher absence due to mental health difficulties, as well as emotional instability and aggression on the part of teachers. This could be particularly attributed to traumatic stress resulting from working in an unsafe environment and ongoing repeated exposure to the suffering of others.

---

further down by a church and shops selling religious memorabilia, and ends in the school, surrounded by degraded buildings and visible human suffering.

Chronic underinvestment in education has meant that teachers are underpaid and overworked. At the time of research, the salary for a medium level teacher in the São Paulo municipal education network with a workload of 40 hours per week was R$1187.08 per month (approx. US$585.66) (Prefeitura de São Paulo 2016b). In the same year, the minimum salary needed to meet an individual's basic needs in São Paulo was calculated at R$2329.35 (approx. US$1147.73) (DIEESE 2012). Because of this, many teachers had to work more than one job in order to survive. The Prefecture's rules state that teachers can accumulate teaching workloads up to 70 hours per week and many did so, working up to three shifts a day across different schools (Jacomini and Minhoto 2012). Low pay and overworking impacted teachers in a number of ways, including an inability to meet basic needs, disaffection, and feeling undervalued professionally $(M2 \rightarrow P \rightarrow Q \rightarrow R/S)$:

A teacher came in and said that she and other teachers had been watching the video testimony of Amanda Gurgel, a teacher from Rio Grande do Norte. The video had 151, 404 views in five days. Gurgel spoke about the challenges of being a teacher in the Brazilian public school system, about the low salary and poor working conditions. Three DCX teachers were discussing how they related to her talk:

Teacher 1: She said that in 15 or 20 years' time there won't be any more teachers, nobody will want to become a teacher and all the teachers will become ill.
   Teacher 2: There really won't be [any more teachers].

They started discussing the increase in teaching days due to come, and the government's proposal to abolish summer holidays:

Teacher 2: It's the only rest we get, the only thing that makes us survive. If they take away the holidays what do we have? We won't be able to stand it. [To teacher 3] Are you going to get a different job?
   Teacher 3: I'm going to prostitute myself! [Laughter].
   Teacher 2: I will! I already live next door to the red light district, I won't even need to commute! (Observation notes 19 May 2011)

The teacher said that unfortunately teachers are often seen as bad people, because recently teachers in the public school system have had a terrible reputation. But this doesn't take into account the great devaluing of teachers, because the teacher, like we saw yesterday in the conversation about salaries which are very low, is not paid for what they do. They spend a lot of time studying, gaining qualifications and doing teacher training. But sometimes the teacher training courses are really poor quality, so the teachers are not equipped nor paid, and most of them completed their basic [primary and secondary] education in the public school system too [which has a reputation for poor quality]. (Conversation with teacher 29 March 2011)

Aside from frustration at being underpaid for the work they already do, teachers were also concerned about the impending implementation of the government's plans to increase the required daily school attendance for each child from four hours to a full day (A→B→D):

She said that Brazil has a chronic problem, which the government is trying to resolve with the '*Programa Mais Educação*' ['More Education' programme] and the creation of full school days, because they don't know what to do with all the children who are in the street, at the traffic lights,[6] etc., and they want to 'intern' them in schools to get them off the streets. This creates a big problem because the teacher is expected to do the work of parents, but is not paid for this, and she is not even sure whether it is the teacher's role to do this. (Conversation with teacher 29 March 2011)

Having to work such long hours meant that teachers struggled to carry out tasks of daily living outside of work, had very little family time, and suffered from severe exhaustion. Having to rush from one school to another meant that teachers lacked time to communicate with one another about essential work-related matters and fatigue impacted on the quality of teaching (M2→P):

And then she said 'since I teach in two schools' and she said 'it's a lie, whoever says that you can teach two shifts of quality lessons'. Is that not true? You can start the day teaching a lesson, you know, lalala, because you just woke up … the day goes on, you don't have the same motivation anymore. (Teacher 23 May 2011)

Rushing from another school often meant that teachers arrived late at DCX, causing disruption to students and other teachers:

One teacher said that there needed to be more cooperation between teachers. She said that on the 3rd floor the teachers cooperate, and they don't have problems with students loose in the corridors, messing around, because

---

[6] In Brazil, it is common for children from poor families to spend the time they are not in school selling items at traffic lights on busy intersections of highway.

if a teacher arrives late because they're coming from another school, she leaves her classroom and goes into the other class, tells the students that the teacher is on their way, and puts an activity for them to do up on the blackboard. She said that she talks to students who aren't her students, makes friends with them and if they are loose in the corridors chats with them and keeps an eye on them. She said 'you have to be friends with the student, even if they're not your student. If you don't have this partnership they kick our doors, swear at us, etc.' Another teacher said that this is difficult to do, and there needs to be some way to deal with the absence of teachers, because to leave your classroom to go and look after another teacher's class is complicated. Perhaps a staff member should stay with the class downstairs until the teacher arrives. The School Director said there weren't enough staff for this, and that if the class didn't go upstairs the rest of the students would refuse to go too. She said the only solution was for teachers to arrive on time. (Pedagogical meeting 19 May 2011)

Another issue for teachers is the complexity and in some cases precarity of how their work is contracted. Municipal law stipulates a complex system of different types and combinations of employment contracts for teachers which include different combinations of 'in-class' hours and 'supplementary activity' hours, and different criteria for pay and career progression. While some teachers are contracted for a set number of hours and time-tabled to specific classes, others who are at school carrying out 'complementary activities' to an allocated workload (called 'CJ's, short for completação de jornada [completion of contractual hours]) are not time-tabled to specific classes but required to substitute the absences of other teachers, often with no notice or knowledge of what the students have been working on (Americano 2011). The combination of the complexity of this system, disaffection, and CJ contracting contributes to confusion, instability, difficulty planning activities, low motivation, and high levels of absenteeism which have a cyclical knock-on effect (M2→P):

> The teachers who teach the 5th years in the afternoon don't have contracted hours, so it's really easy for them to be absent. Sometimes in the afternoons there is only one teacher to teach [four simultaneous classes]. (Teacher comment 15 June 2011)

Having to work such long hours in order to survive, in such challenging circumstances, often left teachers without the time or energy to pursue personal and professional development activities (M2→P):

Teacher 1: You don't manage to read what you would like to, it's no good. And she said 'teachers don't manage to study'. The teacher works and spends time studying? What time? When? Right?

Teacher 2: Between midnight and 6am.

Teacher 1: Right. I, I at least get exhausted, if I teach … last year when I taught morning, afternoon and night two days a week… I was EXHAUSTED during the last shift. There's nothing else you can do. You get on the bus home and you want to SLEEP. Understand? You don't want to read, you don't even want to concentrate! (Conversation between teachers 23 May 2011)

This, coupled with often poor quality, technicistic pre-service training (characterised by the separation of theory and philosophy of education from practice based on the 'simple' transmission of 'facts, skills and competencies'), left teachers unprepared to provide a quality education which students could engage with. Teachers also lacked training in dealing with students' challenging behaviour, and in looking after their own wellbeing when exposed to the demands, stresses, and 'trauma inputs' (Rothschild 2006) of the Baixada and the DCX School. As a result, many teachers experienced high levels of anxiety in relation to their roles (A→B→D→E). To provide an illustrative example, in the teachers' meeting of 15 June 2011, not one of the five scheduled agenda items were discussed, because the meeting time was used by the teachers to vent about the difficulties they were having in managing students' behaviour. Lack of training in managing difficult behaviour put the teachers in a vulnerable position and also increased the risk of them responding to such behaviour with aggression (A→B→D→E→G→I):

Another teacher said that she wouldn't know how to respond if a student attacked her. Once a student tried to attack her a few years ago. The student threatened her and she just said 'come on, come on, you can attack me and you'll end up in hospital and I'll end up in prison'. (Conversation with teachers 11 April 2011)

Despite the difficult circumstances of the Baixada and DCX School, teachers were not provided with emotional or psychological support, or any kind of professional or clinical supervision. As a result, teachers often showed signs of emotional overwhelm, compassion, fatigue, and secondary or vicarious traumatisation. In a state of exhaustion and saturation, teachers struggled to control these emotions which would often spill out in interactions with students (A→B→D→E→G→I). While there were some opportunities for teachers on a certain type of contract to collectively reflect on practice, these sessions were reserved only for these teachers and were often dominated by the pedagogical coordinator who subscribed to a particularly strong 'banking' style pedagogy. As a result, formal opportunities for genuine reflection on practice were not available, and this was visible in the broad disparities between different teachers' pedagogical styles and approaches to curriculum, as well as in inconsistencies in individual teachers' own practice (M2).

The physical and emotional impact of working at DCX took its toll on teachers, resulting in both short and extended sickness absences. This increased pressure on other teachers, who felt unable to manage the workload or keep the students safe with low staffing levels ($A \rightarrow B \rightarrow D \rightarrow E$):

> This third year boy that was being beaten up today, I don't know who it was attacking him, he didn't want to say but he got really scared, his heart was nearly coming out of his mouth when I went there to defend him. Oh, that one … from 5C whose name I can't remember right now, punched him too. The fight wasn't even with him, but he went there too, to pick on him. You know? If we leave them alone they LYNCH each other! If we leave them they lynch each other! And there is nobody in break time, nobody is watching. Nobody … you know? The day I die people, touch wood, but the day that the worst disgrace happens here in the school that gets in the news, who knows, people will demand that the school be closed. They'll say 'There aren't the conditions to work here in the Baixada. Close DCX'. I know that I'm indignant people, it's impossible … it's impossible… [Voice fades away to a tired, defeated tone] soon I'm going to ask for medical leave… (Teacher comments 9 May 2011)

As illustrated in this quote, high rates of medical leave increased pressure on remaining staff. As so many lessons were cancelled due to teacher absence, students struggled to get into a routine and would act out more. Aside from the extra workload, remaining teachers struggled to manage student behaviour and in turn felt the need to take medical leave themselves. In effort to maintain staffing levels, the School Director actively discouraged staff from taking sick leave:

> The school director said 'we're all in the same ship, we all run the risk of getting ill, so don't take time off'. (Pedagogical meeting 19 May 2011)

This culture in which self-care was not fostered or promoted, coupled with the lack of appropriate training, further impacted on staff who, unable to cope sustainably would reach breaking point and be forced to take medical leave whether the director approved or not ($M2{\to}P{\to}Q{\to}R/S$):

> The teachers said that many teachers don't know how to deal with seeing violence every day, with being attacked and threatened and such. One teacher spoke about another teacher who had tried to intervene with a girl who had brought a knife to school to kill another girl. He had seen the other teacher arrive at school, open the cupboard, then drop to his knees and sit there, staring into the cupboard. Then he closed the cupboard and left without coming back. Now he is on medical leave. (Field notes 11 April 2011)

Another factor that impacted on staff wellbeing was sensory overload from the school environment. The large, concrete quad-style building acted as a sound amplifier. The smallest noises echoed and bounced off the shiny concrete floors, walls, and metal doors. Sound from all floors flowed up the central staircase filling the rest of the building, and heavy traffic noise from the street filtered in through the thin single glazing. All of the audio recorded during data collection contained very high levels of background noise—banging, shouting, buzzers, chair legs screeching on concrete floors, sirens, and booming, rumbling traffic. Shouting was a particularly common background noise and stress factor for teachers ($A{\to}B{\to}D{\to}E{\to}G{\to}I$):

> There is a noise outside of a mother and son shouting ferociously at each other in the corridor, a heated argument. The teachers go quiet ... then teacher 3 says 'it's really distressing'. (Field diary 13 June 2011)

> We heard shouts coming from the corridor. One of the teachers flinched. 'Are they calling me?' Then she relaxed a little, laughing... 'I thought they were calling me, because they haven't called me yet!' The shouts continued, it was a teacher shouting in despair at her students. The teacher who had flinched said to the other teacher 'you go out there, you have more strength than me'. (Field notes 25 May 2011)

The above quote also illustrates how teachers were often on 'high alert', ready to spring into action at any time due to the necessities of a high risk, chaotic environment ($A{\to}B{\to}D$). Research has shown that the stress levels associated with being in this state for long periods can be detrimental to health (Rothschild 2006).

The result of the above factors (being overworked, low staffing, challenging student behaviour, sensory overload, unpredictable working environment, high levels of trauma inputs, lack of appropriate training and supervision, and being discouraged from practising self-care), was that teachers demonstrated many symptoms of stress, compassion fatigue, secondary and vicarious traumatisation, and burnout. These symptoms included physical exhaustion, headaches, insomnia, increased susceptibility to illness, somatisation, absenteeism, anger and irritability, exaggerated sense of responsibility, compromised care for students, attrition, emotional exhaustion, depression, reduced ability to empathise, cynicism and embitterment, resentment, dread of working with certain students, feelings of professional helplessness, diminished sense of career enjoyment, disruption of worldview, increased sense of personal vulnerability, inability to tolerate strong feelings, hypervigilance, hypersensitivity, or insensitivity to emotional material, loss of hope, difficulty separating professional and personal lives, and failure to nurture non-work-related aspects of life[7] (Mathieu 2011, pp. 49–62). One particular symptom was emotional instability and overreactions to student behaviour (124) (M2→P→Q→R):

> Teacher 1: I agree with LTC that each teacher has their limit. Am I not fierce sometimes?
> Girls: You are.
> Teacher 1: I have my limits too. Always for my reasons, in truth. Teacher 2 has too, for his reasons. I think that within their own reasons, teachers do end up becoming saturated. Right? Are there not days when … how was it on Monday in 5D, G[8]?
> G: My god, it was terrible.
> Teacher 1: It was terrible, it was.
> G: It was horrible.
> Teacher 1: It was horrible. And the other day in 5C, when I ended up saying a whole load of crazy things. (Conversation between teacher and students 16 June 2011)

As a result of all of the above, the overall atmosphere among the teachers was one of anger, despondency, powerlessness, and resignation. There was a feeling that burnout and illness was an inevitable consequence of working at DCX, and that they were stuck in an endless self-perpetuating cycle from which there was no way out (M2→P→Q→R/S):

---

[7] All of the above are clinically recognised symptoms of prolonged exposure to stress and 'trauma inputs' (Mathieu 2011).

[8] G is a student.

Are we unbalanced? Are we? I arrived at this school balanced and healthy, and now I'm ill, they're ill, and you're going to get ill. (Teacher comment 15 June 2011)

M [a CJ teacher] had a problem. She was covering all the Portuguese, Science and English night classes because all three teachers are on medical leave. And today Z [another teacher] hadn't arrived yet. She was stressed because she couldn't cover all the teachers who were absent today. She went to teach a class. When the first night class finished we saw her in the corridor. Z had arrived and they were debating rapidly who would take which class. As I passed, Z looked at me with anger in his eyes and said 'this school is going to hell, Beth'. (Field notes 23 May 2011)

Somebody enters to tell teacher 3 that EDL (a teacher) is in hospital and Z (another teacher) is late because he comes running from another school. So teacher 3 has to go cover EDL's class:

Teacher 3: So, let's finish up here quickly ... and the blog ... and I, I'll lead the blog [trying to make plans for the following day, gets flustered].
　　Teacher 1: Calm down, calm down, calm down, who, who is EDL?
　　Teacher 3: EDL ... she's hospitalised and is going to stay hospitalised...
　　Teacher 1: And there's no activity at all right? [for EDL's students]
　　Teacher 3: Nobody ever leaves any activity [for them to do].
　　Teacher 1: Ah, ok.
　　Teacher 3: Never.
　　Teacher 1: This is a problem.
　　Teacher 2: But you know what I do [teacher 3]? When I am going to enter a maths class, for example, I take the textbook that is there, take a theoretical part and give it to them [the students]. One, two exercises and one text. For Geography I do the same thing—I take something from the end of the book and give it to them.

　　Teacher 3 asked teacher 2 to finish a task for her that she now wouldn't have time to do, and got up to leave the room, flustered and unhappy saying 'now I won't be able to do it'.

Teacher 1: Calm down, calm down.
　　Teacher 3: I don't know, they tell us to do the project but we can't do it and the project is going to be left for Beth [to do alone]
　　Teacher 1: Because it's not possible, not possible to do anything.
　　Teacher 3: I don't know, any class that doesn't have a teacher, I take. I can't do it... [Leaves room]
　　Teacher 1: And, there's nobody left [teaching] the night classes now, there's practically only her because, Z must be arriving soon in truth, but PL [another teacher] has moved to teach Geography now, right? I know that

soon nobody ... look people, soon nobody is going to want to be a teacher, for real. (Conversation between teachers 2 May 2011)

Teacher 1: [...] Today our problem is cyclical.
    Teacher 1: Ummmm [in agreement]
    Teacher 3: These days we are in a ... vicious cycle.
    Teacher 1: Ummmmm [in agreement]
    Teacher 3: You know, that we can't break out of. (Conversation between teachers 23 May 2011)

The feeling expressed by teachers of being stuck in a self-perpetuating cycle which they couldn't break out of, was exacerbated by a number of factors. One of these was a difficulty imagining alternatives for society, for the school, and for dealing with the issues that they faced. This is illustrated by the following discussion between teachers as they worked on a video about their perspective of the school:

Teacher 3: Shall I stick with 'See us'? Or should I put a different phrase there? What do you think?
    Teacher 2: I'm going to do a literary interpretation. 'See us' is a cry for help, isn't it? 'Look at me here please, look at me'—'See us'.
    Teacher 3: Yeah, I watched it with a lot of the atmosphere that we have here that, that I think we're in.
    Teacher 1: I like it. I don't think you need to change anything, just build on it. You could put 'What alternative?' This 'I'm still alive' is great.
    Teacher 3: But, for how long?
    Teacher 1: Yeah, for how long? If you put after 'Alternative society', 'What alternative?' Understand? So, I think this idea of 'I'm still alive' was a great observation, understand? Because despite everything that goes on here, we're still alive right! I would put 'This is not a fiction' [...] Ummm [...] But I think, in the worst case scenario, I would put after 'Alternative society' things like 'What?' 'What alternative?' I would play with this thing of 'What alternative?' Right? I would put, like this, 'What alternative?' 'How?' 'When?' Understand? Like, to show, I mean, ok, is there really an alternative for society? 'Alternative society.' Is there an alternative? What alternative?
    Teacher 2: And this alternative isn't ours, right? This alternative is social.
    Teacher 1: Yeah... It's not ours. Because we even have the alternative of getting out of here, let's say. Right? So I mean, others don't have this alternative. Right? Others, by which I mean the children. It's not even us. Right? I think they have even fewer alternatives than us Right? Most of them. (Conversation between teachers 23 May 2011)

This can be seen as an illustration of how the collective affirmation of ideology fosters social circumstances in which the only forms of social organisation and practice that are valued, are those perceived to serve predominant ideologies. At the same time, the possibility of alternatives is negated, resulting in a 'limit situation' in which 'the ordinary person is crushed, diminished, converted to a spectator, manoeuvred by the myths which powerful social forces have created' (Freire 2003, p. 5). As highlighted in Chap. 4, phenomenological freedom means that no ideology can be absolute. However, when teachers did come up with ideas for alternative ways of working, they had significant difficulty putting these into practice due to the restrictions imposed by non-conducive circumstances (M2):

> Teacher 1: But I think it can be really heavy too, this thing of how hard it is, to work, to do things, to make things happen. (Conversation between teachers 23 May 2011)

These difficulties were also connected to a fear of 'doing differently' to the collectively affirmed practices that prevailed, shaped by the ideological schema on which Brazilian schooling is built. This included a fear of losing one's job and a fear of being judged (A→B→D). Teachers' feeling of being undervalued also translated into a lack of motivation to reflect on their own practice (M2→P→Q→R/S). Brazil's long history of state sanctioned repression of dissent, often through the use of police violence, also translated into a lack of political mobilisation when it came to fighting for change (A→B→D):

> I mean, the Spanish went to the streets, to demonstrate their indignation, right? The teachers. And the Greeks, and Egyptians, and Libyans … so. And we hardly ever go to the streets. Right? And when we go, what happened on Saturday happens.[9] (Teacher 23 May 2011)

Lack of resources and difficulty investing time and energy into projects also made it difficult for teachers to respond to challenges effectively, which resulted in despondency and low motivation when it came to implementing ideas for change (M2→P→Q→R/S):

[9] The previous Saturday a planned public march against the criminalisation of cannabis had been prohibited by the government. One thousand citizens marched peacefully in protest of this prohibition and were repressed by the military police with rubber bullets, stun bombs, tear gas, and pepper spray (Abos 2011).

When the teacher suggested introducing a programme to reduce violence, she highlighted that implementation would require the cooperation of the whole school. The only response was from one teacher, who said 'will we need a photocopier? Because if we need to have a photocopier, if we need to have everything photocopied, if the school doesn't have a photocopier then don't even bother thinking about doing anything'. (Pedagogical meeting 19 May 2011)

One teacher said he was disappointed because the others had promised to support his project of making dolls out of bottle tops, but they hadn't done so. He said his hand is all burnt from making holes in bottle tops in his own time at home, the school didn't give him any budget nor support, and people complained about the smell of burning plastic when he used a tool to make the holes, which is the third tool that he has bought with his own money, and now he thinks he will give up on the project. (Teacher meeting 15 June 2011)

Another major factor that impacted on teachers' ability to work effectively and to come up with and implement ideas for change, was an overall lack of mutual support and co-working between staff at all levels within the school (A→B→D→E→G→I & M2→P→Q→R/S):

Beth: Do you think one factor is a lack of coherence amongst the teachers?
    Teacher 1: There's that too … a LOT of that.
    Teacher 2: But not only amongst the teachers—amongst the teachers, amongst the management…
    Teacher 1: We make agreements in meetings, and afterwards those agreements disappear. You understand? I don't know what happens with the agreements that we make in meetings. (Conversation with teachers 9 May 2011)

I asked how the teachers communicate, to resolve the types of problems that were discussed in the meeting. One teacher laughed, 'they don't communicate! This is the biggest problem. Sometimes they call a meeting but people don't come because of their schedules, or they disagree in the meeting, or make agreements but nothing happens'. 'So there isn't a regular meeting unless someone calls one?' I asked. 'There are collective times' said the teacher, but many of us can't attend because of the time' she replied. (Conversation with teacher 9 May 2011)

There's no such thing as team work, no such thing as interdisciplinary work… (Teacher comment 15 June 2011)

There was a discussion about tensions between teachers, who helps who, who doesn't, and disagreements about who works when. Then teacher 3 said: 'It's that I'm feeling like we're really lacking in partnerships ... it's so horrible ... [...] It's serious, we're really isolated [teacher 2], don't you have this feeling? We are really isolated...' (Field diary 27 June 2011)

And another thing, there are people who don't even care ... people who don't even care... I can't see the kids fighting and not go there and separate them. I think that it could be my son being beaten up there ... but the others ... there are people who pass by, 'ah, they're not in my class' and simply go away! I can't see how people can be like this... I can't. They should be living in caves. (Teacher comments 9 May 2011)

On the walk to the Metro, the two teachers said that they thought that the discourse presented by the School Director at the teachers' meeting is very disconnected from reality, up in the clouds, and that the School Director must be counting the days until she retires. One teacher said 'She is on another planet completely'. During the teachers' meeting, while the School Director had been speaking, I had noticed the two teachers' expressions of disbelief numerous times and also noticed them smiling sceptically. (Field notes 15 June 2011)

I think we need to take responsibility for certain things, because things aren't working. I take responsibility too so ... but it's like this: there comes a time when ... why do we even have management? Why do we even have directors? (Teacher 9 May 2011)

This lack of mutual support and co-working was often mirrored by students, and also extended to relations between the school and parents, the school and the Regional Directorate of Education (DRE), and the school and other agencies:

The teacher said that [...] unfortunately, there are parents who think that the teachers are enemies, like today, she had seen a mother at the school, ranting about a teacher. And there are teachers who think everything is the parents' fault. (Conversation with teacher 29 March 2011)

Teacher 1: I am a Think Quest[10] of nerves, it's a Think Quest of nerves, because, it's useless, I don't know what to do.
   Teacher 3: You have to talk to the people at the DRE.
   Teacher 1: No, they won't come here. She said that she won't come here. (Conversation between teachers 13 June 2011)

[10] Think Quest is an online learning platform which the school was required by the DRE to use with the students.

The meeting began with a visit from a government worker, who spoke about the inclusion of people with learning disabilities. She explained that her team (a psychologist, a therapist, a nurse, and six other workers) evaluate and monitor students with possible or diagnosed disabilities. The teachers wanted to know if they should refer students to her that they suspected might have a learning disability, and she said yes. The teachers started talking about a student at DCX who they think has autism, and who isn't receiving any kind of specialist support. The lady said that she knows this student and that he is already being supported by CAPS Infantil.[11] The teachers said that they didn't know this [and] they spoke about the fragmentation between the school and specialist support services. (Staff meeting 19 May 2011)

The impact of all of the factors cited in this section was that teachers found it very difficult to work effectively and as a result lacked a sense of personal efficacy (M2→P→Q→R/S):

[The teachers] commented on the quantity of teachers in public schools who have depression. 'It's a hard job' said the art teacher, 'I think if teachers felt like they were making some difference in people's lives then they wouldn't feel depressed. There are days and moments that make up for the rest, but the rest is truly difficult. Sometimes it seems that we're not getting anywhere at all […]. The new teacher who can't deal with the class must feel like they're not getting anywhere at all. And the teacher who doesn't recognise himself in his work…' 'It's because it's very alienated work' said the IT teacher, 'It's very sad, feeling alienated in your work, someone said we should be happy when we're not at school, otherwise we can't stand it, but I think we should be happy here at school as well because we spend a large part of our lives here, and if we can't manage to be happy here inside … and we have to be happy with the students too, right? Feel like we're making some difference. (Field notes 6 May 2011)

I think it's a tragedy, because the potential that exists that [the students] sometimes have, and […] we don't broaden anything, they continue, you know, going round in circles, […]. It's a tragedy! […] Of course, this is alienated work. We don't have mastery of [the students]. […] So, these things create a certain anguish, right? In us, […] in what happens in the day to day of the school, right? Because [the students] have potential, and we can't manage […]. How many philosophers, how many historians, how many masters, how many judges, how many teachers are there? And we can't manage … to make [the students] flourish. (Teacher comment 2 May 2011)

---

[11] A psychosocial support service for children with severe emotional troubles.

This section has illustrated the multiple and complex ways in which the violent epistemology of collectively affirmed ideology, translated into policy and practice, constitutes non-conducive circumstances which thwart the self-actualisation and healthy subject development of teachers. Many of these factors can be seen as symptomatic of the prevalence of positivistic, rationalistic, and efficiency-related aims in schooling, in which there is little room for things like work-life balance, secure employment contracts, adequate pay, self-care, and psychological and emotional wellbeing. The outcome, however, is widespread physical and mental ill-health and the perpetuation of non-conducive circumstances, as well as the further enactment and manifestation of violent epistemology.

7.4 How Structurally Engrained Violent Epistemology Affects Teacher and Student Subject Development and Interpersonal Relations

Aside from the non-conducive social circumstances of the Baixada neighbourhood, and the non-conducive employment circumstances in which teachers operated, the presence and impact of violent epistemology could also be strongly seen in the organisational structure of the school and the collectively affirmed ideological premises upon which it functioned. This impacted the subject development of both teachers and students and shaped interpersonal relating between the two.

As is common in many schools, particularly in post-colonial contexts, the DCX School operated according to traits inherited from the nineteenth century European schooling model with its control of bodily movement and activity within time, positivist, rationalistic, 'civilising', authoritarian, and domesticating tendencies, as well as the emphasis on technicism and efficiency of more recent years. Based in ideological schema which hold the cognitive dimension—associated with the learning of 'facts' and basic skills such as reading, writing, arithmetic, and computing—above all other dimensions of being (such as the physical, emotional, and psychological), a traditional 'banking' style pedagogy was largely employed, in which teachers aimed to 'transmit' such facts and skills to students via the use of 'chalk and talk' teaching methods. Bare-walled classrooms were laid out with chairs and desks in rows facing a large blackboard at the front, from where teachers would be encouraged to read aloud from textbooks and set exercises for students to copy.

As is common in this model of schooling, an official hierarchy of power was in place, with the most 'knowledgeable' individuals expected to command over the least—the school director being at the top and students at the bottom. This hierarchy was maintained via a number of methods. One notable method was the strict vigilance and control of student movement, both within the classroom and around the building. One example of this is how entrance to the building and its different interior levels was controlled via a series of padlocked gates. Movement through these gates was strictly controlled by staff members:

> Going upstairs to the project room, I saw G5 sitting by the locked metal gate that allowed access to the upper floors of the school. The lady that guards the gate (and holds the keys to its padlock) was refusing to let him upstairs. I saw IG and he asked me if he could go upstairs with me to the project. He said his lesson had been cancelled. I said yes, but then another teacher came and said sternly to him no, telling him to go back down to the patio and wait. (Field notes 31 May 2011)

The school also had a strict policy that no student should be outside the classroom during lesson times, and many teachers held the view that students needed to remain under surveillance at all times:

> It's no use saying 'Ai, how bad they are', like I heard today. The alternative is that firstly, they can't be left, in any scenario, by themselves. (Teacher comment 23 May 2011)

Teachers also exerted significant control over students' bodies and movement within the classrooms:

> 'Where's A?' the teacher said. 'A, come here!' A came back to the computer but remained standing. He leant over the back of the chair to type the corrections that the teacher instructed him to. I asked him if he wanted to sit down. 'No', he replied. 'Sit down' the teacher said. 'I don't want to', said A. 'Sit down PLEASE' said the teacher in a forceful tone. A sat down. (Observation notes 12 May 2011)

This strict control over student movement can be seen as an expression of dimension M2 of the theoretical model, because the ability to self-actualise (which includes meeting physical needs) relies on freedom of movement.

Another method by which hierarchies between teachers and students were maintained was the restriction of space for students to express their own thoughts and needs. This was embedded in the structure of the chalk and talk pedagogy in which teachers controlled when students were permitted to speak and what they were allowed to say:

> Teacher 1: So, it's written there … right girls I'm going to separate you, you hear? Oh, pay attention here, oh. [Reading from the screen] 'I am one of the 'different people', and you?'
> IG: I'm one
> Teacher 1: Could it be that B is one of the 'different people'? He's chatting just like a little rich girl—now is not the time for you to be playing—go and sit there with the teacher.
> Teacher 2: B. Sit here by my side. (Dialogue between teachers and students 18 May 2011)

The silencing of students was also embedded in teachers' approaches to resolving problems or conflicts. These interactions focussed largely on discipline and punishment rather than on teachers inviting students to express their needs:

> The teacher told AP off today. AP hadn't gone straight home yesterday, and her father had come to complain again. AP was silent while the teacher asked why she didn't go home. She sat there fidgeting with her hands, then mumbled that she had gone to eat dinner in the canteen. The teacher said 'you're losing your father's trust and today you lost even more. You can't just sit there with a face like 'scared Maria', you have to use your head and react. If things aren't going well you have to react because the world doesn't go round on its own. I have told you many times already [voice getting angrier] and it looks like you're not thinking about what I say, like it's not going in to your head. How long have you been in Sao Paulo?' AP said that she didn't know. 'How old are you?' asked the teacher. '13' said AP. 'And at 13 years of age you have no notion of time? How many months?' 'I arrived when I was 12' said AP. 'One year then' said the teacher. 'You have to earn your father's trust and think about what you do because people are coming to complain about you every day, wanting to claim money from you and all kinds of things, and your father has already come to speak to me. I won't involve myself in family things anymore because I'm promising things to your father that you are not fulfilling, so you need to think now and decide what you're going to do'. AP looked furious, but stayed silent. The teacher looked despairing. 'Think about what I said. You're going away aren't you?

You have a lot to think about during your trip and afterwards. And if I speak to you again, say something in response'. The teacher stopped talking, and AP asked me in a quiet, timid voice whether I had saved her work from yesterday. I sat with her and spent some time trying to teach her to correct her own work. She hardly knew how to use the computer, and could barely type. (Field notes 10 June 2011)

While in this example the teacher expressed frustration that AP had remained largely silent, her demeanour and language demonstrated a closure to considering AP's perspective, and a predetermined assumption that AP was 'to blame'. This behaviour is indicative of the holding of rigid schema, maintained through type α behaviour and a lack of imaginative labour. Such epistemology was also reflected in how teachers tended to ask questions in ways that expected students to give the 'correct' answer or say what the teacher expected of them, rather than expressing their own particular thoughts. This resulted in students being fearful of saying the 'wrong' thing or making mistakes ($A{\rightarrow}B{\rightarrow}D{\rightarrow}E{\rightarrow}G{\rightarrow}I$):

The students were asked whether they felt free to express their opinions in group discussions:

EST: I feel too ashamed. [...] I'm afraid of getting something wrong.
LC: And of people laughing in your face.
EST: Yeah. (Conversation between teacher and students 28 June 2011)

The general 'silencing' of students can be seen as a manifestation of violent epistemology because it involves a 'closure' to, and suppression of, the particularities and diversity that students could express (dimension G of the theoretical model) whether this takes the form of type α behaviour, identity thinking, a lack of imaginative labour, or a self-protective 'everyday consciousness'. This silencing resulted in students feeling unheard, which led to frustrations being expressed through agitated and aggressive behaviour ($M2{\rightarrow}P{\rightarrow}Q{\rightarrow}R$):

MR was agitated today—picking things up and putting them down, picking up the register and flicking through it, laughing in a strange sort of disconnected way, saying that she wanted to join the blog group because the radio group was rubbish, getting up to talk to AP in the blog group, etc. Then I saw her write on the desk 'Thank you JB [a teacher] for not letting me collect an invite, MR'. Then she rubbed out her name and re-wrote it with the letters jumbled up. (Observation notes 16 May 2011)

G: But teacher, rarely when you say [who did something], [...] rarely will [the teachers] do anything... One day I said, and nobody heard me, and it seemed like me against everyone, nobody heard me. I said 'But it wasn't me that did it' and everyone said 'Ai but you were there, you went there' and I ended up losing it with a friend. (Student comment 28 June 2011)

While some teachers wanted to encourage students to express themselves more freely but struggled to do so, others subscribed to the ideology of 'banking' style education and liked being authoritarian because it helped them to achieve the goal of transmitting information:

'I personally don't agree very much with the way the other teacher does things' said one teacher to me in private. 'She defends the students a lot. I'm not very accustomed to doing things this way. I'm more authoritarian, or dictatorial you could say. I'm sterner with the students and this works for me—I manage to pass the information that I need to them. (Conversation with teacher 26 April 2011)

The hierarchical system fostered a general expectation that teachers should control the students and their behaviour (M1→M2):

Teacher 2: She came one day and asked me to remove a student from her class, which is a really horrible thing.
    Teacher 1: It is. The other day [another teacher] came and asked me, she said it like this 'Ai, I'm going to 5B, can you help me?' I said 'It's just that I'm going to 5D right now' and she said 'Ai, but can you...' and so I went there, got them inside, made them sit down ... but, like, people, it's really ... it's more or less ... it's what the people from the Assistencia[12] say, if you do this, it takes away the authority of the teacher, no?
    Teacher 3: It does.
    Teacher 1: It's not cool, you understand? So when [the School Director] said 'look people, you can't call for help all the time, because it takes the authority away from the teacher!' So how can I go... I mean, I go into HER lesson to make the students sit down. I think that up to a certain point—tell one off ... say 'Get inside!' to whoever's in the corridor still, because I'm there by the door still, waiting for my students, but... It's ok for her to say 'I need help', but then what? When I go and turn my back, it'll just continue! Right? It's the teacher that will have to take that on ... with [the students] ... understand? So I went there but ... it doesn't resolve the problem... (Conversation between teachers 27 June 2011)

---

[12] Municipal Education Department.

The impact of this was that students expected to be controlled by the teacher, and would 'lose control' whenever teachers were not present (K):

> If I enter the classroom, everybody maintains a certain attitude because I am there. As soon as I leave it turns into mayhem because I'm not there anymore. (Teacher comment 06 June 2011)

Students also showed more 'respect' for more authoritarian teachers and tended to bully teachers who were not perceived as 'strict' or 'cool' (K):

> G: [...] Why do the students disrespect teacher AR and don't disrespect teacher 2 for example?
>
> BR: Because he arrives in the classroom and it looks like he is afraid of the students. Because if the students mess around, knock over the desks, he doesn't say anything right? He just resolves these things with the School Director, and the others throw chalk, swear at him, and he doesn't say anything... [...]
>
> Student: If you ask him why he lets the students mess around, he says like this that he's tired... [...]
>
> Student: They take the chalk box and throw [chalk] at him, once a boy threw it right at his glasses.
>
> Teacher 1: But let me ask you, you're not answering, I mean BR answered G's question, why do they disrespect...
>
> JSC: Because he comes in the classroom and he stays, kind of quiet in his corner and everyone thinks 'he's not fierce' because teacher 2, when he arrived on the first day of classes he already arrived more ... with more ... but not AR.
>
> PL: Because he arrives and he arrives throwing chalk and he doesn't say anything right?
>
> Teacher 1: A teacher throwing chalk?
>
> PL: No [lots of giggling]
>
> Teacher 1: Calm down.
>
> PL: The students.
>
> Teacher 1: The students, ok.
>
> PL: The students throw chalk and there was that day when he got really upset with the students wasn't there? (Conversation between teacher and students 28 June 2011)

Another impact of teachers being expected to be 'in control' was that students became accustomed to being told what to do and how to do it, and to being asked to copy from the blackboard rather than using their own creativity or initiative. This resulted in students lacking intrinsic self-motivation and ability to act autonomously (M2):

> 'So, we could make a film about recycling in general, using the recordings from the fair and other things too' I suggested. FLP and N appeared to like the idea. FLP got up and said goodbye. I explained to N that he attends night classes and had to go to these. There were 10 minutes left, and N looked at me with an expression that said 'I don't know what to do now', pen hovering over the notebook in her hand. I said 'let's note down our ideas then?', and she looked at me with the same expression. 'Let's write 'Recycling' as our idea?' I prompted. 'Where?' she asked, not sure where on the page she should write. 'Anywhere is fine' I said. 'Here?' she asked. 'There's fine' I replied. (Observation notes 4 May 2011)

Because students were not free to move around or leave the classroom, and due to the lack of materials for stimulation, they would become bored and agitated when they had completed tasks set by the teacher (M2→P→Q→R/S). This resulted in a pressure on teachers to keep students occupied within the classrooms at all times, reminiscent of how perceived 'vacuums of leisure' were 'filled' with educational activities during Brazil's military dictatorship in order to suppress dissent:

> They have finished their work really quickly and ended up hanging around, really idle haven't they? Really idle, and agitated, driving us crazy at times up there, understand? So we have to give them as much work as possible so they don't get agi ... idle. (Teacher comment 13 June 2011)

Another impact of the hierarchical structure in which teachers were expected to maintain control over students was that students understood 'respect' to mean obedience and pleasing the teacher (another expression of the 'civilising' aims of schooling). Teachers saw this kind of 'respect' as something to be imposed, and students tended to reproduce this authoritarian rhetoric:

> [Our behaviour is] our responsibility because there are a lot of people messing around and each teacher has their limit. AR, he has his limit because he has more patience, but RB doesn't. And I arrived and the boys said that JL had taken NTS' sandal, and the teacher asked 'whose sandal is this?' she said 'It's mine' and he threw it in her face. (Student comment 28 June 2011)

The art teacher said that he thinks the students respect the teachers with contracted hours more, with whom they have regular contact, and not the teachers who are just filling gaps in the curriculum (like him). He wanted to know whether the teachers with contracted hours could work with or talk with the students, to try to get them to respect the fill-in teachers. (Field notes 15 June 2011)

Discussing the script, MR and another student were thinking about phrases to say to the younger students over the radio during break time, such as 'don't mess around in the classroom, it's not worth it'. MR said 'but we need to remember that they're small children', at which another student suggested 'Don't mess around in the classroom, always obey your teachers'. (Observation notes 16 May 2011)

Students struggled to understand who was responsible for their behaviour and its impact. Some saw their parents, their teachers, or themselves as solely responsible, while others believed there was a shared responsibility. Many demonstrated a belief that they were accountable to authority rather than responsible for acknowledging the impact of their own actions, and tended to curb their own behaviour based on what teachers had told them was 'wrong' or that they 'shouldn't do', rather than an understanding of the impact of this behaviour on others:

BR: It's our responsibility [to control our behaviour when the teacher isn't there] because nobody is going to say that you're doing something wrong but you're doing something that you shouldn't, right? (Student comment 28 June 2011)

The expectation that teachers 'control' students can be seen as an expression of domination over some human beings by others in the name of ideology. As discussed in Chap. 4, because of how ideologies hold certain dimensions of life above others, creating conditions of worth that correspond to this hierarchy of particularities, social organisation based on such ideologies also tends to take a corresponding hierarchical form. In such circumstances, those higher up in the hierarchy tend to employ an instrumental reason to dominate over those lower down, in order to serve the perpetuation of that ideology. In schools, domination over students by teachers can be seen to impact student subject development, as students come to see themselves as subjects without autonomy or responsibility for their own actions. The development of such self-schema can be seen as an example of learnt violent epistemology that contributes to the de-formation of subjectivity.

The emphasis on authority-based behaviour monitoring also represents violent epistemology through its focus on looking to a 'higher power' for guidance on how to act in the world (which risks negating the particular demands of the situation at hand), rather than a focus on being open and responsive to the particularities of phenomena that present themselves to our awareness in any given situation. Some teachers felt that this stemmed from a punitive approach to social control rooted in society as a whole, and which they were forced to reproduce:

> So their need is the same need as the whole of society, for the guy to be obligated for example not to racially discriminate against others, because there's a law that will have him arrested. Not because he has to understand that all people are equal blablabla. No, because there's a law. 'Ah, if I do this the law will have me arrested'. So I don't... I understand ... they live according to this overarching idea ... this is why we have to tell them to sit down, have to tell them to do this, do that. It's not that we agree. Shall we invent another way? But then it would have to be a different school. It can't be this one. (Teacher comment 27 June 2011)

Pressures on teachers to keep students in the classroom, quiet, sitting still, and occupied at all times were often too much for teachers to handle, especially considering the high levels of student agitation and teacher burnout. This often resulted in angry outbursts on the part of teachers (A→B→D→E→G→I) and the fostering of hostile and disruptive interpersonal relations within the classroom. This, in turn, impacted on students' ability to engage in classroom activities and learn (M2):

> At the beginning of the session a teacher was screaming at one of her third year students out in the corridor, in front of the rest of her class. She grabbed the student aggressively and shouted. One of the project teachers shut the door and commented that she was shocked by this teacher, because her class didn't learn anything throughout the entire year and she didn't know how this was possible. She said the school management never did any kind of evaluation in the classrooms and simply let this happen. Another project teacher said that this teacher's students didn't have any autonomy at all in the classroom, and were only allowed to copy from the blackboard. She said she thought third year students should have some autonomy already, and that this class was the only one this year that didn't learn anything. (Conversation with teachers 8 April 2011)

After witnessing countless fractious interactions in the school environment, it was interesting to perceive how the distant, hierarchical relationships between teachers and students transformed into warm, friendly, and egalitarian interactions when taken outside of the rigidly structured school environment, highlighting the strength of influence that the 'non-conducive' circumstances of the hierarchical school environment had on interpersonal relating. Within the school, teachers tended to take disciplinary or coercive approaches to managing student behaviour that involved blaming, disapproving, combative, and intimidating tactics rather than fostering an intersubjective understanding of particular situations, individual feelings, and needs:

> Teacher 2: I don't know, I think that we need to take measures that are a bit more drastic, at least now, we need to take one of them, and make him sit outside for a week to appear as if he is being punished because he provoked such and such. Was it just him? No. It was ALL of them without exception. But we will have to take one to be an example to try...
>   Teacher 1: Because if we... I'm not in favour of physical aggression so punishment is, is the only way out people. I say this to my son... I put him there, sat down, I take away his toys, understand? Make him think about his life, right? (Conversation between teachers 9 May 2011)

> Today as I arrived the two project teachers were outside the IT room with B. He was standing with his back to the wall, his whole body pressed up against the wall, with the teachers standing over him, hands on hips. He looked as if he had been backed into a corner and was trying to melt backwards through the wall to get away. 'Think about what we said. Go home and think about it' said one of the teachers to him. B was silent, and the teachers looked stressed. (Observation notes 30 April 2011)

The epistemic closure inherent to such disciplinary approaches appeared to foster alienated and mutually objectifying relations in which students and teachers developed and maintained rigid and limited identity schema in relation to one another. On one hand, teachers held schema about students in which they were seen to be deviant and in need of control. On the other hand, students held schema about teachers as being authority figures to rebel against, rather than people trying to carry out educational work (A→B→D→E→G→I, M2→P→Q→R/S):

> The teacher told me that once there was a boy in his class, and when he asked him to read out loud the young man had said 'I won't read'. The teacher had replied 'Here there is no such thing as 'want', the only thing

that exists is you doing what I tell you so you will read', and the young man had whispered 'I don't know how to read'. 'I wanted to cry!' said the teacher. 'I felt so bad'. (Conversation with teacher 2 June 2011)

The teachers were talking about the school coordinator, who the children have nicknamed 'Panettone'. When the rebellion happened the other week, all the students ran out of the classrooms and shouted 'Panettone, Panettone!' (Conversation with teachers 6 April 2011)

They don't see us as workers right? When I said 'you treat us badly ... or ... do you want your parents to be treated badly in their work?' [They said] 'No teacher' [and I asked] 'So why do you mistreat us workers?' So, sometimes there's this alienation that they don't see sometimes, they see us as something else and not as someone who is carrying out his or her work'. (Teacher comment 18 April 2011)

Some students showed signs of having internalised teacher reprimands into a rigidified schema of self as 'bad', playing out this self-schema as a type of 'hardened', callous (Horkheimer and Adorno 2002) subjectivity (K):

During the group discussion, B sat the whole time with a half-smile on his face, looking as if he was being permanently told off. He had a 'naughty boy' expression on his face, but in the depth of his eyes I felt like I could see another expression—something which suggested a profound insecurity. He sat with a catapult made from an elastic band on his fingers, and spent the whole session threatening people with it with that wry—yet also ashamed looking—half-smile. The teacher made him move places and sat behind him for a long while, monitoring his behaviour. (Observation notes, 16 May 2011)

Another impact of being held accountable to authority rather than encouraged to understand and take responsibility for their own behaviour was that students would often do anything to avoid accountability, which signified punishment from teachers or parents. Students would threaten each other, use bribes, and form strategic 'friendships' in order to keep each other silent about indiscretions (A→B→D→E→G→I):

Teacher 2: [To PL] Do you think it's fair for you to take the blame for the person who threw chalk? Or do you think you should have said who it was?
    PL: I should have said, but in the moment when I told the teacher I got scared.
    Teacher 2: [To all students] Would you say who it was, in this situation?
    [Some students said they would, others said 'sometimes'].

AP: You should say. If you say they threaten to hit you or something else, to do something wrong.

Other students: Yeah.

PL: Like AP said, there are people who threaten, right? And if there were two people that threw [chalk], and if they threaten you, then if I tell the teacher it will be everyone against me, and the teacher will say that it was the other person, and then what will I do? (Conversation between teacher and students 28 June 2011)

This self-censorship can be seen as an example of how non-conducive circumstances can foster a situation in which subjects close themselves down, motivated by a desire for self-preservation in a world in which they cannot 'afford to be open' (Sherman 2007). This kind of threatenedness was visible in interpersonal relating across the school, which was marked by the types of self-preservation motivated behaviours of response pathway A→B→D→E→G→I, such as physical violence, bullying, and threats:

I saw who it was but I don't want to say. I won't say because otherwise afterwards they'll want to make me pay. (Student comment 9 May 2011)

T was smacking another girl in the face, and she started to lose her patience and T swore at her, and she pushed T to the floor and started hitting her. (Student comment 16 June 2011)

People this public school looks like hell and nobody notices. Our inspector walked around with a piece of wood in his hands this big, banging on the doors. It's horrible, it looks like a FEBEM[13] [...] which is crazy. (Teacher comment 9 May 2011)

'You threaten the boy but what does he have? [...] there's no point saying that you're armed because he'll say he has a bigger gun'. (Pedagogical coordinator 19 May 2011)

This defensiveness in response to threat also extended to the physicality of the school, with its locks, gates, and guards:

This school is horrible, it reproduces those tower blocks there, where they live confined. (Teacher comment 13 June 2011)

As we left I saw 5 or 6 policemen wearing bullet proof vests, guarding the school gate. We said goodbye to them and went on our way. As we passed I

---

[13] Young offenders' institution.

saw a policeman get out the police car, take a gun and tuck it into his belt. I noticed that all of them were armed. (Field diary 30 March 2011)

A teacher was leaving at the same time as I entered [the school gate], and gave me an untrusting look. I smiled at him but he continued with this expression. I went upstairs and the barred gate halfway up the stairs was locked with a padlock. A lady came to open it for me. I explained who I was and went through. (Field diary 22 March 2011)

This can be seen as the response pathway A→B→D→E→G→I, manifest in the physicality of the school's architecture and security structure, and motivated by a desire for self-preservation in a world seen as filled with threat.

Another significant manifestation of violent epistemology in the DCX School was homogeneity. Not in terms of teachers or students, but in its 'one size fits all' approach to school organisation, rules, curricula, and teaching methods. One example is the implementation of universal policies based on the instrumental reason of local and international governing bodies rather than particular student needs. This was evident in areas such as the use of 'Think Quest', an information technology learning platform which was imposed by the DRE but too challenging for DCX students, and the introduction of extended school days imposed by the government with a mind to meet international development goals, but which did not take into account the ability of teachers to provide this service, nor the family and home life obligations of the poorest students. Also, while the Brazilian public school system has expanded dramatically in order to meet the global development goal of universal matriculation, in doing so the existing model of schooling was simply multiplied, rather than adapted with a consideration for the particular needs of a new student demographic. The impacts of this were exacerbated by inadequate infrastructure, Brazil's long history of underinvestment in teacher training, and insufficient consideration of the suitability of efficiency-based, technicistic education for this new demographic:

'No', responded the IT teacher, 'I think the students do have to learn. We shouldn't forget content. But I think it's not everything'.

'And when they made the inclusive school' the art teacher added, 'they only made half of it. Yes, there are people going to school all together, we have people with disabilities, autism…'

'Yes' said the IT teacher, 'which is democratic access—everyone has the same access to school—which is more than what we had in Brazil in the past'.

'Yes' said the art teacher, 'but it doesn't stop there. The school, I believe, will only work when it becomes a cultural centre, a health centre, you know? [For now] things remain fragmented'. (Discussion between teachers 6 May 2011)

This can be seen as a manifestation of the response pathway A→B→D→E→G→I on a national level. Brazil signed up for the international Education for All goals out of perceived need for economic self-preservation. The traditional nineteenth century model of schooling which had been imported from Europe to serve the needs of wealthier classes who aspired to a vision of European-style 'progress' was simply expanded to allow for the matriculation of rapidly increasing numbers of poorer students, representing a 'closure' to the particular needs of this demographic. The imposition of policy reforms in Brazil by international financial and governing bodies can also be seen as the domination of some people over others through the employment of instrumental reason, in the name of strengthening globalised neoliberal economic ideology.

Significant aspects of the traditional model of schooling that has become established in Brazil are the homogenisation of the use of time and space and the standardisation of class sizes. Throughout the course of the Educommunication project at DCX, the teachers and students came up with many wonderful plans for interesting and meaningful projects. However, unfortunately due to the rigid time constraints of the school day there was only time to start some of these projects, and none were completed (M2):

Sometimes the time is too short, right? On Thursday there was a load of tasks and things [to do] and we couldn't manage [to complete them]. (Teacher comment 18 April 2011)

Classroom spaces at DCX were also homogenised, and could not be adapted to meet student needs (M2):

I asked the teacher if she thought the physical organisation of the class made any difference to student behaviour. She said that in the past, when there were classrooms designated for specific subjects, she had the geography classroom, with all of the geography materials, and she put the chairs in a circle, and saw that it worked really well with some groups, and not so well with others. Sometimes the students would crawl around under the chairs in a line, and it was difficult to catch them. Now that they no longer have subject-specific classrooms she gave up doing this, because she would lose a lot of time arranging the chairs and then rearranging them. 'You have to leave the classroom back how it was, for the next teacher'. (Conversation with teacher 15 June 2011)

As in schools around the world, children were grouped in classes of approximately 30 students, according to age. This was problematic for two reasons. Firstly, many children at DCX had missed out on parts of their schooling or struggled to learn at school, and therefore had different needs from other children of the same age. Secondly, many children required 1:1 emotional, behavioural, and learning support which was not possible in large class sizes. Teachers struggled to meet these needs:

A teacher told me about a girl who 'freaked out' in his classroom. 'She punched me, and shouted and such. We took her to her parents, to talk, and she lived in a tiny room, 3×3, with no water, no bathroom, and no kitchen. They cooked and did everything in that same space, and they were living, eight people in this room. The poor mother, and the uncles, they were all drunk. There was no food at all in the house, no food at all! So, these people have really difficult lives. We complain that life is difficult but they have a really difficult life. But I don't think that, even like this, I can go accepting any old behaviour in the classroom!' (Conversation with teacher 2 May 2011)

There were three teachers and me in the classroom, with less than 20 students, and it was really difficult to meet the needs of the group. (Field diary 3 May 2011)

The teachers said that they can't give individual attention to all the students, as much as they need, which leads to them dispersing during classroom activities. The teachers said the students need guidance, and when it doesn't arrive they start messing around. (Field diary 3 May 2011)

Speaking about JF, a student who needs extra support with reading and writing, the teachers said that even though taking part in the Educommunication project could help him a little, it wasn't enough to meet his needs. He needed extra support. They said there should be a SAP [Pedagogical Support Class] to provide reinforcement classes for those students that haven't learnt to read and write yet, but there isn't one. I asked if there is any support available to him and they said 'there's nothing'. They said the school is going to start providing a class to support students with special educational needs, the plan was to have 20 students in the class. One teacher said 'imagine 20 students with special needs in the same class, is it going to help? No—because all of them need the type of attention that you saw just now where I sat the entire time with JF. It's not going to work'. (Conversation with teachers 1 May 2011)

Another factor was that, being conditioned to teach in a standardised system, teachers were not accustomed to considering and adapting for particular student needs:

After students complained about teachers not making lessons interesting, the teacher said that what was important was to learn the content, and that when the test or exam time came they would see just how much they had lost, just because they didn't want to make the effort to pay attention in the lessons of the teachers who didn't teach in the way they liked, and that they should try harder to pay attention. (Observation notes 24 March 2011)

I argued with the school director recently, because I sent a student home to fetch his book. And the guy came back and said 'I lost the book'. I said 'Deal with it. Get your mum and take her to the bookshop to buy another one'. Is a guy who doesn't even eat going to buy a book? That's his problem, it's not my responsibility! [...] I say 'You haven't got a book? Then come here to the front, you sit here, you there, you here. You do times tables, you...' Today they sat writing a text. The entire time. Not even allowed to get up from the table. Writing a text. (Teacher comment 9 May 2011)

Such standardisation can be seen as a manifestation of violent epistemology because it represents a system built on the universalisation of particularities (such as age) under which all other particularities are subsumed (such as the particular needs of individual students). This led, as is common in Brazil, to many students leaving school only semi-literate, and developing schema relating to 'self-as-failure' as a result of struggling to engage with an educational institution that could not meet their needs (M2):

50% of students who left DCX School last year didn't finish high school. They were recorded as having abandoned their schooling, because they didn't know how to read and write. (School Director 15 June 2011)

The teacher gave the print-out of information about genre to JSU, and said 'read the explanation there about video clips and documentaries for us'. He sat with the paper in his hands, doing nothing. 'Read it loudly' said the teacher. 'Read it loudly' JSU repeated back. 'Eeesh, but I'm really bad'. He sat for a few seconds looking at the paper as if he was trying to make out the text in his head. Then he said 'I need to go to study class' and left. (Observation notes 11 May 2011)

These examples also illustrate the dangers of how neoliberal ideology places the responsibility for 'success' mostly on individuals, whilst largely negating the social, historical, and economic context that shapes the availability of opportunities and the ability of individuals to engage in these opportunities.

Another aspect of school life marked by the drive for homogeneity was how students were expected to behave in a standardised manner (viz. by remaining calm, quiet, and largely stationary). Students found these expectations hard to meet. However, rather than considering the reasons for this or reflecting on whether these expectations were reasonable, teachers tended to reprimand and suppress behaviours that didn't meet these expectations:

> Trying to find solutions to the problem of children running around and becoming agitated during break times, the teachers discussed how the radio could be used for this purpose. 'What would be good for this group of fifth years during break? Just listen to music? Just dance to funk which didn't work very well before? Or have, for example, for the first and second year students, to stop them running around, you could have circle songs, in this radio programme, which encourages them to play [in a structured game] or charades […] we could make a 'radio corner' downstairs on the patio, with tables for people to sit and listen to the radio to stop them running around so much'. (Conversation with teachers 18 April 2011)

With standardised expectations of behaviour also came an expectation that staff and students leave dimensions of their selves outside the school gate:

> Talking with a teacher about the relationship between school and society, the teacher said 'The school is not separate from society, the two need to change together. We say 'here at school you can't do this' but I don't understand how they don't want violence in school, as if it were something separate from society. They want the students to say goodbye to aspects of their being to come into school, and the teachers demand this. They demand this, but the school directors also demand that the teachers say goodbye to the social aspects of their being. Only when we have parents, students and society all together will things change, because they are society'. (Conversation with teacher 27 April 2011)

This rejection of particularity was also visible in the standardisation of curriculum content, which can be seen as an example of the same violent epistemology behind the 'civilising', nationalising, and homogenising aims of Brazilian schooling from the colonial through to the republican era; the prosecution of teachers who taught students in their mother tongue during the Vargas era; the nationalism and political repression of the military dictatorship; and the developmentalist goals of Education for All:

> Our students suffer linguistic prejudice all the time [...]. All the time. Understand? All the time. Last year I worked on a project 'the different ways of speaking in the writing of letters'. A teacher reported me for it. She called it absurd because I was reinforcing 'incorrect speech'. No. It was the contrary. I was giving an example to our student to show that it isn't that he speaks incorrectly, but that he has a REGIONAL speech of his own. [...] if you don't understand this and don't help the student to understand this, you work from the presupposition of linguistic prejudice [...]. Now if you treat grammar as the be all and end all, without understanding that it is part of a historical process, that it's a synthesis of a historical process, that language is something ALIVE, is a historical process ... understand? This is something that most people don't discuss. [...] How did the purist Portuguese of Brazil begin? When the economic and political power was transferred from Salvador, to the Central-South. From the Northeast to the Central-South. [...] Because when you talk about accents, and about speaking incorrectly and speaking correctly, people don't include the Paulista or Carioca accents, they include the North Eastern. [...] But the Paulistano thinks he's the only right one, because of this history, which we don't teach. So I work on this with my students, and it's interesting, when I teach this, like I was going to last year here at DCX, I was going to work with a text, but the proposal of the teachers working with this text in the classroom, they didn't embrace the idea. Much to the contrary, they boycotted it. And one day the students said they didn't want me to teach them this anymore because I was reinforcing ... they said I wanted them to speak incorrectly, and they wanted to speak correctly. (Teacher comments 23 May 2011)

This emphasis on reinforcing nationalised 'standards' rather than integrating the particularities of regional histories and student experience into the curriculum fostered the development in certain students of a schema relating so 'self-as-sub-standard':

> When RF spoke he looked at the floor and fumbled his words. He spoke with a very strong North Eastern accent. (Observation notes 16 May 2011)

Again, the standardisation of behavioural expectations and curriculum content represent violent epistemology as select particularities are made universal, and all other particularities are either subsumed beneath these universalised schema or negated and suppressed.

The cumulative impact of hierarchical and dominating relations, and the experience of standardised schooling that did not meet their needs, meant that many students felt alienated from schooling and as if the school space was not genuinely *theirs*. This often manifest in frustration and aggression and in students intentionally damaging or 'messing up' parts of the school building, furniture, spaces, or learning materials (P→Q→R/S). Teachers interpreted this as a lack of respect for the school space and learning materials, but gave little consideration to the possible reasons for this behaviour.

Another expression of violent epistemology could be seen in the language teachers used to describe students. Teachers would often refer to students as *Danado* [Damned], *Da pá virada* [Useless], *Marginal* [Marginal/Criminal], *Mal* [Bad], *Idiota* [Idiot], *Terrível* [Terrible], *Problema* [Problem], *Aquela Raça* [That race], or *Cobra criada* [Scoundrel]. These terms were expressed in specifically objectifying language, as they were often prefixed by the permanent form of the verb 'to be'. Portuguese has two forms of this verb. *É* is used to refer to something being in a long-term or permanent state, such as *ela é alta* [she is tall], whereas *está* is used to refer to something being in a temporary state, such as *ele está cansado* [he is tired]. By prefixing these terms with *é* in statements like *ele é danado* [he is damned], teachers promoted the subsumption of the many and changing particularities of a student under a single, rigidified scheme that both neglected to consider the underlying reasons for their behaviour, and objectified them 'into character' (Sherman 2007).

Students also showed signs of having learnt, from schooling, to reproduce violent epistemology. Aside from the internalisation of violent epistemic self-schema discussed earlier, learnt violent epistemology was also expressed in the use of the same kind of objectifying language used by teachers, as well as in expressions of homophobia and racism that appeared to be learnt through schooling. Students would also often interpret the epistemically violent language of teachers as a promotion of physical violence:

Teacher 2 encourages the students to stop associating themselves with the students who lead the messing around in class, until those students become isolated:

Teacher 1 [to students]: Teacher 2 said that you need to ISOLATE this minority. Let's do this [...]

> Student: There was a time when I was arriving at school and a boy was harassing me. I told him to stop, he didn't stop. I told my brother and my brother went there and gave him a kick [proud tone]. Then on Monday, NR was taking my keys […] and I hit her [still with proud tone]. (Conversation between students and teachers 16 June 2011)

When teachers behaved violently towards students, student would also mimic this by responding violently in return:

> It's like the students are saying 'we can be violent in the classroom too. We turn into monsters if the teacher shouts at us'. (Teacher comment 15 June 2011)

Teachers' use of objectifying language and the encouragement of student to 'isolate' peers who do not conform to behavioural expectations is exemplary of how violent epistemology maintains rigid schema and rejects particularities that do not conform. These behaviours could also be seen as expressions of neoliberal ideology in how it posits individuals who are unable to 'succeed' by conforming to societal expectations, as deficient or lazy subjecting them to stigmatisation and social exclusion.

Not all teachers intended to be authoritarian or perpetuate violent epistemology, and some explicitly tried to practice a more Freirian style pedagogy. However, these intentions were often overridden by the overall hierarchical structure of the school, resulting in epistemic contradictions in teacher practice. Teachers would struggle over allowing students choice, freedom, and responsibility; demonstrated limited understanding of what student autonomy might look like in practice; and found it difficult to resist the expectation that they be 'in control', causing them to act in an authoritarian manner one moment, and anti-authoritarian the next. This illustrates the continuing prevalence of both traditional and neotechnicistic tendencies in schooling which make coherent, progressive, or transformative practice virtually impossible.

Regardless of how hard they tried not to be violent, the cumulative impact of all of the factors discussed above (including being overworked, underpaid, insufficiently trained, and expected to maintain control over large groups of students with complex needs, without appropriate support structures in place), meant that teachers were often in a state of such high anxiety, stress, and exhaustion that they would lose control of their emotions and act in explicitly violent ways ($A \rightarrow B \rightarrow D \rightarrow E \rightarrow G \rightarrow I$, $M2 \rightarrow P \rightarrow Q \rightarrow R$):

We have a discipline of shouting. (Teacher comment 15 June 2011)

AP: There was a day when the history teacher said something to LC, I don't know what they did, I was at the back, and I saw that the history teacher said just like this [puts on a threatening, aggressive tone in imitation] 'I'm going to cut your throat'. And he got so angry that he shouted because he got, I don't know what he got but he said just like this 'I'm going to cut your throat'. Whenever the students don't return [something to him] he says something like that.

BR: He said like this, that if he was his son he would want to kill him and throw him in the trash. (Student comments 28 June 2011)

JSC: [...] Once IG was messing around, weren't you?

IG: I was

BR: [The teacher] took a thing off the wall and started to throw it at IG. IG was complaining about the teacher and the teacher said he would put him outside and IG got up on the desk and started harassing him through the window, and the teacher took a thing off the wall and started to throw it at IG.

JSC: And the teacher couldn't write with his hand because he [IG] made him break his arm, Because he went to take IG outside and he broke his arm, and he went for an operation, and he said he broke his arm because of IG. He lost the movement in his hand. He [IG] was banging on the chair and he [the teacher] said 'this is serious, I should hit him'. Because he was banging on the chair, and he'd broken all the chairs during the semester, and he said 'teacher, I've lost my patience'. And the teacher ran after him and knocked over everything in his path. He even pushed the chair over. (Student comments 28 June 2011)

The phenomenon of teacher violence appeared to contradict the schema that teachers held about themselves and the school. This made it difficult for them to acknowledge their own violent behaviour and adapt these schemas accordingly. The result was that teachers often negated their own and their colleagues' violent behaviour, and blamed students for disruptions in class (A→B→D→E→G→I). This could be seen to further perpetuate violence, as student disclosures of teacher violence were not openly acknowledged or responded to (K→M1→M2):

Student: There was a teacher and [...] he said to [lists some girls' names], he was trying to explain, and he said that if anyone said they didn't understand he would give them a smack in the face.

Another student: A smack in the face.

Teacher 1 [without acknowledging what students just said]: But can you answer Beth's question? (Conversation with students and teacher 28 June 2011)

As long as only certain manifestations of violence are acknowledged whilst others are negated, we can imagine that such collective 'type α behaviour' will act to prevent the establishment and success of any project that intends to address violence in schooling at its root causes.

7.5   CONCLUSION

As this chapter has illustrated, DCX School can be seen in the context of a schooling system built on a long history of collectively affirmed violent epistemology. The chapter has demonstrated the many ways in which violent epistemology can manifest in schooling. This has included how non-conducive social circumstances (also established through a long history of collectively affirmed violent epistemology) outside of the school itself can impact on student and teacher subject development and engagement with prescribed roles in schooling. I have also illustrated how non-conducive employment circumstances as well as hierarchical and homogenising tendencies in schooling can foster teacher burnout and violent, alienating relations between teachers and students, contributing to a self-perpetuating cycle which teachers struggle to break out of.

Let us return again to the phrase highlighted in Chap. 1, expressed in the teachers' meeting: '*I put tables against the door so that they don't leave*' (Teacher comment 15 June 2011). At that time, existing theories of violence in schooling could not fully explain how such circumstances could have arisen. By reviewing concepts from a variety of disciplines and carrying out a detailed sociohistorical and case-study analysis, this book has presented a holistic and comprehensive framework for understanding the multiple factors that can lead to situations like the one in which this teacher found herself—a framework for understanding the root causes of violence in schooling.

While manifestations of violent epistemology (as this book has shown) can take many different forms, in this particular context its overwhelming expression was in the shaping of a multi-layered context in which 'the world of desires, of feelings, of social and biological needs, has been conditioned and contaminated by the economic dimension' (Clovis de Azevedo 2007, p. 94). In a world shaped by a globalised capitalist economy, this is likely to be the case in many contexts. However, this book demonstrates how we should not see economic ideology in itself as the root cause of violence, but rather the underlying violent epistemology upon which such ideology is built.

I will end this chapter with two pieces of data that particularly motivated the writing of this book:

> We watched M's video again. She had added some words superimposed over the images. J [another teacher] said she liked the shot with the word 'Lack' superimposed. 'Because what is lacking, right? So many things. Lack of teachers, lack of education, lack of salary, lack of discipline'. JB [another teacher] said he liked the scene with 'See us' superimposed. 'It's as if we're asking to be seen—'look at us' he said. (Conversation between teachers 30 May 2011)

> I see the state of education as a silent scream; we shout and shout and nobody hears. (Teacher comment 15 June 2011)

I hope that this book goes some way towards seeing and hearing the challenges faced by teachers and their students, and to beginning to find ways of breaking out of such 'vicious cycles' of violent epistemology and non-conducive circumstances.

REFERENCES

Abos, M. (2011). *Marcha da Maconha Acaba em Conflito com a Policia Militar*. Retrieved April 25, 2016, from http://oglobo.globo.com/brasil/marcha-da-maconha-acaba-em-conflito-com-policia-militar-2789220.

Americano, V. R. (2011). *Os Professores em Completação de Jornada (CJ) na Rede Municipal de Educação de São Paulo (2011): Condições do trabalho e implicações no currículo*. Dissertation. Pontifícia Universidade Católica de São Paulo.

Clovis de Azevedo, J. (2007). *Reconversão Cultural da Escola: Mercoescola e Escola Cidadã*. Porto Alegre: Suline.

DIEESE. (2012). *Salario Mínimo Nominal e Necessária*. Retrieved October 18, 2016, from http://www.dieese.org.br/rel/rac/salminMenu09-05.xml.

Freire, P. (2003). *Education for Critical Consciousness*. London: Bloomsbury.

Globo. (2015). *Após PM Matar Jovem, Moradores Entram em Confronto com Policiais*. Retrieved April 10, 2016, from http://g1.globo.com/sao-paulo/noticia/2015/03/moradores-do-centro-de-sp-entram-em-confronto-com-policiais.html.

Horkheimer, M., & Adorno, T. W. (2002). *Dialectic of Enlightenment*. Stanford: Stanford University Press.

Jacomini, M. A., & Minhoto, M. A. P. (2012). *Remuneração dos Professores da Rede Municipal de São Paulo (1996–2010): Considerações Preliminares.* Third Iberoamerican Conference on Education Policy and Administration, 14th–17th November, Zaragonza. Retrieved April 18, 2016, from http://www.anpae.org.br/iberoamericano2012/Trabalhos/MarciaAparecidaJacomini_res_int_GT6.pdf.

Kohara, L. (2009). *Relação Entre as Condições de Moradia e Desempenho Escolar: Estudo com crianças residentes em cortiços.* São Paulo: University of São Paulo.

Mathieu, F. (2011). *The Compassion Fatigue Workbook: Creative Tools for Transforming Compassion Fatigue and Vicarious Traumatisation.* London: Routledge.

Prefeitura de São Paulo. (2016a). *Atualização da Estrutura Administrativa da Secretaria Municipal de Educação.* Retrieved April 9, 2016, from http://sao-pauloaberta.prefeitura.sp.gov.br/index.php/minuta/estrutura-administrativa-da-secretaria-municipal-de-educacao/.

Prefeitura de São Paulo. (2016b). *Planos de Cargas, Carreiras e Salários.* Retrieved April 18, 2016, from http://www.prefeitura.sp.gov.br/cidade/secretarias/gestao/portal_do_servidor/pccs/index.php?p=13836.

Rothschild, B. (2006). *Help for the Helper: The Psychophysiology of Compassion Fatigue and Vicarious Trauma.* New York: Norton.

Sherman, D. (2007). *Sartre and Adorno: The Dialectics of Subjectivity.* Albany: SUNY Press.

Titchiner, B. M. (2017). *The Epistemology of Violence: Understanding the Root Causes of Violence and Non-conducive Social Circumstances in Schooling, with a Case-Study from Brazil.* Doctoral Thesis, University of East Anglia. Retrieved October 21, 2018, from https://ueaeprints.uea.ac.uk/63644/.

CHAPTER 8

Moving Forwards

8.1   Working Towards a Non-violent Epistemology

At this stage, I imagine that the question for practitioners is 'what can we do now?' or as Holt (1970) says—'what do I do Monday?' As this book has shown, violence in schooling is a complex phenomenon, rooted in the interactions between individual subjectivity, collectivised ideology, and non-conducive circumstances. This demonstrates the need to develop far more complex and sophisticated approaches to addressing the issue—approaches which are likely to require significant changes at a societal level and involve rethinking the depths of our own ways of relating with the world, ourselves, and others, as well as the fundamental ideas, policies, and practices upon which societies and schools operate. This is no easy task, since, as I have demonstrated, violent epistemology is historically and deeply engrained in human subjectivity and social structures, tending to be self-perpetuated in cyclical feedback loops.

Despite the enormity of this challenge, I propose that the most useful starting point would be to address the issue at its root cause—by beginning to consider how we might enact less violent epistemology, and consequently how we might begin to foster circumstances conducive to its enactment. Throughout the remainder of this chapter, and to conclude the book, I will outline some thoughts regarding what such an epistemology and its conducive conditions might look like. I will then provide some

© The Author(s) 2019   229
B. M. Titchiner, *The Epistemology of Violence*, Critical Political Theory
and Radical Practice, https://doi.org/10.1007/978-3-030-12911-8_8

brief thoughts on the challenge of fostering change, ending with some comments on possible avenues for future research.

To begin thinking about how we might enact non-violent epistemology, we can start with the question of choice or agency since, as the concept of phenomenological freedom implies, this is the one dimension over which we each possess a degree of control. As discussed in Chap. 3, we can determine two interconnected points of *epistemic agency* within our cognition. The first lies within our ability to control attenuation—to choose what to focus on and what to push to the margins of awareness (James 1918; Broadbent 1958; Treisman 1964; Posner 1978). The second lies in the interplay between our immediate, prereflective consciousness of sensory experience and our reflective consciousness. This interplay (what Sherman (2007) calls 'mediating subjectivity') can be seen as a site of agency because it enables us to choose what to think about the particularities of our experience. As previously outlined, this has been called 'phenomenological freedom' (Sartre 1956; Sherman 2007). Therefore, the starting point for considering how we might enact a non-violent epistemology is remembering that we possess epistemic agency, and therefore the ability to make epistemic choices when cognitively processing our experiences. This means that however deeply engrained a subject is in enacting violent epistemology, the possibility always exists of changing one's epistemic behaviour. As I will discuss in a moment, certain factors can make this extremely difficult to achieve, but the epistemic agency within us all makes it theoretically possible in any circumstance.[1]

We will also remember the assertion in Chap. 3 that our sensory experience (both interoceptive and exteroceptive) is multidimensional (encompassing sight, sound, touch, smell, taste, feeling, and emotion), and that the phenomenal world is also multidimensional and fluid (ever-changing). As discussed, our epistemic agency enables us to enact violent epistemology by choosing to push certain dimensions and particularities of this complex, multidimensional experience to the margins of our awareness (and to reject them from our schema or allow them to be subsumed). However, and crucially, it is also our epistemic agency that enables us to try to do justice to the particularities of our experience by attending towards them and integrating them into our schema formulations—in other words, to learn from them (Jarvis 2009; Illeris 2009). Drawing on

---

[1] Except perhaps for those with certain forms and degrees of cognitive impairment. More research would be necessary to explore the impact of this on epistemic agency.

the concept of phenomenological freedom (Sherman 2007), we can consider the possibility of choosing and consciously monitoring how we use this agency.

Considering the formulations presented in this book of the cognitive behaviours that I have argued constitute violent epistemology, I propose that choosing to use our epistemic agency to enact non-violent epistemology would require a particular attitude towards the experience of being 'disoriented' (Jarvis 2009; Piaget 1977), the process of 'orientating' (Merleau-Ponty 2012; Husserl 1973; Heidegger 1962) ourselves towards phenomena, and the ways in which we construct our schema or 'orientations' (Ahmed 2006). In Chap. 3, I proposed that the unsettled feeling of disorientation or disequilibrium (Piaget 1977) that occurs when the particularities of our experience do not match up with our pre-existing schema (ibid.) can be a motivating factor for the enactment of violent epistemology. In light of this, we can suggest that enacting non-violent epistemology would require a shift in how we respond to these unsettling feelings. As Illeris (2007) writes, disequilibrium is a natural and inescapable part of the learning process, because as I have discussed, our pre-existing schema can never absolutely match the particularities of our experience. However, Piaget's (1977) work demonstrates that there *are* different ways in which we can respond to the experience of disequilibrium.

In Chap. 3, I discussed one of these—type α behaviour. We will remember that this is characterised by the rejection or negation of particularities that do not fit with pre-existing schema, so that a sense of orientation or equilibrium can be maintained without having to adapt one's schema. This is what Adorno (1973) referred to as 'guarding the old particularity' (pp. 283–284). As this book has discussed and demonstrated, the ethical implication of this is that type α behaviour does not fully acknowledge the particularities of a phenomenon, which can result in the development of violent epistemic schema in relation to that phenomenon and since, as discussed in Chap. 3, schema operate as guides for acting in the world (Trevarthen and Reddy 2007), violent epistemic schema can guide violent behaviour (as demonstrated by the case-study presented in this book). However, Piaget identified another type of epistemic behaviour in his research, which gives some indication of a less violent approach to equilibration.

After type α behaviour, Piaget (1977) discussed what he calls type β behaviour. Rather than rejecting or negating particularities of experience that do not match up to pre-existing schema, type β behaviour consists 'of integrating into the system the disturbing element arising from without [through behaviour which] no longer consists in cancelling the disturbance or in rejecting the new element, so that it will not intervene within the whole set already organised, but in modifying the system [by] alter[ing] the […] scheme itself to accommodate the object and follow its orientation' (ibid., pp. 67–68). In other words, rather than rejecting or negating new particularities, in type β behaviour these are integrated into existing schema by adjusting the schema to account for the new particularities. Rather than 'guarding the old particularity' (Adorno 1973), in type β behaviour the subject re-orientates themselves towards the phenomenon, reworking aspects of existing schema to accommodate new particularities.

Compared with type α behaviour, we can argue that type β epistemic behaviour is much less violent since it does not negate or reject particularities of experience. However, as Piaget (ibid.) argues, in type β behaviour, pre-existing schema sets are left largely intact with new experiences being integrated as variables of pre-existing concepts:

> [T]here is, therefore, equilibrium displacement but with minimisation of the cost (as much as possible of the […] scheme is conserved and with maximal gain the disturbance is integrated as a new variation of the scheme). (p. 68)

In this way, entire schema sets are not deconstructed and reconstructed in a different form, but rather dimensions of the schema set are simply 'adjusted' to accommodate new particularities. While, according to the definition of violent epistemology presented in Chap. 3, we can argue that type β behaviour would be less violent than type α behaviour, it is also evident that type β behaviour carries with it some risk of conceptual subsumption—another characteristic of violent epistemology. As discussed in Chap. 3, conceptual subsumption (Polanyi 1969; Adorno 1973) occurs when the subject subsumes particularities of experience under conceptual categories that do not fully acknowledge the complexity, multidimensionality, and particularity of phenomena (what Adorno (1973) called 'identity thinking'). Assessing Piaget's statement above, this can be interpreted as meaning that in this behaviour there is minimal 'cost' for the subject because accommodating most phenomena into its pre-existing schema sets, with only minor experiences of disequilibrium (which can be easily resolved through minor adjustments to schema), does not demand great amounts of mental and emotional energy.

Piaget (1977) considers schema maintained through type α behaviour to be unstable because they 'concern a very restricted field [and because] their organisation continues to be incomplete and neglects a whole set of observables capable of intervening, it is obvious that these observables, precisely to the extent that they are neglected, are the sources of possible great alterations' (p. 74). In other words, to the extent that many particularities are rejected, these particularities are likely to continue presenting themselves to the subject as challenges to the stability of that schema, and if acknowledged and incorporated by the subject, would result in a substantial reconstruction of the schema. We can assume based on the discussion above, that this would involve significant 'cost' (ibid.) to the subject, in the form of overcoming a marked sense of disequilibrium through considerable mental and emotional effort.

Piaget (ibid.) argues that schema maintained through type β behaviour are more stable than those maintained through type α, but still not particularly stable because 'the disturbance factors conserve a great modification power as compared to the cognitive system considered but less than in type α, since they are integrated by the compensating reaction and result in changes of equilibrium which retain a part of the initial form and remove from the alterations their disturbance character' (p. 74). In other words, particularities which appear to the subject as close but not identical to existing schema sets cause minimal disequilibrium and can easily be integrated into the existing schema by tweaking or reworking part of the schema or schema set.[2] However, a particularity, phenomenon, or combination of such could still present themselves to the subject in a way that challenges the validity of an entire set of schema, throwing the subject into a more unsettling sense of disequilibrium or disorientation.[3]

Remembering that the subject can be seen to possess epistemic agency, it can be argued that at this stage, the subject has a choice: to engage in type α behaviour and regain equilibrium by negating the disturbing phenomena and maintaining the old schema, or to deconstruct the entire schema set and construct a new one that does better justice to the

[2] For example, noticing that a child needs more help with learning than previously thought can easily be integrated into a teacher's existing schema related to that child by acknowledging this and making a mental note to spend a bit more time with them on the topic or to look into additional learning support. However, this is very unlikely to cause significant disequilibrium by challenging the validity of everything the teacher knows about teaching and learning.

[3] For example, when a teacher is required by a phenomenon to call into question the validity of an entire pedagogical philosophy into which their career and sense of self may be heavily invested.

phenomena at hand. As Fromm (2013) writes, 'once the individual faces the world outside of himself [...] two courses are open to him [...]. By one course he can progress to "positive freedom"; he can relate himself spontaneously to the world [...] in the genuine expression of his emotional, sensuous and intellectual capacities; he can thus become one again with man, nature and himself, without giving up the [...] integrity of his individual self' (pp. 165–166). Piaget does not deal with the latter scenario. However, Illeris (2007) addresses this with the concept of 'transformative learning', which he defines as 'learning that takes place when a large number of schemes are reorganised at the same time' (p. 44). Rogers (1969) speaks of something similar which he calls 'significant learning', which comprises a 'change in the organisation of the self', that is 'pervasive' in how it involves the 'whole person' reaching out to illuminate the 'dark area of ignorance she is experiencing' (p. 20).

Bearing in mind the definition of violent epistemology as that which rejects particularities that do not fit comfortably into existing schema, we can argue that the act of deconstructing existing schema sets and constructing new ones to better incorporate the particularities of the disturbing phenomena would be the less epistemically violent choice. However, as Rogers (1969) states, 'any significant learning involves a certain amount of pain, either pain connected with the learning itself or distress connected with giving up certain previous learnings. [It] involves turbulence, within the individual and within the [cognitive] system' (pp. 157–158 & 339), and can even reach the level of existential crisis (Illeris 2007). This indicates that while the choice to enact non-violent epistemology may be arguably the most ethical (based on the proposition that as guidelines for acting in the world, less violent schema would likely inform less violent behaviour), it may also be a painful and challenging process requiring a significant degree of courage and effort from the individual.

Chapter 3 outlined how violent epistemology can be characterised by an attitude of closure to new particularities (Jarvis 1987; Illeris 2007; Rogers 1961; Leithäuser 1976; Adorno 1973; Piaget 1977) which, motivated by fear or anxiety, can constitute a form of 'self-imposed regression' (Sherman 2007) and even a 'hardened' or 'callous' subjectivity (Horkheimer and Adorno 2002). In light of this, I propose that the enactment of a less violent epistemology would require a more 'open' (Rogers 1959) attitude towards the process of orientating ourselves towards phenomena. Piaget's formulation of type β behaviour indicates a more open attitude to newness, particularity, and diversity and a willingness to adjust existing schema to integrate such particularity into learning. Going beyond this, transformative learning can be seen to require courage and willingness to endure the pain and effort involved in letting go of large parts of previous schema sets and in constructing new ones. Arguably, both types of epistemic behaviour require the subject to be willing to let go of the 'old particularity' (Adorno 1973) and to overcome emotional blocks to learning.

Rogers (1959) proposes that this is more than just a cognitive process, because it involves a transformation of the whole person and is therefore intricately entwined with our emotional and psychological development. He describes this as a process of moving from 'fixity to changingness, from rigid structure to flow, from stasis to process' (Rogers 1961, p. 131). As mentioned in Chap. 3, he defines a person in a state of fixity (or at Stage One) in the following way:

> The ways in which he construes experience have been set by his past, and are rigidly unaffected by the actualities of present. He is [...] structure-bound in his manner of experiencing. [...] He reacts "to the situation of now by finding it to be like a past experience and then reacting to that past, feeling *it*". (ibid., p. 133)

Flowingness, on the other hand, is described as a way of living in which:

> The self and personality emerge *from* experience, rather than experience being translated or twisted to fit a preconceived self-structure. [It means] an absence of rigidity, [and] of the imposition of structure on experience. It means instead a maximum of adaptability, a discovery of structure *in* experience, a flowing, changing organisation of self and personality'. (ibid., p. 189)

According to Rogers (1959), a shift away from the former and towards the latter can at times involve transformative or significant learning, characterised by what he calls 'the process of breakdown and disorganisation'. As in the experience of disequilibrium, when schema maintained by type α or β behaviour are significantly challenged, Rogers describes how:

> If the individual has a large or significant degree of incongruence between self and experience and if a significant experience demonstrating this incongruence occurs suddenly, or with a high degree of obviousness, then the organism's process of defence [re-equilibration through type α or β behaviour] is unable to operate successfully. As a result anxiety is experi-

enced as the incongruence is subceived. The degree of anxiety is dependent upon the extent of the self-structure which is threatened. The process of defence being unsuccessful, the experience is accurately symbolized in awareness, and the gestalt of the self-structure is broken by this experience of the incongruence in awareness. A state of disorganization results. (ibid., pp. 228–229)

Rogers (ibid.) goes on to outline how (often with the support of appropriate therapy) the individual can recover from this state of disorganisation through a 'process of reintegration' (p. 230), moving towards a more flowing and 'fully functioning' engagement with experience. Reintegration, he writes, is a process of 'increasing the *congruence* between *self* and *experience*' by reversing the 'process of *defence*' (i.e. type α behaviour) and allowing *threatening experiences* to be '*accurately symbolized* in *awareness* and assimilated into the *self-structure*' (ibid.).

Two key concepts in this process from 'fixity' to 'flowingness' are 'openness to experience' and 'congruence between self and experience'. The former he outlines thus:

> When the individual is in no way threatened, then he is open to his experience. To be open to experience is the polar opposite of defensiveness. The term may be used in regard to some area of experience or in regard to the total experience of the organism. It signifies that every stimulus, whether originating within the organism or in the environment, is freely relayed through the nervous system without being distorted or channelled off by any defensive mechanism. [...] In the hypothetical person who is completely open to his experience, his concept of self would be a symbolization in awareness which would be completely congruent with his experience. (ibid., p. 206)

Rogers describes such 'congruence with experience' as a scenario in which 'the individual appears to be revising his concept of self to bring it into congruence with his experience, accurately symbolized' (ibid., pp. 205–206).

As we can see, the process of moving from more defensive, 'type α' epistemic behaviour to more open, integrative and congruent epistemic behaviour can be thought of not just as a simple practice that can be quickly learnt, but as something that, depending on the degree of fixity or 'neurosis' (Rogers 1961), could also involve a rather unsettling process of disintegration and reintegration of schema and self-concept which could even trigger existential crisis and/or result in a significant change of personality (ibid.). Of course, as Rogers highlights, each of us sits somewhere on a continuum between 'fixity' and 'flowingness', and the experience of moving away from the former and towards the latter will be different for each person. What Rogers brings to discussions about moving away from violent epistemology towards less violent epistemic practice is the idea that non-violent epistemology cannot simply be 'adopted' but is rather a complex, whole-person approach which can have a deep and potentially transformative impact on how we relate with ourselves, others, and the phenomenal world.

Returning to Chap. 3, and as mentioned above, we can remember that one dimension of my formulation of violent epistemology was based on Adorno's (1973) concept of 'identity thinking'. This can be summarised as imposing general categories or schema onto diverse phenomena in a manner that tries to make phenomena identical to our concepts of them. In such thought, phenomena are subsumed by their concepts 'without leaving a remainder' (ibid., pp. 4–5). This was considered in Chap. 3 to be a form of violent epistemology, because it involves negating or distorting any particularities which do not fit neatly into our concepts.

As an alternative to identity thinking, Adorno (ibid.) proposed the concepts of 'non-identity thinking' and 'mimesis'. 'Non-identity', he proposes, 'is the secret telos of identification [...]. Dialectically, cognition of non-identity also lies in the fact that this very cognition identifies—that it identifies to a greater extent, and in other ways, than identity thinking' (ibid., p. 149). By this Adorno means that if we recognise phenomena as not being identical to our concepts of them, we do more justice to their particularity and are thus able to understand or 'identify' them better. Adorno argued 'the need for conceptual fluidity to adequately (and therefore never completely) describe the actual [phenomena] of a fluid reality' (Sherman 2007, p. 240). This type of conceptual fluidity that Adorno advocates, brings to mind Rogers' (1959) state of fluidity in that, like Polanyi's (1969) 'open-textured' concept, it implies a constant reworking of our schema through 'felt contact with objects [phenomena]' (Adorno 2005, p. 247). Like Piaget's type β behaviour and Rogers' fluidity, Adorno's non-identity thinking requires of the subject an openness to experience that 'respect[s] the non-identity of objects [phenomena] with concepts' (Cook 2005, p. 24).

Adorno's conceptualisation of 'mimesis' is complex and a full discussion of it is beyond the scope of this book. However, a few key elements can be highlighted as relevant to a discussion of non-violent epistemology.

Mimesis appears to be presented by Adorno as both an epistemic attitude and method. As with the other concepts outlined above, it rests on the conditions of 'openness' to experience and 'felt contact' with phenomena. He writes, 'in mimesis, the subject immerses itself in the things it attempts to present' (1973, p. 189). Further, Cook (2008) explains that 'mimesis is an attitude towards things; it is affected by an *epoché* [a temporary suspension of preconceptions] which allows things themselves to come into view' (p. 92). This phenomenological attitude speaks to Adorno's refusal to subsume phenomena under concepts. However, in the concept of mimesis he does not appear to be arguing that all previous concepts be suspended *all the time*, but rather that this suspension is something that we should normatively return to as a protective factor against slipping into identity thought (as I have attempted to do in this research with the dialectical approach to 'bracketing' (Waring 2012) outlined in Chap. 2).

Rather than a pure subjectivity or objectivity, through the concept of mimesis Adorno is also arguing for a normative, dialectical interrelation or dialogue between subject and object [phenomenon], in which neither dominates over the other:

> In its proper place, even epistemologically, the relationship of subject and object would lie in the realization of peace among men as well as between men and their Other. Peace is the state of distinctness without domination, with the distinct participating in each other. (Adorno 1978, pp. 499–500)

In Chap. 4, I discussed how the desire for control and domination over ourselves (internal nature), the phenomenal world (external nature), and over others can be seen as a core motivating factor for the forming of rigid conceptualisations, in an attempt to tie phenomena down and hold them in a 'safe' place within a rigidified world view. Mimesis is presented as an alternative to this. By reconciling 'the world and consciousness, [...] objectivity and subjectivity [...] mimetic rationality seeks to find ways in which the subject's experience of the world is not merely instrumental' but is rather marked by an 'undistorted' form of relating 'with nature, with [...] inner nature, and with fellow human beings' (Verdeja 2009, pp. 500–503) that respects the particularity of all phenomena without trying to dominate them by subsuming them under rigid 'identity' concepts. Even though Adorno speaks of reconciliation between the subject and phenomena, he does not propose that some ideal 'end point' exists in which the subject forms a perfect, accurate conceptualisation of a phenomenon. Rather, because both our own subjectivity and the phenomenal world are in constant flux, in order to maintain a non-violent epistemic practice he argues that we must also maintain an 'interminable dialectic' (ibid.) between phenomena and our conceptualisation of them, in which neither is permanently 'fixed'.

A final point to consider in relation to conceptualising a non-violent epistemology, concerns the role of the imagination. So far, I have largely been concerned with the importance of attempting to remain open to, and to fully acknowledge what *is*, but a number of authors also argue that there is an important role for the imagination in considering what *could be*. Three important functions of the imagination appear relevant to a conceptualisation of non-violent epistemology: firstly, the ability to imagine what another person may be thinking or feeling, a central aspect of empathy; secondly, the ability to imagine what may be occurring or what may occur in a given situation, allowing for decisions to be made about action; and finally, the ability to imagine how things might be better as a starting point for overcoming oppressive, violent, or generally 'non-conducive' circumstances. An important point to be made in relation to the first two functions is the importance of recognising the difference between imaginings and observations—considering the arguments made above, to assume that what we are imagining is identical to what is actually happening would be equivalent to enacting identity thinking. However, this is not to say that it isn't possible (or worthwhile) to make educated guesses (whilst acknowledging that they are guesses and therefore provisional), based on past experience.

We can consider that doing this 'without velleity or violence' (Adorno 2005, p. 247) however, would require a number of factors. When it comes to imagining what might be happening in a given situation, Piaget argues that we require 'structures for prediction' (1977, p. 68), the reliability of which, he argues, are far superior in people whose schema are maintained through type β behaviour (and which are therefore broader in scope and closer to the reality of phenomena) than those maintained through type α behaviour which tend to be restricted and distanced from phenomena (ibid.). When it comes to empathy, we can imagine that schema sets created and maintained through transformative and mimetic learning would also contain more accurate and sophisticated structures for prediction, because the epistemic behaviour associated with such schema sets entails an openness to considering and integrating the diversities and particularities of phenomena (which can of course include other human beings).

As discussed in Chap. 3, Graeber (2011) also argues that we must undertake 'imaginative labour'—the work that we do to try to understand what our fellow human beings are thinking and feeling (which can be seen as central to empathy), rather than merely applying simple schema or concepts (prejudices and stereotypes especially) onto others, thus subsuming their particularity. This, he argues, takes care and energy. Rogers (1961) also argues that empathy is a core condition of therapeutic processes which aim to bring the client from a state of fixity to fluidity. In this process, therapists are encouraged to foster an empathic understanding of the client's internal frame of reference. If we consider empathy as imaginative labour (rather than identity-thinking assumption), we can see that this necessarily requires openness to the other, as one aims to gain as accurate an insight as possible into another's frame of reference without assuming absolute knowledge. In this way we can perceive the importance of imaginative labour as a constituent of non-violent epistemology, which as we have discussed, requires the same attitude of openness—whether it be the teacher trying to understand the perspective of a student (or vice-versa); the politician trying to understand the perspective of those in poverty; or the therapist trying to understand a client.

Finally, we can consider the important role that imagination can play in envisioning a different way of being in the world. Schick (2009) argues that while it is not often recognised, Adorno proposed that such imaginings can 'perceive [...] the world as it is, fully aware of the contradictions and oppression that permeate existence, but [...] also see [...] beyond these failings to what could be, remaining alive to the possibility of beauty and kindness' (p. 155). This highlights the potentially important role that imagination could play when it comes to imagining a less violent epistemic practice, to finding ways out of 'limit situations' (Freire 1996) such as that experienced by the teachers at DCX School, and to imagining alternatives for greater societal change.

I discussed earlier how moving towards the enactment of non-violent epistemology can involve a deconstruction and reconstruction of a large part of the subject, even resulting in personality change. To close this section I will offer some ideas regarding what such a non-violent personality might look like. In Chap. 4, I discussed the notion of the subject who has undergone processes of de-formation as a result of enacting violent epistemology, thus becoming self-alienated (Horkheimer and Adorno 2002), 'blocked in realising his sensuous, emotional and intellectual potentialities' (Fromm 2013, pp. 213–214) and 'crippled by [...] terror of the new and unexpected, carrying its sameness with it wherever it goes' (Sherman 2007). As an alternative to this mode of being, Adorno (1973) presents the concept of the 'right human being', who he proposes 'would be nothing like the person, that consecrated duplicate of its own self-preservation' (p. 277). Rather, this subject would 'give the object [phenomenon] its due instead of being content with the false copy' by 'resist[ing] the average value of such objectivity [it would] free itself as a subject' (ibid., pp. 170–171).

Similarly, Rogers (1959) presents the concept of the 'fully functioning person', which he sees as possessing the following characteristics:

> An inherent tendency toward actualizing his organism [...] the capacity and tendency to symbolize experiences accurately in awareness [...] the capacity and tendency to keep his self-concept congruent with his experience [...] He will be open to his experience [...] he will exhibit no defensiveness [...] Hence all experiences will be available to awareness [...] All symbolizations will be as accurate as the experiential data will permit [...] His self-structure will be a fluid gestalt, changing flexibly in the process of assimilation of new experience [...] He will meet each situation with behaviour which is a unique and creative adaptation to the newness of that moment [...] He will find his organismic valuing a trustworthy guide to the most satisfying behaviours, because [a]ll available experiential data will be available to awareness and used [and] no datum of experience will be distorted in, or denied to, awareness. (Rogers 1959, pp. 234–235)

Rogers makes a specific point of highlighting that 'the fully functioning person' would be a 'person-in-process, a person continually changing' and 'continually in a process of further self-actualisation' (ibid.).

Lastly, Sherman (2007) presents the concept of the 'free flourishing' or 'liberated' subject:

> The free individual (in a free society) would not be "guarding the old particularity" [but] would be a work of art ceaselessly in progress. And, indeed, it is each individual constantly reworking his self (and, impliedly, the collective of which he is a part), that is the essence of the notion of a mediating subject. In contrast, what impels the individual to hypostatize the "old particularity" in its presently existing form—that is, to undertake the "bad faith" project of making himself into a thing—is the fear that by not making himself into a thing [...] he will die under the weight of an indifferent economic system. Under the right state of affairs, there would be no such fear,

and the individual would feel free to open himself up to the world, which would mean that self-identity would become more fluid, the individual would be in a position, as Nietzsche states, to become who he is. Openness to a world in which the individual can actually afford to be open is therefore the very condition of the liberated subject. (p. 281)

We can see immediate similarities between all three authors' concepts, and between these and the concept of non-violent epistemology formulated above. This includes an emphasis on openness to new experiences; a rejection of identity thinking or of 'guarding the old particularity'; the constant reworking of schema including concepts of self; and freedom from thwarting—freedom to self-actualise. Sherman's concept in particular emphasises not only the importance of a certain emotional, psychological, and (what we could formulate as non-violent) epistemic attitude on the part of the individual, but also the importance of the social and economic context surrounding the individual being such that they can 'actually afford to be open'. This brings us again to the importance of considering the conducivity of circumstances, which I will address in the next section.

8.2   THE PROSPECT OF CHANGE AND IMAGINING MORE CONDUCIVE CIRCUMSTANCES

As this book has demonstrated, violence is not only a matter of individual subjectivity. It is also deeply engrained in how individual epistemic behaviour and non-conducive social circumstances co-constitute each other. With this in mind, it is not sufficient to address the issue of violence at the level of individual epistemic agency alone. We must also consider how we might foster *social circumstances* that are more conducive to healthy subject development and the enactment of non-violent epistemology.

As formulated in Chap. 4 and illustrated in Chaps. 5, 6, and 7, non-conducive circumstances can be seen as those economic, social, political, and institutional conditions which have been designed, built, or developed on the back of, or fostered by, violent epistemology (manifest as collectively affirmed ideology). As the case-study analysis has demonstrated, such circumstances tend to foster multiple manifestations of violence, the de-formation of subjectivity, and the enactment of violent epistemology. Contrary to this scenario, we can imagine that circumstances that are designed, built, or developed on the back of, or fostered by, *non-violent* epistemology would be more conducive to healthy subject development, and would also foster the continued enactment of non-violent epistemology through similar co-constituting interactions.

As the case-study has shown, non-conducive circumstances operate at all levels of a nested system, from the globalisation of economic ideologies, down to interpersonal classroom dynamics. This indicates a rather daunting conclusion: that to truly address the issue of self-perpetuating cycles of violence (without simply fostering an 'oppressive peace'), it is necessary to coordinate fundamental epistemic and systemic change on a global scale. This is an enormous, complex, and perhaps insurmountable task, which as both a concept and a project would likely meet with multiple barriers and contestations. Even at a national, local, or school level, such a project is likely to face similar barriers, and would require an impressive degree of coordination to achieve. Some schools have tried to overcome these issues by fostering their own islands of more conducive, less violent circumstances (A. S. Neill's Summerhill School is one example[4]). However, this does not get away from the fact that as soon as staff and students leave the school grounds, those broader non-conducive circumstances remain.

If we can conclude, based on the findings of this research, that breaking the current cycles of violent epistemology ↔ non-conducive circumstances and establishing healthier cycles of conducive circumstances ↔ non-violent epistemology would require fundamental, structural, and societal change *and* changes in individual epistemic behaviour (that may require deep personal learning and transformation), then we can fully appreciate the enormity of the challenge that addressing violence at its root causes truly presents. In this way, the current global state of affairs (as well as the context in which the DCX case-study analysis is located) can be seen to represent something of a 'limit situation'. Pinto (1960) defines a limit situation as the boundary which separates simply being, from being *more* (i.e. being in flowingness or self-actualisation as Rogers (1959) would say, or being open in a world in which one can 'actually afford to be open', as Sherman (2007) writes). While such barriers may appear insurmountable on a broad scale, as highlighted above we can still consider a role for the imagination as one particular means to visualise what overcoming such a limit situation might look like.

---

[4] This is not to say that Summerhill School is a perfect example of conducive circumstances, but is rather an example of a school that aims to break away from many of the characteristics of traditional schooling that can be seen to constitute non-conducive circumstances.

As I have already proposed, a core characteristic of non-violent episte-mology can be considered to be its openness and adaptability to the par-ticularities of any given phenomenon or situation. Therefore, it is not possible to propose a 'one-size-fits-all' recommendation for the develop-ment of more conducive circumstances, whether at the global, national, local, or individual school level. Actions stemming from a truly non-violent epistemology would need to be responsive to the specific context for which they are designed. Therefore, outlining a detailed scheme of specific recommendations is far beyond the scope of this book. However, I will offer some thoughts on what the general characteristics of more conducive circumstances might look like, with reference to both the theoretical for-mulation of non-conducive circumstances and the example of the DCX case-study.

As already discussed, the core driver of non-conducive social circum-stances can be seen as the collective affirmation of ideological thought. As I have shown through the DCX case-study, although not absolute, ideol-ogy in today's world has become all-pervasive and cannot simply be done away with overnight. However, as Fiske (1987) argues, one way in which we could begin to address this (even on a minute scale) could be for indi-viduals to 'withhold consent' by refusing to subscribe to collectivised ideo-logical schema, aiming instead to honour the particularities of experience.

As I have also discussed, Adorno (2005), Fromm (2013), and Sherman (2007) propose that the collective affirmation of ideology stems from the loneliness, isolation, and 'stunting' of subjectivity often needed to survive in society, which motivates individuals to seek out a sense of comfort and community in the ideological collective. Aside from the need to foster social circumstances in which individuals are not reduced to enacting violent *self*-preservation as a means to survive, this also raises the question of whether other forms of collectivising can be fostered in a manner that can provide a sense of human solidarity and community, but without the need for a central ideological scheme. Rather than thwarting subject development, we might imagine that such collectives would operate so as to allow room for diversity, particu-larity, and the ongoing development of individual subjectivity without the need for social exclusion. Some interesting discussions in this area can be found in Edgerton (2010) and Smith (2017).

A key characteristic of the thought governing ideological collectives is its hierarchical structure, which tends to suppress and attenuate phenom-ena or dimensions of phenomena that are seen to be of lesser importance than those held up within the scheme. A core function of this is the operation of instrumental reason, which serves to facilitate such repression and also fosters the domination and control of all other dimensions so as to pull them into the service of these elevated dimension(s) (Horkheimer 1947; Horkheimer and Adorno 2002). As discussed in Chap. 4, this tends to foster social hierarchies (Sidanius and Pratto 2001), as well as the domination and repression of internal nature (ourselves), external nature (the phenomenal world), and others. While, as I have argued, the core underlying issue here is the epistemic structure of ideology, this does also highlight the importance of identifying and examining the operation of instrumental reason within the many different spheres of life. We might ask questions in our personal and professional lives about where such reason is operating, take some time to examine its impact, and consider what we could do to challenge or change this.

As I have already discussed, another characteristic of ideological social circumstances is the way in which they tend to assign 'conditions of worth' (Rogers 1959) to individuals and activities, which can foster the adaptation, sublimation, suppression, and appropriation of the self (Honneth 1995; Rogers 1959) as individuals are compelled, coerced, or forced to conform to the expectations of ideological society. This in turn can foster the de-formation of subjectivity through the stunting of self-development (Sherman 2007) and the development of a 'fixed' (Rogers 1961) or 'hardened' subjectivity (Horkheimer and Adorno 2002). All of the above can thwart self-actualisation and encourage the enactment of violent epistemology in relation to both the self and others. As already stated, I have proposed that the underlying issue here is violent epistemic ideology. However, we can also examine the ways in which we consent to, perpetuate, or ascribe conditions of worth onto ourselves and others. As above, we could consider the impact of this and what we could do to 'withhold consent', challenge, or change such epistemic behaviour.

In relation to the DCX case-study, two core manifestations of violent epistemic ideology were seen to run throughout the entire context in which the school and individuals are situated, from the level of the globo-system down to the microsystem of the school: globalised economic ideologies and a particular vision of development grounded in ideals of whiteness, cleanliness, order, and rational positivism. Since these ideologies are globally entrenched, they are not easy to overcome. However, it is possible to imagine other ways. There are a number of interesting proposals for alternative views and models of economic practice (cf. De Graaff 2016;

Smith 2013, 2017; Castells 2017; Dohndt 2014; Weiss 2013—to name just a few). While such texts can offer ideas for alternative ways of doing things, a crucial point is that it is not the model itself which is important, so much as its underlying epistemic structure and the ability of global society to implement any new model in a manner that does not revert to a re-enactment of ideology. This is certainly not an easy challenge.

Many authors have also challenged the specific ideological visions of development and 'progress' that have come to dominate since the era of European colonisation (cf. Fanon 1963; Foucault 1980; Said 1994; Spivak 1988; Bhabha 1994; Chakrabarty 2000; Young 2001). However, the critiques that I made of post-structuralism in Chap. 2, and of the concepts of epistemic violence and epistemic injustice in Chaps. 2 and 3, also apply to much of this literature. What the points I raised in these critiques ask of us in relation to this issue is to consider what non-ideological visions of the future might look like. How can we recognise the enduring harm caused by colonial ideology and foster a future which embraces the rich diversity and particularity of humanity, without reverting to a pure subjectivism that does not consider the underlying violent structures of certain forms of epistemology, regardless of who is enacting them? Aside from a form of epistemic relativism, post-colonial discourse often revolves around issues of identity politics (ibid.). However, this book indicates that rigid 'identity' schema can be repressive and foster violence. This raises the need to differentiate between the underlying epistemic structure of violent and non-violent forms of self- and identity-schema, and to carefully consider in each situation whether a cultural or identity category is operating as a violent epistemic scheme. I would propose that 'progress' in relation to these issues might entail a shift away from cultural and identity politics, towards a vision of fostering the free self-actualisation and healthy subject development of all, regardless of such categories as race/class/gender/culture and so on.[5]

As the case-study has shown, in Brazil these global ideologies have manifest as a long history of economic exploitation spanning from slavery, through the industrial era, to the precarious labour market conditions of the neoliberal era—a history marked by social suffering and exclusion, mass poverty, rapid urbanisation without adequate infrastructure, poor living conditions, and the exploitation and criminalisation of those unable to

---

[5] This is not to say that such categories should be done away with altogether, but simply to caution against their use as a form of violent epistemic 'identity thinking' (cf. Adorno 1973).

access the formal labour market (such as was the case for many of the families whose children attended DCX School). These ideologies have also fostered a society in which those of lighter skin colour continue to be afforded higher social status and increased access to opportunities, where disproportionate rates of police violence against those with darker skin continue, and where entire sectors of society continue to face socio-spatial segregation, criminalisation, and exclusion.

The nested system model demonstrates the importance of addressing these ideologies on a global level in order to effect the most systemic change. However, bearing in mind the enormity and long-term nature of this challenge, there are practical measures that can be considered on a national level that might alleviate (rather than solve) some of these problems in the meantime. These might include evaluating the degree to which economic exploitation, precarious contracting and excluding sectors of the population from economic activity is actually beneficial to society (assessing the real outcomes of neoliberal economic policy). Since the Lula administration, there has been some recognition of the need to alleviate poverty, resulting in the introduction of cash-transfer programmes such as Bolsa Família and Bolsa Escola (Rasella et al. 2013). Other measures to consider could include developing ways to value and integrate street commerce into city centres rather than marginalising itinerant vendors; investing in degraded neighbourhoods such as the Baixada with measures to improve housing conditions and provide public services (there have been some examples of this in the favelas (cf. Atuesta and Soares 2016)); introducing measures to foster the use of more stable employment contracting; exploring new ways to support people into employment or self-employment[6]; and considering the potential for rolling out alternative approaches such as Universal Basic Income (De Wispelaere 2016) and/or worker's co-ops (Vieta et al. 2016; Cheney et al. 2014).

Some measures have been taken to address inequality of opportunities between people of different skin colours, such as the operation of a quota system for admissions to public universities to increase non-white student numbers (Telles and Paixão 2013). However, this remains a controversial issue. Political and police corruption is widespread, meaning those responsible for violence (such as police and vigilante killings or the diversion of funds away from public schools) are often not held to account (Willis

---

[6] While recognising that simply integrating more people into the existing economic system does nothing to challenge its underlying ideology.

2015; Ferraz et al. 2013). Since mid-2011, Brazil has seen an increase in public protests (in which teachers and students have been very active). However, these have been consistently met with police repression, and the country has also faced significant political upheaval with a resurgence of the political right in recent years (Cannon 2016). This indicates that while there is a strong public desire for change, this is also a fragile and contested process which may not result in any significant reduction in violence. This also means that the suggestions made above may not hold much traction with current political leaders.

In Chap. 6, I demonstrated how the history and development of schooling in Brazil can be seen as shaped by the instrumental reason of the ideologies discussed above. Particular characteristics of this can be seen to have run throughout most of the development of Brazil's education system and remain predominant in the structures and practices of schooling today. These include 'civilising' (Faria Filho and Vidal 2007), repressive (Dockhorn 2002), pacifying (Rosa 2006), depoliticising (Leodoro 2001), standardising, and homogenising (Schwartzman 2003) tendencies. The instrumental reason of such ideologies has also resulted in the implementation of policy reforms without sufficient consideration of the particularities and needs not only for adequate investment in infrastructure and resources, but also of an overstretched teacher population and a diverse student population (Marcílio 2005), as well as the use of force to repress teacher and student dissent (Schwartzman 2003).

Considering what education might look like, if designed with the aim of creating environments conducive to the enactment of healthy subject development and non-violent epistemology, indicates that this would likely involve a complete deconstruction of the current structures and practices of mainstream traditional schooling, and perhaps even of current notions of 'teacher', 'student', and 'school'. We can imagine that such a schooling would be open and responsive to the ever-changing particularity, diversity, and needs of all involved; would value all dimensions of phenomena and being; and would foster rather than thwart self-actualisation. We can also imagine that such schooling would avoid ascribing conditions of worth and would not require the domination and repression of others, ourselves, or the phenomenal world.

However, as the DCX case-study has shown, schools also exist as part of a nested system, and such wholesale deconstruction and reconstruction into different form is unlikely to occur on a broad scale unless the predominant social and economic ideologies are also deconstructed, allowing for the grip of their instrumental reason to be released. This, of course, brings us back to the question of wholesale, global and societal, and epistemic and structural change. As I have already discussed, such change (if possible) would likely involve a long, complex, and contested process. In the meantime, therefore, we can again consider some potential actions that might alleviate some of the issues evidenced in DCX School, bearing in mind that these do not fully address the issue.

To begin, particular issues stemming from the neglect of the Baixada and its residents had an impact within the school. These included the impact on children and teachers of traumatisation resulting from witnessing or being a victim of violence, the impact on children's self-esteem of struggling to develop basic skills; and children behaving in a hyperactive, agitated, and aggressive manner at school as a means to release pent-up physical and emotional energy. Without forgetting the need to address these issues outside of the school itself, and to reconsider the structures and practices of schooling as a whole, in the meantime the provision of access to psychological therapies may help teachers and students to process and manage difficult experiences (without, as Edkins (2002) cautions against, simply aiming to reinsert them back into the established social order while encouraging them to forget their suffering or label them with mental illness). Teachers and school management could also consider introducing alternative means for students to release energy and frustrations. This could include, for example, the introduction of more variety and physical activity into lesson plans; using alternative spaces for learning such as the large open patio and yards that comprise the school building's lower levels; and providing increased opportunities for self-expression and physical self-actualisation through, for example, music, performance poetry, dance, theatre, capoeira, and/or sports.[7] The introduction of extra support to develop reading and basic skills, perhaps in small, supportive group or 1:1 sessions, may also help students to increase their self-esteem.[8]

---

[7] However, previous attempts to introduce such activities have perpetuated the exclusion of students who live in tenements. As Kohara (2009) found, these students would not participate because the activity required them to remove their shoes, and lacking access to adequate sanitary facilities, the children were embarrassed about the smell of their feet. This highlights yet again the importance of addressing broader contextual factors. As analysis of the Educommunication project also found (cf. Titchiner 2017), simply increasing opportunities for self-expression is also not sufficient.

[8] However, this would not address the fact that low self-esteem is often a product of subject de-formations fostered by struggling to conform to conditions of worth ascribed by an ideological society. Therefore, such actions do not address this underlying issue.

All of the above suggestions would place extra demands on teachers and require time, energy, and resources. As my analysis has shown these have all been in short supply at DCX. Measures would need to be taken to secure the necessary resources, and addressing some of the other issues faced by teachers would likely make introducing new practices and trying new ideas more realistic. While this is beyond the control of individual schools, increasing pay by a sufficient amount to enable teachers to work in just one school and for fewer hours overall would allow for a better work-life balance and more rest time. This, in turn, may decrease exhaustion and stress levels, enabling teachers to invest more energy into their work and to provide higher quality learning opportunities for students. This would also allow teachers more time to pursue personal and professional development goals which, if coupled with the provision of pre-service and in-service training that is designed to meet individuals' particular needs and interests, might enable teachers to feel more self-actualised (thus reducing feelings of despondency and desperation).

Other structures and practices at DCX shaped by the instrumental reason of nineteenth century and neoliberal education ideologies included official hierarchies of power and the suppression of deviance and dissent using various forms of discipline, intimidation, and coercion. Introducing less hierarchical forms of organisation and governance might foster an environment in which relations between managers, teachers, and students become less alienated, as individuals have more say in how operations are run. This might increase the ability of the school to listen to the ideas and experiences of diverse individuals, and to respond more effectively to teachers' and students' needs, potentially reducing the need for violent forms of dissent. There are many examples of democratic school governance which can be seen to foster this (Appleton 2002; Biesta 2015). Alternative methods for resolving conflicts could also be considered. Restorative Justice practices have been used in many schools (Song and Swearer 2016), while others have used democratic tribunals (Appleton 2002; Biesta 2015) or peer mediation (Politeia 2016; Evans and Vaandering 2016) to resolve disputes without using traditional punitive methods.

Aside from the above, structures and practices resulting from the aforementioned instrumental reason have included the standardisation and enforcement of homogeneity in terms of class groupings, classroom layout, curricula, teaching methods, use of time, and expectations of behaviour. These practices tended to foster strict vigilance and control over student movement and expression, and to make it very difficult for teachers to meet students' diverse needs. The introduction of more flexibility in how students are grouped, for example allowing for different group sizes and for students of different ages to work together, might allow for teaching to be better tailored to individual students' interests and needs.[9]

Curricula could also take a more multidimensional approach to subject matter, by valuing and exploring the diversity (such as the different regional dialects of Portuguese) and different dimensions (such as the emotional, visual, physical, and aural dimensions (cf. De Graaff 2011)) of phenomena. This could also foster increased participation from students in the learning process and afford more opportunities for students to contribute with their own ideas, feelings, and experiences. Such an approach would encourage an epistemically less violent mode of learning. It might also foster increased self-actualisation by affording more space for student expression, and by incorporating the exploration of dimensions of life that better reflect the multidimensional nature of student experience. This, in turn, might reduce students' feelings of alienation from schooling (bearing in mind that such an approach will always be limited while the underlying structural embeddedness of violent epistemology remains).

As already discussed, rigid use of time and control of student movement are commonly used to manage the project of transmitting 'skills' and 'knowledge' as quickly, cheaply, and efficiently (Ghiraldelli 2000) as possible. However, examples exist of other approaches to the use of time and to the control of movement and activity within the school space. Class Two at Summerhill School (which is designed for students of a similar age to the majority of those who participated in this research) is one example. Rather than being arranged in the traditional manner, the 'classroom' is a series of three adjoining rooms, each designed to be used in a different way (e.g. one room for messy activities, another for quieter, more focussed activity and tutorials, and another room for rest or quiet reading).

Rather than enforcing a strict timetable of lessons throughout the day, many different activities and resources are made available to students who

---

[9] This would need to be implemented with caution so as not to assign conditions of worth to placement in particular groups, which could simply reinforce students' self-schema as 'bad', or 'sub-standard' if placed in a group which is seen to be for students of lower ability, for example.

are free to move around between the rooms and from activity to activity, spending as much or as little time on an activity as dictated by interest, motivation, and need. The teacher organises workshops and lessons, but rather than expecting all children to sit down quietly and participate at the same time, students who are interested are free to join the lesson, while those who are not can continue with other projects. As I witnessed when visiting the class in 2013 and 2014, this allows for a much greater degree of student self-actualisation and self-determination, and for the teacher to maintain an observational and supportive interaction with students without the need to uphold strict vigilance and control over all movement and activity—thus greatly reducing the need for the teacher to employ dominating, coercive, punitive, or aggressive tactics in order to maintain control (in fact, the teacher was not concerned with maintaining control, but with finding ways to create and foster an environment to meet the learning needs and interests of each individual student). This also encouraged students to take responsibility for their own behaviour and choices.

Finally, as previously discussed, violent epistemology could also be seen at DCX in how teachers would often fail to openly acknowledge their own and colleagues' violent behaviour, which did not match their self-schema or schema about schooling. This prevented violence perpetrated by the school and teachers from being addressed. In line with the concept of non-violent epistemology outlined above, which emphasises the importance of acknowledging all particularities of a phenomenon and integrating them into our schema, this raises the importance of teachers and school management acknowledging their own violent behaviour and the violence inherent to certain structures and practices of schooling. One provision which might help teachers to develop less violent professional practice and process emotional responses to the difficult realities of teaching at DCX might include clinical supervision. There are a number of different approaches to using clinical supervision in education settings (Pajak 2002), and Dussault's (1970) Rogerian inspired approach may provide a starting point for the development of a method that is compatible with the concept of non-violent epistemic practice presented in this chapter.

The practical suggestions made above are not intended to be read as direct recommendations. As this book has argued, it is the epistemology which underlies and shapes an intervention that is important. Crucially, although implementing any of the above suggestions might alleviate some of the impacts of violent epistemology (and might foster slightly more conducive circumstances for healthy subject development, and for the enactment of non-violent epistemology), simply applying an intervention without broad scale epistemic and systemic change, is likely to have limited impact. As this book demonstrates, the non-conducive circumstances and overarching structure, practices, and ideologies operating in schools may mean that even the suggestions made above might be unrealistic. This brings us back once again to the difficult question of the realistic possibilities of mediating and negotiating change, and if change is possible, what might constitute a realistic and effective starting point?

While recognising the clear need for broader epistemic and systemic change, if we consider Harich's (2010) argument that identifying a root cause is equal to identifying the point in a causal chain at which an intervention can effectively be targeted, then we can consider (as mentioned in the previous section) the most fundamental linchpin for change to be the epistemic behaviour of individuals. As Sherman (2007) states, and as I have formulated in this book, 'although subjectivity is plainly mediated by the existing sociohistorical structures, it also has the capacity to affect these very structures' (p. 6). However, 'the idea that individuals can truly be raised free from coercive tendencies under the existing sociohistorical conditions is a mistaken one' (ibid., p. 233). Therefore, while we can take comfort in the power of our epistemic agency to effect change, we must also strive to become aware of the de-formations in our own subjectivity, and be mindful of how these may impact on our attempts to do so.

Marx also took hope in human agency, stating that '[People] make their own history' (1978, p. 595). However, he cautioned (and as this book has demonstrated), 'they do not make it just as they please; they do not make it under circumstances chosen by themselves, but under circumstances directly found, given and transmitted from the past' (ibid.). In this sense, we must conclude that we can only begin with the facticity in which we find ourselves by striving to understand the complexities of the circumstances that we have inherited and created, and acknowledging that we are forever working from, and on, these circumstances. This process can begin with a 'de-masking' of the realities of these circumstances. Morgan (2013) writes of how this can occur 'when the gap between what is proclaimed and what actually exists is too great for the ideology to mask any longer' (no page). I hope that this book can go some way towards 'de-masking' ideologies by highlighting the gaps between 'what is proclaimed and what actually exists', creating a disequilibrium or disintegration of discourse and providing a starting point for the reconstruction of schema about our societies and models of schooling, based on a less violent epistemology.

However, as I have made clear above, the 'deconstruction and reconstruction' that I am referring to is epistemic at its core. Because of this, the idea of change brought about by a flash revolution has no use because as I have discussed, the process of epistemic change rests on the slow and effortful transformation of individual subjectivity which involves not only a change in epistemic attitude and behaviour, but also a healing from previous de-formations of subjectivity. As Graeber (2011) writes, 'our customary conception of revolution is insurrectionary: the idea is to brush aside existing realities of violence by overthrowing the state, then, to unleash the powers of popular imagination and creativity to overcome the structures that create alienation' (p. 42). The problem with this view is that, unless underpinned by a change in epistemic practice at the level of individual subjects, any change in regime or introduction of new social structures, practices, and ideologies is likely to perpetuate violent epistemology—just in a different outer manifestation.

Graeber (ibid.) argues that it has become 'apparent that the real problem [i]s how to institutionalise such creativity without creating new, often even more violent and alienating structures'. He asks, 'what does revolution mean once one no longer expects a single, cataclysmic break with past structures of oppression?' (p. 42). In response to this, and in line with Adorno, I propose that while we cannot produce instant '"solutions" for the ills of modernity', in the meantime we can still strive 'towards a different kind of being that might ameliorate its worst excesses'—a political and intellectual reorientation 'directed at changing our fundamental ways of being and thinking, rather than at particular concrete projects' (Schick 2009, p. 150). As Smith (2015) affirms, 'any theory of systemic change worth its salt has to look structurally at the need for societal transformation, while also considering societal transformation on the level of the subject [involving] *a many-sided human transformation process*' (no page).

It is in relation to this 'process of human transformation' that the concept of non-violent epistemology holds so much value, because it provides a clear concept of what we could strive towards. However, we are still faced with the fact that engagement in this process hinges on the choice and commitment of individuals through the enactment of individual agency. Our capacity to choose between enacting violent or non-violent epistemology lies in our phenomenological freedom. While it has become cliché, Eleanor Roosevelt's famous saying, 'with great freedom, comes great responsibility', brings us to reflect on the following question: if phenomenological freedom implies epistemic freedom, ought we to be thinking more about epistemic responsibility?

We have established that engaging in a process of personal transformation from the habitual enactment of violent to non-violent epistemology can be difficult and painful. In light of this, we must ask not just whether we want to change our epistemic practices, considering the potential pain and effort involved, but also to what extent we have a responsibility to change them, if we truly want to see a reduction in violence and suffering. Code (1987, 1988) proposes a concept of epistemic responsibility that is largely compatible with, and could be expanded by, the concept of non-violent epistemology presented above. While she comes from a feminist perspective, she is clear that epistemic responsibility is relevant to all contexts, and the outcomes of the analysis presented in this book suggest that individual and collective epistemic responsibility is something that needs to be taken seriously when considering our roles as individuals in processes of change.

For those who might understandably argue that individual change might be too challenging, because our current society is often not one in which people can 'actually afford to be open' (Sherman 2007, p. 281), I propose that this highlights the importance (as discussed above) not just of individual change, but also of creating circumstances which are conducive to such change. This may need to include, as Fiumara (2015) proposes, the development of a 'new culture of healing and therapy' in order to collectively overcome a long history of violence, trauma, and subject de-formation. Some might argue that the above seems impossible in our current social circumstances, permeated as they are by the all-pervasive reach of violent epistemology. In response to this, I propose we begin by creating or looking for 'cracks' (Holloway 2010) in that ideology's reach (however small), and use the spaces afforded by such cracks to start opening up, examining our own epistemic practice, and fostering non-violent epistemic ways of relating with the world, ourselves, and each other.

8.3   TAKING THIS BOOK FORWARDS

I hope that this book has made a meaningful contribution to better understanding the root causes of violence in schooling, and to forming preliminary conceptualisations of non-violent epistemology/conducive circumstances. However, there is much scope for further research. This includes further investigation and refinement of the concepts of violent epistemology and subject de-formation presented herein, particularly from the perspectives of psychology, learning theory, child development, and lifelong learning. Such investigations could further explore the cognitive, emotional, and motivational dimensions of violent epistemology. There is also scope for further development of the concept of non-conducive circumstances in terms of how these impact on subject development and foster the enactment of violent epistemology, as well as in relation to how such circumstances are formed and maintained. Both the concepts of violent epistemology and non-conducive circumstances could also be refined through further research into their presence, operation, and impact in different contexts.

Aside from this, the proposed conceptual model of non-violent epistemology presented in this chapter can be developed further, with emphasis on better understanding not only its cognitive, emotional, and motivational dimensions, but also its interrelation with subject development. A particularly interesting area of investigation could be the processes by which an individual comes to initiate and undergo a significant and lasting change in epistemic behaviour, and the conditions that might foster such a process. Likewise, there is also much room for research into the concept of conducive circumstances, in terms of conceptualising the necessary characteristics of such circumstances, as well as how they might be developed and maintained.

Finally, in direct relation to the field of education, this book provides a starting point for the development of a new area of research focussed on the interactions between schooling and violent/non-violent epistemology, subject development, and the role of education in fostering violent and non-violent ways of relating with the world, ourselves, and each other. This could include research into how educational institutions and practices can be designed and developed with the concepts of non-violent epistemology and conducive circumstances in mind, and also ways in which non-violent epistemology and healthy subject development might be fostered through specific curriculum approaches, pedagogical practices, and organisational structures. Ultimately, if this book is correct in its proposal that a fundamental shift in epistemic practice is necessary for addressing violence at all societal levels, then, due to its formative influence, the role of education in this process is of vital importance.

However, although through the DCX case-study this book has emphasised understanding the root causes of violence in schooling, this book is
not just about schools or education in the traditional sense. The problem
of violent epistemology is one that pervades every aspect of human existence, from the intimacy of individual consciousness, to the vastness of
global structures and ideologies. There is, therefore, much scope for the
further development and application of the concepts presented herein, to
a very wide range of contexts and fields. It is my hope that others will take
this further.

References

Adorno, T. W. (1973). *Negative Dialectics*. London: Routledge.

Adorno, T. W. (1978). Subject and Object. In A. Arato & E. Gebhardt (Eds.), *The Essential Frankfurt School Reader* (pp. 497–511). New York: Urizen Books.

Adorno, T. W. (2005). *Minima Moralia: Reflections from Damaged Life*. London: Verso.

Ahmed, S. (2006). *Queer Phenomenology: Orientations, Objects, Others*. Durham: Duke University Press.

Appleton, M. (2002). *Summerhill: A Free Range Childhood*. Loughton: Gale Centre Publications.

Atuesta, L. H., & Soares, Y. (2016). Urban Upgrading in Rio de Janeiro: Evidence from the Favela-Bairro Programme. *Urban Studies, 55*(1), 53–70.

Bhabha, H. K. (1994). *The Location of Culture*. London: Routledge.

Biesta, G. J. (2015). *Beyond Learning: Democratic Education for a Human Future*. London: Routledge.

Broadbent, D. (1958). *Perception and Communication*. London: Pergamon Press.

Cannon, B. (2016). Inside the Mind of Latin America's New Right: If the Rhetoric of Latin American Elites Is Any Evidence, Neoliberalism Is Alive and Well, Despite a Decade and a Half of Left Governance. *NACLA Report on the Americas, 48*(4), 328–333.

Castells, M. (2017). *Another Economy Is Possible: Culture and Economy in a Time of Crisis*. Cambridge: Polity.

Chakrabarty, D. (2000). *Provincializing Europe: Postcolonial Thought and Historical Difference*. Princeton: Princeton University Press.

Cheney, G., Santa Cruz, I., Peredo, A. M., & Nazareno, E. (2014). Worker Cooperatives as an Organizational Alternative: Challenges, Achievements and Promise in Business Governance and Ownership. *Organization, 21*(5), 591–603.

Code, L. (1987). *Epistemic Responsibility*. Lebanon: University Press of New England.

Code, L. (1988). Experience, Knowledge and Responsibility. In M. Griffiths & M. Whitford (Eds.), *Feminist Perspectives in Philosophy* (pp. 187–204). Bloomington: Indiana University Press.

Cook, D. (2005). From the Actual to the Possible: Nonidentity Thinking. *Constellations, 12*(1), 21–35.

Cook, D. (2008). *Theodor Adorno: Key Concepts.* Stocksfield: Acumen.

De Graaff, A. (2011). *Backwards into the Future: Chaos in the Classroom.* Holt: Heathwood Press.

De Graaff, A. (2016). *The Gods in Whom They Trusted: The Disintegrative Effects of Capitalism: A Foundation for Transitioning to a New Social World.* Holt: Heathwood Press.

De Wispelaere, J. (2016). Basic Income in Our Time: Improving Political Prospects Through Policy Learning? *Journal of Social Policy, 45*(4), 617–634.

Dockhorn, G. V. (2002). *Quando a Ordem é Segurança e o Progresso é Desenvolvimento (1964–1974).* Porto Alegre: EDIPUCRS.

Dohndt, G. (2014). *Participatory Economics: A Theoretical Alternative to Capitalism.* Retrieved June 27, 2015, from http://www.heathwoodpress.com/monthly-guest-article-jan-participatory-economics-a-theoretical-alternative-to-capitalism-by-geert-dhondt/.

Dussault, G. (1970). *Theory of Supervision in Teacher Education.* New York: Teacher's College Press.

Edgerton, R. (2010). *Sick Societies.* New York: The Free Press.

Edkins, J. (2002). Forget Trauma? Responses to September 11. *International Relations, 16*(2), 243–256.

Evans, K., & Vaandering, D. (2016). *The Little Book of Restorative Justice in Education: Fostering Responsibility, Healing and Hope in Schools.* Brattleboro: Good Books.

Fanon, F. (1963). *The Wretched of the Earth.* New York: Grove Press.

Faria Filho, L. M., & Vidal, D. G. (2007). History of Urban Education in Brazil: Time and Space in Primary Schools. In W. T. Pink & G. W. Noblit (Eds.), *International Handbook of Urban Education* (pp. 581–600). Dordrecht: Springer.

Ferraz, C., Finan, F., & Moreira, D. B. (2013). Corrupting Learning: Evidence from Missing Federal Education Funds in Brazil. *Journal of Public Economics, 96*, 712–726.

Fiske, J. (1987). *Television Culture.* London: Methuen.

Fiumara, G. C. (2015). *Psychic Suffering: From Pain to Growth.* London: Karnac.

Foucault, M. (1980). *Power/Knowledge: Selected Interviews and Other Writings, 1972–1977.* New York: Pantheon.

Freire, P. (1996). *Pedagogy of the Oppressed.* London: Penguin Books.

Fromm, E. (2013). *Escape from Freedom.* New York: Open Road Media.

Ghiraldelli, P. (2000). *História da Educação.* São Paulo: Cortes.

Graeber, D. (2011). *Revolutions in Reverse: Essays on Politics, Violence, Art, and Imagination.* London: Minor Compositions.

Harich, J. (2010). Change Resistance as the Crux of the Environmental Sustainability Problem. *System Dynamics Review, 26*(1), 35–72.

Heidegger, M. (1962). *Being and Time.* New York: Harper & Row.

Holloway, J. (2010). *Crack Capitalism.* London: Pluto Press.

Holt, J. (1970). *What Do I Do Monday?* New York: E. P. Dutton & Co..

Honneth, A. (1995). *The Fragmented World of the Social: Essays in Social and Political Philosophy.* New York: SUNY Press.

Horkheimer, M. (1947). *Eclipse of Reason.* New York: Oxford University Press.

Horkheimer, M., & Adorno, T. W. (2002). *Dialectic of Enlightenment.* Stanford: Stanford University Press.

Husserl, E. (1973). *Experience and Judgement.* London: Routledge.

Illeris, K. (2007). *How We Learn: Learning and Non-learning in School and Beyond.* London: Routledge.

Illeris, K. (2009). A Comprehensive Understanding of Human Learning. In K. Illeris (Ed.), *Contemporary Theories of Learning: Learning Theorists … In Their Own Words* (pp. 7–20). London: Routledge.

James, W. (1918). *The Principles of Psychology* (Vol. 1). New York: Dover.

Jarvis, P. (1987). Learning from Everyday Life. *Human and Social Studies Research and Practice, 1*(1), 1–20.

Jarvis, P. (2009). Learning to Be a Person in Society: Learning to Be Me. In K. Illeris (Ed.), *Contemporary Theories of Learning: Learning Theorists … In Their Own Words* (pp. 21–32). London: Routledge.

Kohara, L. (2009). *Relação Entre as Condições de Moradia e Desempenho Escolar: Estudo com crianças residentes em cortiços.* São Paulo: University of São Paulo.

Leithäuser, T. (1976). *Formen des Alltagsbewusstseins.* Frankfurt: Campus.

Leodoro, M. P. (2001). *Educação Científica e Cultura Material: os artefatos lúdicos.* São Paulo: University of São Paulo.

Marcílio, M. L. (2005). História da Escola em São Paulo e no Brasil. *Revista FAEEBA, 14*(24), 103–112.

Marx, K. (1978). The Eighteenth Brumaire of Louis Bonaparte. In R. C. Tucker (Ed.), *The Marx-Engels Reader.* New York: W. W. Norton and Co.

Merleau-Ponty, M. (2012). *Phenomenology of Perception.* New York: Routledge.

Morgan, M. (2013). *The Paradoxical Perpetuation of Neoliberalism: How Ideologies Are Formed and Dissolved.* Retrieved November 30, 2014, from http://www.heathwoodpress.com/the-paradoxical-perpetuation-of-neoliberalism-how-ideologies-are-formed-and-dissolved/.

Pajak, E. (2002). Clinical Supervision and Psychological Functions: A New Direction for Theory and Practice. *Journal of Curriculum and Supervision, 17*(3), 189–205.

Piaget, J. (1977). *The Development of Thought: Equilibration of Cognitive Structures.* New York: Viking Press.

Pinto, A. V. (1960). *Consciência e Realidade Nacional.* Rio de Janeiro: ISEB.

Polanyi, M. (1969). Sense-Giving and Sense-Reading. In M. Green (Ed.), *Knowing and Being: Essays by Michael Polanyi* (pp. 181–207). London: Routledge & Kegan Paul.

Politeia. (2016). *Nossa Proposta.* Retrieved July 11, 2016, from http://escolapoliteia.com.br/a-politeia/.

Posner, M. I. (1978). *Chronometric Explorations of Mind.* Oxford: Lawrence Erlbaum.

Rasella, D., Aquino, R., Santos, C. A., Paes-Sousa, R., & Barreto, M. L. (2013). Effect of a Conditional Cash Transfer Programme on Childhood Mortality: A Nationwide Analysis of Brazilian Municipalities. *The Lancet, 382*(9886), 57–64.

Rogers, C. R. (1959). A Theory of Therapy, Personality and Interpersonal Relationships as Developed in the Client-Centered Framework. In S. Koch (Ed.), *Psychology: A Study of a Science Vol. 3–Formulations of the Person and the Social Context.* New York: McGraw Hill.

Rogers, C. R. (1961). *On Becoming a Person.* London: Constable.

Rogers, C. R. (1969). *Freedom to Learn: A View of What Education Might Become.* Columbus: Charles E. Merrill.

Rosa, J. M. (2006). *As vozes de um mesmo tempo: A educação física institucionalizada no período da Ditadura Militar em Cacequi.* Santa Maria: UFSM.

Said, E. (1994). *Culture and Imperialism.* London: Vintage.

Sartre, J. P. (1956). *Being and Nothingness: An Essay in Phenomenological Ontology.* New York: Washington Square Press.

Schick, K. (2009). To Lend a Voice to Suffering Is a Condition for All Truth: Adorno and International Political Thought. *Journal of International Political Theory, 5*(2), 138–160.

Schwartzman, S. (2003). *The Challenges of Education in Brazil.* Retrieved August 26, 2016, from https://www.researchgate.net/profile/Simon_Schwartzman/publication/225088750_The_Challenges_of_Education_in_Brazil/links/0912f5064693c5c575000000.pdf.

Sherman, D. (2007). *Sartre and Adorno: The Dialectics of Subjectivity.* Albany: SUNY Press.

Sidanius, J., & Pratto, F. (2001). *Social Dominance: An Intergroup Theory of Social Domination.* Cambridge: Cambridge University Press.

Smith, R. C. (2013). *On the Basic Income Law, Economic Democracy, Participatory Economics, and the Importance of the Commons in the 21st Century: Further Thoughts on an Alternative Philosophy of Social Change.* Retrieved May 2, 2017, from http://www.heathwoodpress.com/basic-income-law-economic-democracy-participatory-economics-importance-commons-21st-century-thoughts-alternative-philosophy-social-change/.

Smith, R. C. (2015). *Systemic Cycles of Domination and Imagining the Horizon of Liberation: An Engagement with Dialectic of Enlightenment.* Retrieved July 24, 2016, from http://www.heathwoodpress.com/dialectic-of-enlightenment-a-critique-of-cycles-of-systemic-domination-imaging-the-horizon-of-liberation/.

Smith, R. C. (2017). *Society and Social Pathology: A Framework for Progress.* Basingstoke: Palgrave Macmillan.

Song, S., & Swearer, S. (2016). The Cart Before the Horse: The Challenge and Promise of Restorative Justice Consultation in Schools. *Journal of Educational and Psychological Consultation, 26*(4), 313–324.

Spivak, G. C. (1988). Can the Subaltern Speak? In C. Nelson & L. Grossberg (Eds.), *Marxism and the Interpretation of Culture* (pp. 271–313). Chicago: University of Illinois Press.

Telles, E., & Paixão, M. (2013). Affirmative Action in Brazil. *Lasa Forum, 44*(2), 10–12.

Titchiner, B. M. (2017). *The Epistemology of Violence: Understanding the Root Causes of Violence and Non-Conducive Social Circumstances in Schooling, with a Case-Study from Brazil.* Digital Thesis, University of East Anglia. Retrieved from https://ueaeprints.uea.ac.uk/63644/.

Treisman, A. (1964). Selective Attention in Man. *British Medical Bulletin, 20,* 12–16.

Trevarthen, C., & Reddy, V. (2007). Consciousness in Infants. In M. Velmans & S. Schneider (Eds.), *The Blackwell Companion to Consciousness* (pp. 41–57). Oxford: Blackwell Publishing.

Verdeja, E. (2009). Adorno's Mimesis and Its Limitations for Critical Social Thought. *European Journal of Political Theory, 8*(4), 493–511.

Vieta, M., Quarter, J., Spear, R., & Moskovskaya, A. (2016). Participation in Worker Cooperatives. In D. H. Smith, R. A. Stebbins, & J. Grotz (Eds.), *The Palgrave Handbook of Volunteering, Civic Participation, and Nonprofit Associations* (pp. 436–453). Basingstoke: Palgrave Macmillan.

Waring, M. (2012). Grounded Theory. In J. Arthur, M. Waring, R. Coe, & L. V. Hedges (Eds.), *Research Methods and Methodologies in Education* (pp. 297–308). London: Sage.

Weiss, A. (2013). *A Comparison of Economic Democracy and Participatory Economics.* Retrieved May 2, 2017, from http://www.heathwoodpress.com/comparison-economic-democracy-participatory-economics/.

Willis, G. D. (2015). *The Killing Consensus: Police, Organized Crime, and the Regulation of Life and Death in Urban Brazil.* Berkeley: University of California Press.

Young, R. J. C. (2001). *Postcolonialism: An Historical Introduction.* Oxford: Blackwell.

Index[1]

[1] Note: Page numbers followed by 'n' refer to notes.

© The Author(s) 2019
B. M. Titchiner, *The Epistemology of Violence*, Critical Political Theory
and Radical Practice, https://doi.org/10.1007/978-3-030-12911-8

.

Printed by Printforce, the Netherlands